THE SOCIAL PSYCHOLOGY OF ORGANIZATIONS

Healthy and successful organizations require the people who work within them to be happy, healthy and creative. Just as a human body is undermined if it suffers from sickness, so an organization can only function fully if its 'working relationships' bring engagement and well-being, and any toxic influences which shape or burden their working lives are resolved.

This important new title provides a much-needed overview not only of what it means for an organization to be weakened by pervasive psychosocial influences within the working environment, but also how this dysfunction can be addressed through psychological interventions. The book is split into three core sections:

- **Toxicity and dysfunction in the workplace**, outlining structural, behavioural, emotional and cognitive sources of toxicity that undermine organizations.
- **Diagnosis and intervention in the workplace**, outlining core concepts of belonging, contribution and meaning.
- **Creating the healthy workplace**, outlining a range of approaches to address organizational toxicity, including design thinking, positive psychology, and evidence-based approaches.

Written by a practising organizational psychologist, and including case studies to illustrate how toxicity at the micro level can impact upon wider organizational goals, the book draws on a wide range of literature to provide an accessible, focused understanding of how the psychosocial experiences of working people can have wider consequences for an organization's prosperity, and how interventions within that process can address these issues. It is ideal reading for students and researchers of occupational or organizational psychology, organizational behaviour, business and management and HRM.

Dr Joanna Wilde has over 25 years' evidence-based professional practice in Organization Development and Change at senior levels in FTSE 100 and Fortune 100 companies and is an industrial fellow at Aston Business School, UK. She is on the board of directors for the UK Council for Work and Health and set up the Work and Health Policy Group for the British Psychology Society. She is also the Director of a small organizational psychology practice.

THE SOCIAL PSYCHOLOGY OF ORGANIZATIONS

Diagnosing toxicity and intervening in the workplace

Joanna Wilde

Routledge
Taylor & Francis Group

LONDON AND NEW YORK

First published 2016
by Routledge
2 Park Square, Milton Park, Abingdon, Oxon OX14 4RN

and by Routledge
711 Third Avenue, New York, NY 10017

Routledge is an imprint of the Taylor & Francis Group, an informa business

British Library Cataloguing in Publication Data
A catalogue record for this book is available from the British Library

Library of Congress Cataloging in Publication Data
Names: Wilde, Joanna, author.
Title: The social psychology of organizations : diagnosing toxicity and intervening in the workplace / Joanna Wilde.
Description: Abingdon, Oxon ; New York, NY : Routledge, 2016.
Identifiers: LCCN 2015039753| ISBN 9781138823211 (hardback : alk. paper) | ISBN 9781138823235 (pbk. : alk. paper) | ISBN 9781315742182 (e-book)
Subjects: LCSH: Organizational behavior. | Organizational change. | Organizational effectiveness. | Organizational sociology. | Industrial relations.
Classification: LCC HD58.7 .W529 2016 | DDC 658.4/053—dc23
LC record available at http://lccn.loc.gov/2015039753

ISBN: 978-1-138-82321-1 (hbk)
ISBN: 978-1-138-82323-5 (pbk)
ISBN: 978-1-315-74218-2 (ebk)

Typeset in Bembo Std
by Swales & Willis Ltd, Exeter, Devon, UK
Printed in Great Britain by Ashford Colour Press Ltd

CONTENTS

FIGURES

TABLES

ACKNOWLEDGEMENTS

Rachel and Sophy, because we are three sisters together and nothing is possible without this (and the razor sharp editing pencil that Rachel wields).

Ray and Meri whose practical wisdom and warm support enabled me to get writing and find the right publisher and Russell for being that right publisher who gently and supportively helped me find my voice and unlearn some nasty PhD writing habits.

My friends and close colleagues who have fed this process with thoughts, space and contribution: Fran Laneyrie, Sarah Owusu, Judith Okonkwo, Moira Nangle and Derek Tuitt. Dr Sam Collins and the Aspire women – you know who you are – that inspired me to accept that writing this wasn't something that should be done by some random other, but that must be written by me.

Steve Woolgar and Steve Linstead for being my two intellectual guides when I needed it – thank you.

Paul Tolchinsky, Nick Richmond and the crew at European Organizational Design Forum (EODF). I got to trial my first ideas out in Vienna, at one of the wonderfully safe yet challenging environments this community of practice creates – you know who you are – thank you all.

And all the clients, too numerous to mention, who I have worked with, prototyped with and always learned from.

INTRODUCTION

Intelligent activism and the social psychology of organizations

Our workplaces have lost their humanity. We need to address how we engage with complex organizations to repair this. Underpinning 'how' is the need to engage with what we know about the sources of this workplace toxicity. We also need to find the place for knowledge through practice; the grounded understanding of emergence in complex organizations. We do know better, and it is now time to put what we know into practice.

This book is about psychosocial practice in the workplace, or as I prefer to describe it 'intelligent activism'. Intelligent activism has two parts: first, *intelligent* refers to the work required in translating complex knowledge (for what is now described as impact), and the breadth of knowledge, discipline and insight that can help us do this. Second, *activism* refers to doing, to know-how, to working with uncertainty coupled with a consideration of ethics as the loadstone.

To ground 'intelligent activism' it is important to acknowledge the established place that pragmatism had in early psychology, articulated in the work of pragmatists such as Dewey (1859–1952) (Tiles 1988) and Mead (1863–1931) (Joas 1985) who were both leaders in the American Psychological Association (APA) over a century ago. They articulated that any 'scientific fact' will change with time and that the social was critical to what was taken as fact. In contrast with the dominance of the emerging 'pure science' agenda in other branches of psychology, they suggested that the only sustainable purpose for investment in knowledge development had to be an ethical one: to help shape relationships and communities for the better.

Dewey was particularly focused on using the emerging scientific principles to enable improvement in education and called for a theory of action as the cornerstone of all ethics. Mead, recognized as the founder of social psychology, wrote of the 'imperfections of objectivity' and identified that all perceptions are culturally constituted. This recognition underpinned his ideas of symbolic interactionism, which is considered the launch point for a 'social psychology', the domain within which this book sits. Mead also indicated that as scientific method developed and became increasingly valued, it was troubling that the increasing 'rationality of means' was not being matched with an equivalent increasing rationality of the 'social setting of ends'. He was advocating, over a century ago, that ethical examination of the ends themselves (i.e. what we are creating) was critical.

My work in psychosocial practice for 30 years has brought this challenge to life. Workplace environments have become increasingly toxic to human beings and merely studying this phenomenon is not a sufficient contribution from the psychosocial disciplines we invest in; to restate Dewey, we need an ethics of action in the social psychology of organizations that is prepared to put its name to a purpose, and that purpose needs to be more than merely observing catastrophe. It is time to readjust our focus and state clearly what we are 'for'.

The purpose of this book is to contribute to the knowledge and skills needed for intelligent activism when working as a professional psychologist, consultant or manager wishing to intervene in organizations to make them better places to work. The practice developed and shared in this text is built on breadth rather than depth of study and uses a composite of knowledge from psychology, the sociology of scientific knowledge, anthropology, employment law and studies of organizational life, integrated through 30 years of professional practice, nominally as an organizational psychologist but also and importantly as a human being immersed in and impacted by the workplace environments we have been building for ourselves.

I am a 'doer' but I have realized that without using the techniques of a 'thinker' and 'writer' I cannot share my experience of 'how to do' to a wide enough audience or with sufficient authority. In doing this, I am challenging the current notions of what valid 'knowledge' looks like, by making explicit the alternative 'invisible' work of practice, of 'craft'. I know that the risk I take in doing this, is that my words could be positioned as 'flaky' by those who advocate the predominantly experimental approaches in organizational psychology and as 'naïve' by those who earn their stripes in the fields of critical management. They may well be right, but our workplaces must improve; they must be fairer, kinder and directed towards prosperity not control. Working with this purpose I choose to operate with the courage and commitment of acting in uncertainty coupled with the naivety of hope, even if these do limit 'authority'.

I am not alone here as there have been recent challenges to the gendered nature of psychology (Rutherford et al. 2015) and to the supremacy of the 'white syllabus' (UCL 2014) in academic institutions, both of which point to the dynamics of privilege around what gets taught and what does not. One victim of this dynamic has been the subordination of the complexities of practice (or craft) to a second tier knowledge system. 'Practice' is regularly presented as a sub-set of scientific method and even those studies of the gendered nature of psychology accept 'caring practitioner roles' (Valentine 2010) as being lower in status and in intellectual credit than science.

I believe we need to question the status quo and am concerned that the manner in which social and management sciences are currently taught works to hide the subtleties of social psychology at work and the damage that is done to the fabric of human relationships. I would argue that our contemporary view of science works to validate a heavily gendered, class-ridden and white euro-centric assumption of the dominant importance of control and cognition. The subordinate status of practice is used in service of the 'impact claims' of those who only do 'science', while in parallel, practice is allowed no distinct voice. By contrast my 'position' is that practice, that craft is the 'hard bit', the bit where 'the rubber hits the road', where 'reality bites', where you need 'skin in the game' and where you work with uncertainty in each and every act. The book, in three parts has been designed to provide the overview material needed to engage ethically in the uncertainty of the act; the intelligent activism needed to intervene in work organizations for good. It starts with know-how – the essence of practice. From this point it considers what we know about how our workplaces have lost their humanity and how we need to integrate this knowledge to help us intervene. Finally it considers how we learn from the complexity of practice.

In producing this, and claiming the authority that comes from publishing, I am fully aware that I can only write from a specific cultural, national and professional perspective. Any perspective inherently enables certain ways of seeing and so 'disables' others. I am not the first and I am surely not the last 'writer' to feel the pressure of being trapped in the institutional practices around the way words work:

> I would like us all to recognize that reality is made, not given; to recognize that our seeing and understanding of the world is always 'seeing as' not 'seeing as is'; and to take an ethical and moral responsibility for the personal and collective consequences of the way we see and act in everyday life, difficult though this may be.
>
> *(Morgan 1986: 382)*

To repair organizations means we need to know how to take ethical action in organizations and to understand what is essential for health in the psychological environments that we expect people to work in. For the latter point, the core principle is that psychological safety in the workplace is essential for organizational productivity and human health and we have a poor history in enabling this. Historic examples such as the design and implementation of concentration camps in the Boer War, which formed the model for the (ongoing) World War II atrocities, or the horrors of the 'slave and sugar economy' (Olusoga 2015) indicate that the factors that create organizational toxicity are not new. The continuing hegemony of dysfunction is evidenced in examples such as the shameful abuses in our global supply chains (Klein 2000) and in the epidemic of psychological ill health caused by our toxic workplaces (Hassard et al. 2014). Despite over a century of investment in knowledge development in this area, we have not yet used what we know to redesign the environments we build for ourselves.

Currently there are many practices and habits associated with the way we design and manage workplaces that profoundly compromise the essential requirement for psychological safety, to the detriment of all of us; we experience global financial services organizations that dramatically reduce the value of money and so create and worsen widespread poverty. We are increasingly concerned about health services that cause avoidable harm and death. We are also witness to sporting governance bodies that do not play fair. Effectively translating our psychological and social science knowledge to support beneficial action is therefore an ethical imperative.

Overview of the three parts of this text

Part I: doing intelligent activism – the new social psychology of organizations

This is focused upon the critical practice capabilities needed for system intervention. It considers the model of knowledge translation for practice, which draws upon the Sociology of Scientific Knowledge, the nature of client engagement, considerations of intervention and change, the evidence and methods available for effective practice and practice ethics.

Part II: building an integrated model of organizational toxicity

This covers what we know about the epidemiology of stress, the dynamics of system toxicity and introduces the concept of the toxic dose. It considers the importance of macro factors, micro processes and the interaction between these two levels to provide an integrated model of organizational toxicity. It then covers four macro level sources of toxicity: structural, cognitive, behavioural and symbolic; and four clusters of relevant relationship psychosocial micro processes: accountability, compassion, appreciation and growth.

Part III: learning from practice to intervene in toxic organizations

This starts with an exploration of the practice of diagnosis and outlines the diagnostic themes for assessing the psychological environment in complex organizations. This is based on considerations of contributing, belonging and meaning, each with their associated disorders. Each theme then has a dedicated chapter giving field illustrations of toxicity and its mitigations.

References

Hassard, J., Teoh, K., Cox, T. et al. (2014) *Calculating the Cost of Work-Related Stress and Psychosocial Risk*. European Agency for Safety and Health at Work (EU-OSHA). Luxembourg: Publications Office of the European Union.

Hoffman, D. H. (2015) Report to the Special Committee of the Board of Directors of the American Psychological Association. http://www.apa.org/independent-review/APA-FINAL-Report-7.2.15.pdf.

Joas, H. (1985) *G.H. Mead: A Contemporary Re-Examination of His Thought*. Cambridge: Polity Press.

Klein, N. (2000) *No Logo*. New York: Picador.

Morgan, G. (1986) *Images of Organization*. Los Angeles, CA: SAGE.

Olusoga, D. (2015) Britain's forgotten slave owners. http://www.bbc.co.uk/programmes/b063jzdw.

Rutherford, A., Vaughn-Johnson, K. and Rodkey, E. (2015) Does psychology have a gender? *The Psychologist* 28(6): 508–511.

Tiles, J. E. (1988) Dewey. In T. Honderich (ed.) *The Arguments of the Philosophers Series*. London and New York: Routledge.

UCL (2014) UCL faces race: Why is my curriculum white? https://blogs.ucl.ac.uk/events/2014/11/21/ucl-faces-race-why-is-my-curriculum-white/.

Valentine, E. (2010) Women in early 20th century experimental psychology. *The Psychologist* 23(12): 972–974.

PART I

Doing intelligent activism
The new social psychology of organizations

The purpose of the chapters that form Part I of this text is to address the important know-how or practice to enable organizational detox. The book has started with the know-how as this then feeds ethical and practical understanding into the later explorations of what we know (Part II) and what we are learning from practice (Part III).

Chapter 1 outlines the model for understanding the translation and mobilization of knowledge for practice. Central to this is the use of the literature from the Social Studies of Science Knowledge (SSK) and Actor Network Theory (ANT) outlining what it can teach managers, consultants and organizational psychologists about the phases of knowledge translation for impact.

Chapter 2 gives an overview of the experience of the initial client engagement, focused on addressing the vulnerabilities of asking for help. This covers the variation in topic presentation, the stages in client problem/solution formulation and the different engagement structures that can be set up.

Chapter 3 critiques the conventions of the consulting cycle, covering ideas of intervention and organizational change and outlines the failures of the current orthodoxy around organizational change management and outlining the developing change platform ideas informed by social movement theories.

Chapter 4 explores the types of methodology available to the intelligent activist. It critiques the emerging orthodoxy of decision/cognition ideas about 'evidence-based' practice and outlines four other methodologies that offer more diversity in the way we can approach intervention. All outlined methodologies use evidence but work within very different phases of knowledge translation.

Chapter 5 outlines key ethical capabilities for practice and outlines four ethical considerations for the 'intelligent activist': helping and harm; authority and knowledge; confidentiality and contracting in complex systems; and self-regulation and supervision.

1

KNOWLEDGE TRANSLATION FOR COMPLEX WORKPLACES

Introduction

I would suggest that the purpose of investing in the development of psychology, industrial relations, management studies and other social science knowledge is not merely to know but more importantly to help (Schein 2009). I conceptualize this practice orientation as 'intelligent activism', which covers a distinct set of action-focused capabilities (outlined later in Table 1.2). This shift from knowledge production to knowledge deployment being centre stage could also be characterized as the move from the 'scientist' (root: to know) to the 'engineer' (root: to contrive or devise), designer (root: to mark out) or practitioner (root: to do).

The important issues in this arena are those of tool, action and ethics (Spier 2001) with two distinct and serious sets of ethical questions that need to be faced in day-to-day practice:

- The first set centres on how we 'translate' knowledge into tools, action and practice to help.
- The second set centres on ethical decisions about who to help, whether help for one causes harm to another and what to do about these tensions.

Psychosocial practice, whether by consultants, managers or peers is being made increasingly invisible. Every collaborative endeavour relies on 'invisible work' but the lack of recognition and support for such work is becoming increasingly damaging to organizations. Its removal, most often due to quasi-rational cost-cutting, is a significant source of toxicity (see Chapter 7 on structural sources of toxicity). 'Intelligent activism' is one of these areas of 'invisible work' and we need to have a much clearer, confident and rigorous language to afford this work its proper place.

The impact of this invisibility can be seen in the emerging arguments that 'science-based' methods can be, without problem, transported into client field sites. From my perspective, the different ethics (see Chapter 5) between lab and field is the biggest challenge for the concept of the 'scientist-practitioner' (Hays-Thomas 2006; Muchinsky 2006) currently being advocated and we need a much more robust understanding of practice as distinct from rather than subservient to science. To address this I have used 'lab' generated evidence that explores how knowledge is developed and applied. This knowledge comes from the Social Studies of Knowledge (SSK) and Actor Network Theory (ANT), which provide the insights that help describe and elaborate the phases of knowledge translation for deployment in the 'field'.

Translating knowledge for effective intervention

This body of knowledge uses various concepts that I have found extremely useful in my 30 years of professional practice and illustrative references are given in the further reading section at the end of this chapter:

- The field (Latour 1988) is an abstraction used to describe the day-to-day emergent context we, as practitioners, work within. In the work of professional practice we would describe this as the client context. The critical concept here is that the field is usually focused on addressing a 'wicked problem' (Rittel and Weber 1973). A wicked problem is a complex problem that is changing and cannot be completely 'solved'. It has multiple variables, many of them that are contextual, that mutate through time. A wicked problem is in sharp contrast to a bounded problem required in scientific work.
- The laboratory or 'lab' (Latour and Woolgar 1986) is an abstraction used to describe the controlled social scientific space where 'field' ideas get refined and changed through a set of disciplines using contextually defined knowledge rules. The output from this is 'socially' agreed 'facts'. In our work we would describe this as academia or science.
- Translation (Callon 1986) is a concept used to describe the process of knowledge changing its character between field and laboratory. It refers to the ongoing movement of know-what and know-how between these two environments and is also focused on 'wicked problems'. In our work we would describe this as practice.
- Mobilization (Callon 1986) is a concept used to describe the way in which a wide range of networks and interests get activated to enable translated knowledge to have a wider social impact. In our work we would describe this as policy and practice influence.

To date we have tended to have a fairly polarized view in the psychological and managerial professions of what counts as legitimate knowledge:

- In organizational psychology, there is the tendency to privilege the 'lab', this has been articulated in the concept of the scientist-practitioner role designed to subsume practice as a servant of science. This is supported with assertions of the need to use 'evidence-based' approaches and the rejection of other approaches characterized as 'fads and fashions'.
- In managerial work, which tends to privilege the field, I have encountered the polarization between acceptance of 'common sense' approaches, and the rejection of 'the theoretical'. This encourages the uncritical imposition of normative approaches that are disconnected from our growing understanding of what human environments need to help us thrive and prosper.

These unhelpful acts of polarization work rhetorically to maintain the distance between 'lab and field': science and practice; client and academia. I consider that the tendency to polarize represents a failure to understand the critical importance of the ongoing work of 'translation' between these two distinct and yet equally as disciplined relationships with knowledge. Fundamentally these ignore the evidence of translation and mobilization as psychosocial processes in their own right. The skill to manage polarities without these problems has been recognized as a critical skill for working with complexity (Johnson 1992) and paradox (Handy 1995).

Working in translation for intelligent activism

In Chapter 3, I will briefly critique the current formulation of the consulting cycle used in training practitioners, which is an implicit attempt to import academic method into the field. It has not yet given sufficient consideration to the vicissitudes of practice, so is inherently misleading. I will also demonstrate how a translation-focused approach to intervention subtly alters how we need to describe and teach practice. Instead of it being taught as a 'knowledge driven method' it needs to be formulated and taught as a 'helping-based practice' that enables knowledge translation.

To understand translation, we need to recognize the differences between the knowledge practices used in the client context (field) and academy (lab). Good practice is not merely the transportation of 'laboratory approaches'. However, good practice also does not ignore the value of importing and translating external evidence. Using the formulation of translation from the Social Studies of Knowledge, Science and Technology enables us to conceptualize:

- the difference between field and lab (client context and the academy) and what this *implies for ethical practice*, without succumbing to the temptation to subordinate one approach to the other;
- the process of knowledge translation – developing, refining, elaborating and deploying our knowledge in support of intelligent activism;
- the capabilities required for effective translation.

The difference between client context (field) and academia (lab)

The work of helping through system intervention, using the ideas of translation, is an attempt to work productively with this polarity. I have considerable concern with the way the scientist-practitioner idea appears to uncritically assume that 'lab'-based methods and facts can be 'plonked' into the 'field' and have positive impact. This chapter presents a very different model of knowledge translation to address this problem. The central issue for me is about helping, which combines an acceptance of wicked problems and the ethic of client-centricity. The idea of client-centricity in this text builds on the notion of process consultation (Schein 1998, 2009) but differs in one significant way. Schein (1998) builds client-centricity into his formulation by explicitly displacing the active use of expertise and knowledge to support organizational intervention. Schein's (1998) typology of consulting work is outlined later in this chapter. Given our investment in knowledge development and the important insights generated, I do not consider it acceptable to displace the knowledge and expertise that we have invested so heavily in, when working with the intent to do 'intelligent activism'. To illuminate how to work with this polarity an example from medical practice can help (see Figure 1.1).

The process of knowledge translation

Effective professional practice in response to organizational problems is focused upon helping, which is rarely achieved by merely sharing what is known; just as

---

KNOWLEDGE TRANSLATION TO GIVE HELP

An illustration of ethical and effective helping through knowledge is available in the work of a General Medical Practitioner (GP). When you consult a GP you expect attention to the symptoms and concerns that you bring as an individual, to ensure that they will take action or give advice that will be helpful to you, your health and your situation. You expect an individual focus on diagnosis, advice, prescription and risk assessment:

> The second rule of medicine: No one cares how much you know, until they know how much you care.
>
> *(@GavinPrestonMD)*

You do not expect a GP to use the consultation time to tell you how much they know, defend the validity of their knowledge, delve into the further medical knowledge available to them around any particular symptom or to engage in a research process with you.

The information about you belong to you, and if they choose to run a research or evaluation activity they must get your informed consent before you participate.

FIGURE 1.1 Intelligent activism in action

sharing an account of the causes of cancer or its demography does not help the newly diagnosed cope with the diagnosis, recover from the life threatening disease or handle the process of dying.

Working as a practitioner is therefore not the same as working as a lab/academia-based 'scientist'. It is not simply a matter of exporting teaching and research skills to a different domain. Practice is the process by which knowledge from one situation is converted into a *different form* designed to be effective for the particular situation at hand; it must judge itself by 'impact' and not by the 'facts' it generates.

Education can be an important aspect in enabling impact, but it cannot create client or social impact on its own. For example:

• Teaching managers how in-groups and out-groups operate in organizations does not change unhelpful discrimination and unfairness in the workplace.
• Educating governance boards about cognitive biases does not stop the biases operating.

Undertaking research in any specific organization (which I would conceptualize as the export of laboratory approaches into the field) needs to be undertaken with care. Research can neither *reliably nor validly* change a situation. By *reliably*, I mean in a way that is expected, and by *validly* I mean that it generates the positive impact intended/required. Such imported 'lab' approaches may help uncover how widespread a problem is, how it manifests or how it makes people feel, and so add clarity of understanding to the nature of the problem. However, I have regularly found that the employee experience of being asked to contribute to an organizational research project will increase frustration and toxicity in the system if nothing productive happens for those who are 'subject' to the 'research'. Instead they describe feeling that they have given their ideas and time for nothing and so are aggrieved.

Even when the research methods are described as 'objective', research is an intervention when undertaken in an organization, and hence is 'subjective' in its impact. All interventions impact the system in both intended and unintended ways (Harris and Ogbonna 2002) and research activities are no different. If our psychological, industrial relations, management and social sciences are to have the productive social impact that we seek, we need to get beyond seeing the 'facts' as the point and instead see them as just one step in the whole process of 'intelligent activism'.

Such translation processes can be illustrated in a potted history of penicillin in our society. The storyboard in Table 1.1, built from a simple google search of the topic, helps illustrate the movement of knowledge between 'field' and 'lab'. It shows the interdependence of both field and lab for effectiveness and impact. The reason for my choice is that I was raised on stories about Dorothy Hodgkin (one of my mother's teachers and heroes). It must be noted that of course this 'story' is partial, as all stories are. The 'whole story' is never possible and to attempt it would constitute a complete book in itself. To summarize, the story indicates that without the proper consideration of the 'fad and fashion' of carrying mouldy bread (see Table 1.1) as a treatment for high temperature we would not have the antibiotic technology we rely on today.

TABLE 1.1 The penicillin story board

Date and location	Description
Widely used across Africa, Asia and Europe from 1600s	The storage and use of mouldy bread for treatment of humans and horses – not reliable – depended upon the fungal material used
1870s London	From work on asepsis, it was observed that mould put on a microscope plate would prevent bacterial growth. Lister called this penicillium. Lots of practice-based observations and demonstrations about the positive impact of this 'field' fad
1872 France	Pasteur demonstrated that Anthrax was inhibited by mould, but this was a different agent from penicillium
1890 France	Evidence that typhoid was cured by the use of mould, but wasn't clear what mould it was so could not be replicated
1923 Costa Rica	A Costa Rican scientist at the Institut Pasteur first recorded the fact of the antibiotic effect of penicillium
1928 Scotland	Fleming grew a pure culture of the 'agent' and with help from an unnamed chemist concentrated this and called it penicillin
1930 Sheffield, UK	A pathologist cured a few patients using this concentrate – but with hit and miss impact – the concentrate was unstable and unreliable and only effective on surface/skin problems
1938 Oxford, UK	Work focused on the technology that would stabilize the concentrate
1941 USA	The development of industrial methods for production of concentrated penicillin
1943 USA	The breeding of strains of mould that produced more of the active ingredient
1945 Oxford, UK	Dorothy Hodgkin identified and described the chemical structure of penicillin
1952 Austria	Sandoz developed the first penicillin that could be administered orally and so fully mobilized
1957 USA	MIT produced the first chemically synthesized penicillin (a synthetic)
1960s	The identification of allergies to the synthesized penicillin
2000s (World Health Organization)	The emergence of concerns about anti-microbial resistance and the development of approaches to manage the risks from untreatable infections

For the purposes of this book, it is helpful to extract 12 key 'translation' headlines illustrated through this penicillin story.

1. The underlying drive is to solve a 'wicked problem'; in this case the prevention of death from infection.
2. Common sense or 'field knowledge' is based on broad observation and 'evidence by experience' as there were sustained observations of people getting better some of the time.
3. The field knowledge is intimately connected with the practice of helping: in this case the creation and transport of mouldy bread to cure fever.
4. The contribution of 'science' is in assuming there is a reducible 'cause' for the improvements in health of some of the users: that we did not require all parts of the mouldy bread to be effective.
5. The creativity of science in the control and definition of a problem that can be tested, the social review processes that engage with complex findings all of which combine to generate repeatable and authorized 'facts'.
6. Even with the 'fact' produced from a lab-based 'controlled problem', in practice there was a 'so what?' Despite knowing what the active ingredient is we still needed to travel around with lots of mouldy bread to get the benefits.
7. To move past the 'carry mouldy bread' stage we need skilled and disciplined technological (and in this case pharmaceutical) engagement with the 'wicked problem'.
8. The actual change in *medical practice* did not come until technologists engaged and articulated a different and more elaborated design challenge: 'how do we treat disease in high volumes, in difficult circumstances and across large distances?'
9. Technology/innovation does not work like science – it is a trial and error process focused on impact and scalability rather than a control and test process.
10. What science is able to test changes as contexts and tools change, in this case with the developments in microscopy and chemical synthesis. However the 'wicked problem' remains the same: how do we use what we know to heal people?
11. Translation processes are ongoing – there is not a final end point as 'wicked problems' mutate, and with the growth of resistant strains of bacteria and untreatable infections, the problem mutates.
12. Any 'scaled solution' that delivers impact on the 'wicked problem' will have unintended consequences across impacted populations.

For simplicity we can describe three general processes involved in ensuring that what we know 'helps'.

- Translating field (client problem and response) to 'fact': *from field to lab – mouldy bread to study of mould extracts*. The first process is that from common sense or 'field knowledge' to the creation of the facts we see codified in science and textbooks.
- Translating 'fact' to specific client use: *from lab to single field – the use of mould concentrate in a small hospital practice by a few doctors*. The second process is that

---

PSYCHOSOCIAL TRANSLATION AND MOBILIZATION

Think of an issue in the workplace developed out of 'field' recognition of a problem, that has then been subjected to social science scrutiny. The types of issues could be stress, recruitment, process design, strategy, diversity and inclusion.

- What are the features of this common sense or 'field understanding' about your chosen issue?
- What has the 'science' response been?
- What has the 'practice' response been?
- How many translation steps can you identify in the workplace?
- What mobilization can you see happening around this 'wicked problem'?
- To what extent is this mobilization knowledge-based, or not?
- What has the impact been on people and organizations?
- Which of these is intended and which unintended?

Discuss in groups the questions above based on your chosen topic.

FIGURE 1.2 Discussion: translation points in psychosocial knowledge

involved in taking this 'distilled' or codified set of 'facts' and enabling its focused application context by context. This is where I think we are with psychosocial knowledge.

- Mobilizing by connecting multiple fields: *from single field to multiple fields – the availability of a simple technology that all can access and transport easily*. The third process is that involved in mobilization so taking the embedded fact out into widespread policy and institutional practice.

Figure 1.2 suggests an approach to reflection or group discussion to identify what 'translation' means in day-to-day practice.

This book is specifically focused on the second process itemized above, with full and proper consideration of the current state of knowledge at our disposal from the first process. The history of penicillin outlined in Table 1.1 also points to the strategies, changes and compromises involved in the mobilization of knowledge. Mobilization is not the subject of this text, but is mentioned here for completeness.

Identifying and developing practice capabilities for translation

For the purposes of this book, I have distilled a broad statement of the intervention capabilities that I deploy in day-to-day practice to support ethical change in complex organizations. To outline the full nature of practice capabilities (given our current emphasis on deploying academically driven approaches for intervention) I have undertaken a comparison exercise with the much more widely articulated science capabilities. This comparison exercise serves two purposes. First, it elucidates the very real skills involved in ethical practice. Second, it gives a clear indication that teaching science practices as if they can also be field practices is not appropriate; the two sets of capabilities are quite distinct. By contrast this account, drawn from 30 years of doing such work, describes the capabilities needed by those who would practise in this way.

This comparison is not intended to be critical or to denigrate the importance of science-based practice in knowledge development, but instead to make it clear that translating our knowledge requires a different set of capabilities around problem formulation, how we work with people, how we engage with the collection, processing and storage of evidence and what constitutes good quality output from our work. Of relevance to the emerging research into knowledge-leaders – people who deliberately use knowledge from the academy to change organizations – this 'lab'-based orientation provides a typology of knowledge-leaders, using a research 'oversight' (Fischer et al. 2015).

Table 1.2 indicates that the capabilities required for good practice are distinct from those required for good academic work. I would contend that it is challenging to develop full expertise across both of these different capability sets and the ability to work fully across both domains is very rare. In addition, very often, the ethical use of the capabilities in the left-hand (practice) column, are in conflict with the ethical use of the capabilities in the right-hand (science) column. Such conflicts are not eradicated by subsuming practice as a sub-set of science, but instead by

TABLE 1.2 Comparison of capabilities in practice (field) and academia (lab)

Practice capability overview	*Science capability overview*
1. Engaging with wicked problems, using reflection with awareness of problem mutation	1. Defining bounded problems and setting parameters of control to sustain the focus of inquiry
2. Accessing and using a wide range of evidence from multiple sources	2. Using specific rules about what counts as evidence
3. Working with confidentiality and contracting in the client relationship	3. Complying with informed consent and ethics approval in the research 'subject' relationship
4. Diagnosing client problems for intervention formulation	4. Measurement of research variables against hypothesis
5. Using elaboration and synthesis in the processing of evidence	5. Using reduction and analysis in the collection and processing of data
6 Designing interventions and building a business case for implementation	6. Designing experiments and applying for research funding to run the work
7. Monitoring emergence and enabling course correction	7. Running tests or evaluations
8. Deploying know-how, focused on the tone set in the work	8. Documenting knowledge through peer review and publication
9. Focusing on impact in context	9. Focusing on fact production
The purpose is to help	The purpose is to know

PRACTICE CAPABILITY REVIEW

Based on your experience, compare and contrast practice and science capabilities. Identify two key points of conflict. What are the implications of these conflicts for you in your work?

Choose a potential client need (see Chapter 2, Table 2.1 for ideas). Identify how these practice capabilities would need to be used.

Discuss in pairs/groups the observations you have made and what capabilities are critical.

What are your priority areas of professional development?

FIGURE 1.3 Discussion: practice capability review

treating each as distinct, and developing professionals who manage these ethical and practical tensions as an inherent part of intelligent activism.

As background to this, Schein (1998) outlined three different types of practitioner role:

- the diagnostic role of 'organizational doctor';
- the advisory role of the 'professional expert';
- the inquiry and guidance role of the 'process consultant'.

In his model of different roles, each is seen as bringing a different set of parameters to the helping exchange together with a different set of authorities, boundaries and expectations to manage. The 'organizational doctor' role claims authority from linking data gleaned from the context with a wider knowledge base and indicating what will generate improvement. A 'professional expert' claims authority of knowledge, importing codified professional knowledge into the client context. This pays a much lower level of attention to the context than to the available codified professional knowledge base. Working in a 'process consultant' role assumes that the majority of evidence and relevant knowledge sits with the client and the helping role is one of bringing attention to this, with professional knowledge and facilitation skill directed at enabling the client to take responsibility for the intervention and consequent organizational change.

Schein (1998) considered the process consulting approach to be primary. This approach has been the approach developed in the large consulting firms and in my experience, underpins their use of the leverage model in client growth (Scott 1998). I have considerable experience of people with a broad education, a basic business knowledge being taught how to do process consulting work with little attention to providing them with the knowledge of the factors that can make an organization toxic.

The insights from the translation idea from SSK research suggests that these three are not 'roles', but instead represent phases of knowledge translation all of which need to be at the disposal of a fully capable practitioner. Figure 1.3

provides a reflection exercise to consider the areas of practice capability that you may need to develop.

Fundamentally, when working as a practitioner we need to work with trust in the scientific outputs from the disciplines we draw on. Often I am told that I (as a practitioner) need to undertake a detailed review of each piece of literature that I use in supporting my work with clients. While this may be something that I choose to do when afforded the luxury of Continuing Professional Development (CPD) time, I would suggest that this is not an appropriate use of my time when fully engaged in working with a client need, often associated with some distress or anxiety. There is always extensive evidence from the specific context, and it is more important to engage with this to be able to 'help' appropriately. Instead, I suggest that any practitioner needs to understand and trust, not 'mark the homework', of the academics working in a distinct activity.

A model of the phases of translation for 'intelligent activism'

For the purpose of this textbook, I have generated a simplified model of the work involved in effective translation of 'fact' to client impact, which I have built over my years of professional psychology practice in complex workplaces.

Knowledge translation stages in intelligent activism

The process of intervening in organizations as a psychologist or other practitioner is a process of translating 'fact' into 'practice'. Knowledge must change form and substance from phase to phase of the translation work. In addition, as the content of scientific output develops and the pressures and priorities of clients' organizations change so the substance of what is included needs to change. For those of us that have built a career as practitioners it is the dynamic nature of translating emerging knowledge into changing complex environments that makes the work engaging and rewarding.

Although these six phases of translation work are listed in Table 1.3, this does not imply that any practitioner in any particular client setting would necessarily move in a linear way through them. In each of these phases there are complex multi-stakeholder processes at play. In addition, any practitioner can specialize in any one of these phase of translation and can engage in a full intervention cycle (outlined in Chapter 3) within one aspect of practice. Understanding the different ways in which these aspects can fit together to help a client is addressed in Chapter 3, Figure 3.2. Of critical importance is that you know where you are. The combination of client presentation, resource availability and diagnosis of need will determine what phases of translation are drawn together to provide help.

It is also worth noting that there are various practitioners with different qualifications specializing in different aspects of translation. Designers for example are

TABLE 1.3 Phases of psychosocial knowledge translation

The phases of psychosocial knowledge translation

Help [1]	1. The cry for help *'Knowing why'*
Insight [2]	2. Insight *'Knowing that'*
Design [3]	3. Designing into context *'Knowing what'*
Action [4]	4. Implementation *'Knowing how'*
Adapt [5]	5. Monitoring and course correction *'Adapting to real-time feedback'*
Support [6]	6. Social support *'Coaching how'*

extremely skilled and specialized in phases two and three, professional project managers have codified approaches for phases four and five. Recently, phase six (coaching) has been established as a distinct and stand-alone service.

Being able to understand and work across these different phases of translation is necessary but not sufficient for ethical practice. The other considerations are listed in Table 1.4 as a set of meta-level knowledge practices that also need to factor into the development of practice capabilities.

TABLE 1.4 Meta-level knowledge practices

Meta-level knowledge practices	
7 Build facts	7. Academic literature *Building, agreeing and storing facts*
8 Evaluate	8. Evaluation and best practice *The 'grey' matter*
9 Self in action	9. Self as 'change agent' *Being capably human in a human system*
10 Self in learning	10. Continuing professional development *Sharpening the intellect*

Conclusion

This chapter has covered how knowledge gets translated for impact and the practice capabilities required to do this successfully. I would argue that at this stage psychosocial practice in the workplace needs greater clarity about:

- what makes it distinctive
- how to make it impactful.

If we do not engage with the processes of knowledge translation we are in danger of our 'facts' being nothing more than a point of curiosity from a 'laboratory'. Psychosocial knowledge and practice has tremendous potential to influence the world of work positively and both understanding the knowledge and learning the skills to deploy this are the aims of the remaining text.

Further reading

For the theory behind the way in which science and technology generate impact:

Bijker, W. E., Hughes, T. P. and Pinch, T. J. (eds) (1987) *The Social Construction of Technological Systems: New Directions in the Sociology and History of Technology*. Cambridge, MA: MIT Press.

Callon, M., Law, J. and Rip, A. (eds) (1986) *Mapping the Dynamics of Science and Technology*. London: Macmillan.

Latour, B. and Woolgar, S. (1986) *Laboratory Life: The Construction of Scientific Facts*. Princeton, NJ: Princeton University Press.

References

Callon, M. (1986) The sociology of an actor-network: The case of the electric vehicle. In M. Callon, J. Law and A. Rip (eds) *Mapping the Dynamics of Science and Technology*. London: MacMillan.

Fischer, M. D., Dopson, S., Fitzgerald, L., et al. (2015) Knowledge leadership: Mobilizing management research by becoming the knowledge object. *Human Relations*. Epub ahead of print 14 December 2015. DOI: 10.1177/0018726715619686.

Handy, C. (1995) *The Age of Paradox*. Cambridge, MA: Harvard Business Press.

Harris, L. C. and Ogbonna, E. (2002) The unintended consequences of culture interventions: A study of unexpected outcomes. *British Journal of Management* 13(1): 31–49.

Hays-Thomas, R. (2006) Challenging the scientist–practitioner model: Questions about I-O education and training. http://www.siop.org/UserFiles/Image/TIP/july06/SheridanPDFs/441_047to053.pdf.

Johnson, B. (1992) *Polarity Management: Identifying and Managing Unsolvable Problems*. Amherst, MA: HRD Press.

Latour, B. (1988) *The Pasteurisation of France*. Cambridge, MA: Harvard University Press.

Muchinsky, P. M. (2006) *Psychology Applied to Work* (8th edn). Belmont, CA: Thomson.

Rittel, H. W. J. and Webber, M. (1973) Dilemmas in a general theory of planning. *Policy Sciences* 4: 155–169.

Schein, E. H. (1998) *Process Consultation. Volume 1: Its Role in Organization Development* (2nd edn). Prentice Hall Organizational Development Series. London: FT Press.

Schein, E. H. (2009) *Helping: How to Offer, Give and Receive Help*. San Francisco, CA: Berrett-Koehler Publishers.

Scott, M. C. (1998) *The Intellect Industry*. Chichester: John Wiley.

Spier, R. (2001) *Ethics, Tools, and the Engineer*. London: CRC Press.

2

UNDERSTANDING CLIENT ENGAGEMENT DYNAMICS

Introduction

A critical feature of practice is that the 'problem' is client driven and not defined by the professional practitioner. The engagement dynamic starts with a request for help and the following chapter outlines a set of heuristics (guidelines or rules of thumb) to navigate the complexities of being pulled in to help in complex client contexts. Client expressions of need in such complex contexts will inherently be diffuse, complicated and usually have input from many varied sources.

The cry for help: establishing the client relationship

From the very first client request, usually linked to a complex and diffuse issue, intelligent activism demands a focus on mitigating toxicity through careful attention to the diagnostic approach taken and to the tone that is set in the associated inquiry. Part II of this book covers what we know about organizational toxicity, but intelligent activism is about deploying know-how and it requires psychosocial role modelling (Bandura 1977) of what is healthful, throughout the engagement to ensure intervention does not become a source of unintended toxicity in the client organization.

The engagement encounter is a critical intervention in its own right, regardless of what else emerges through the life span of the client work. While topic considerations are active, it is critical to attend to how practitioner actions and style of inquiry impacts the relevant psychosocial micro processes in the client context: such as asking, what is the impact on perceptions of accountability, compassion, appreciation and growth (see Chapter 8)? This is often referred to as the idea of 'self as change agent' in the Organizational Development (OD) literature (e.g. Cheung-Judge and Holbeche 2011: ch. 10). The issue of self-regulation is explored in Chapter 5 on practice ethics in complex workplaces.

Practically a client request for help comes in a variety of forms: an invitation to tender; a client request for a face-to-face meeting or a telephone call; or via a passing comment with you as an internal colleague. The engagement process is discursive and often partial so requires inquiry and elaboration, and there is rarely a predicable and defined problem that needs to be 'solved'. Handling this first phase requires careful relational work.

The types of help requested

We all find it really difficult to ask for help, particularly if we feel we are exposing a professional or positional vulnerability or weakness. Any attempt to render the client issue quickly down into a defined problem statement is inherently unhelpful. Time and contact with context is needed to be able to work alongside this vulnerability associated with asking for help and so to understand the request sufficiently well. This is critical to identify what help the client is actually asking for. Learning a new context and its history is time consuming and evidence-rich and yet is inherent to effective intervention. Schein (2009: 17) suggests that the 'process of perpetual mutual reinforcement is the essence of society. We have all experienced the tension that arises when we are in a new culture and don't know the rules of mutual acknowledgement.' To define the problem too quickly is to fail in the area of mutual acknowledgement, regardless of the specific topic and so risk being expelled from the social setting. This necessary 'fuzziness' in engaging across the client boundary is a distinct capability for effective practice and is in sharp contrast to the analytic approach used when defining a problem within the bounds of a lab for a research endeavour.

To provide example-based content to bring the engagement process to life, Table 2.1 gives 20 vignettes of first point client 'cries for help', all taken from notes kept during my professional career.

TABLE 2.1 Example client requests for help

1. In a financial services business: the Head of Learning and Development, following the release of a new HR function wide people strategy, stated to her preferred consultant: 'we have no clear pipeline to replace our Heads of Function across the business and don't know what to do about this'.

2. In a construction management firm: a Site Manager finding it difficult to get the necessary people to work on a remote project, comments to an internal OD consultant: 'we are thinking about offering an apprentice scheme and we're not yet clear how this will fit with the capability matrix we are meant to use'.

3. In an engineering company: an Operations Director, who has been criticized for failing to meet her business targets, states to one of her direct reports: 'we need to speed up our rehab from back problems. We never have enough people available.' She calls an HR consultant she knows.

4. In a retail business: the Marketing Director, without making any reference to the work the HR function is doing, calls his preferred consultants and states: 'our customer satisfaction levels are dropping and we think we should invest in an internal brand engagement programme'.

5. In an outsourcing business: the Executive Vice President (EVP) of a global IT function states: 'we are restructuring to take advantage of market changes. We need a new operating model to integrate three regional divisions and need help to design and deliver this' and asks the internal OD function for help.

6. In an IT company: the Head of Corporate Responsibility who is concerned with growing the internal profile of the work says to a small consulting firm 'we need advice on behaviour change and communications approaches around our environmental initiatives'.

7. In a transport business: the Head of the Programme Management Office looks for a consultant who can help because: 'our strategic change budgets have overrun and the senior leadership team (SLT) is complaining about data quality, how do we fix this?'

8. In a construction firm: a senior HR business partner asks his preferred small consulting firm: 'could you arrange some team-building as there is some tension among our commercial division leadership team?'

9. In a financial services business: the Employee Engagement Manager states: 'we are due a re-bid for our staff survey and the SLT want a greater emphasis on what we can do about the output we get from it' and so with the procurement department pulls together a detailed Request for Information (RFI) to be sent to suppliers.

10. In a mining and metals business: the Director of Operations, having already challenged the effectiveness of the resourcing team states to her HR business partner: 'we are not getting the right calibre of candidates and need help'.

11. In a food retail business: the CEO asserts to the SLT: 'we need a leadership development programme because our store managers are not implementing our policies properly and our market share is dropping off a cliff'. The HR director approaches a large consulting firm outlining this, but saying that this is probably not what is needed to solve the actual problem.

12. In an NHS organization: the HR Director asks an external OD consultant: 'our staff survey is showing a dramatic increase in reported bullying in one department and we must do something about it. Maybe we need a coaching programme? Would mindfulness help?'

13. In a logistics business: the Head of Procurement, after being criticized by Sales and Marketing asks for help from a consulting firm saying: 'we have a seven-year contract with one supplier for managing all our customer calls and we are having a real issue with sales conversion rates and escalating complaints. We need to make this a best in class relationship.'

14. In an IT business: the Sales Director, after an organization wide cost saving edict is issued asks an internal consultant: 'cos we have to reduce departmental spend by 10 per cent, it will probably mean job losses and I'm not sure what is the best approach'.

15. In a B2B services firm: the Programme Director responsible for developing a new business led D&I approach asks: 'how do we make our Black Network (BN) work in the UK? The US approach they tried here has failed twice' (see Chapter 11, case two).

16. In a transport sector organization: the OD Director after being criticized for transactional HR spend puts out a tender for: 'a review of the options as we think that it would be much more cost effective to outsource our HR function?'

17. In a construction business: the SLT when reviewing business performance asks the HR Director: 'we think we should implement the Ulrich (1997) model, how do we make that work here?' The HR director then calls her preferred consultant.

(continued)

TABLE 2.1 *(continued)*

18. In a public sector organization: the Employee Relations Manager, after the quarterly negotiation meeting with the three unions active in the organization says to an internal OD consultant: 'our front line supervisors don't know how to manage people, we are really worried about a strike, we need to put something in place quickly to deal with this'.

19. In a fast moving customer goods (FMCG) business: a Marketing Manager asks a small consulting firm: 'we need to be more customer-focused because our customers are leaving many of our brands, what would you suggest, we are thinking about setting up an Invitation to Tender?'

20. In a higher education establishment: after serious student complaints the Dean of Faculty asks an independent consultant: 'I am concerned that we have a serious and exposing issue with department X. Could you provide an independent audit?'

Initial inquiry

It is critical that a practitioner does not move too quickly to categorize and define the 'content' or 'solution', as this action works to silence the client. This can potentially set up a dynamic of client dependency or consultant rejection. It makes it harder to get answers to critical questions, the consequence of which is mis-understanding and a client perception that the practitioner is neither helpful nor informed.

Handling client engagement is not just about understanding the specific issue, but also the context, the likelihood that a piece of work will materialize from the exchange and the probable operating space for the practitioner should the engagement come to fruition. The information about the specific context that any practitioner needs to explicitly listen for when engaging with client requests for help is given in Table 2.2.

Figure 2.1 outlines exercises using the contents of Tables 2.1 and 2.2 to explore how to work with these pressures.

EXERCISES TO EXPLORE THE FIRST STAGES OF CLIENT ENGAGEMENT

Exercise 1: As a group or as an individual, select two of the vignette examples given in Table 2.1. Design the inquiry approach for a first client meeting to take the work forward to get answers to the context questions listed in Table 2.2.

Exercise 2: Go through each of the vignettes given in Table 2.1 and identify what knowledge from the various taught topics that you have encountered needs to influence your approach to the problem and how you think you could broker the knowledge you have into the problem elaboration in a way that could make sense in this context.

FIGURE 2.1 Discussion: exploring client engagement

TABLE 2.2 Tacit context inquiry

Tacit context inquiry questions

1. Where does the client (organization) start in naming the issue? How does this expand?
2. What gets included in (or excluded) in their framing of the need?
3. How flexible is the organization in working with acts of reframing as part of the inquiry process?
4. Who is the budget holder and what are the limits to their authority?
5. What is the authority of the person you are in conversation with?
6. What does the stakeholder landscape look like? Are there any key people you need to speak to?
7. What has been attempted before and what are the organizational stories around this?
8. What form does the request come in and what are the options to convert this into a clear intervention offered by a practitioner?
9. What is the political and positional pressure on the individual who is expressing the need/managing the supply process?
10. What will constitute a good outcome for each person you are engaging with as a practitioner?
11. What will the expectations be on the practitioner from the different stakeholders in the context? How do they vary? Are there any conflicts?
12. What if any ethical issues are raised for you from the initial impressions gained?

Codifying the client engagement structure

Navigating the client political context is an inherent part of working ethically with accountability/authority in complex organizations. How the engagement gets structured is a critical practical part of this initial relationship. Within this, it is necessary to consider whether you are delivering within a consulting style or supply-based engagement structure. Understanding the difference is critical to determining what you can do within the structure and what 'good' looks like. The ethics of contracting and confidentiality associated with client engagements are covered in Chapter 5. The two broad types of engagement structure are:

- Supplier engagement structure: Are you being commissioned to deliver something directly as if you are a function in the organization? This could be offering an assessment function, the delivery of a defined coaching programme for the business or running an annual employee engagement survey for an organization. Very often this can be commissioned as part of business as usual (BAU) (see vignette 13 in Table 2.1) rather than as a change or intervention-focused approach.
- Consulting engagement structure: The key question is are you being commissioned to support others in doing their work? This is based upon the implicit notion of intervening in a situation that needs to change, by working with

those in organizations (see vignette 1 in Table 2.1). This could be through a piece of work or intervention design, facilitation or in outlining the concept designs to develop a new operating model.

This distinction works whether you are commissioned as an employee covered by an employment contract or through a contract for services, in a business-to-business contract. In order to be effective in helping a client, it is critical to be clear which engagement structure you are working in at any one time. Each requires quite a different approach to reporting, monitoring, escalation and change control around the work commissioned and around the contract management discipline. To illustrate the differences, Figure 2.2 applies Jacques' (1991) analysis of two different hierarchically framed delivery mechanisms. One is the idea of 'Delegated Output' and the other is 'Aided Direct Output Support'.

Traps in the engagement dynamics

Schein (2009) identifies the traps in the client–practitioner helping relationship that need to be considered, which have been adapted in Table 2.3. It is at the early stages that these can be most risky as the pattern of the engagement and expectations gets set.

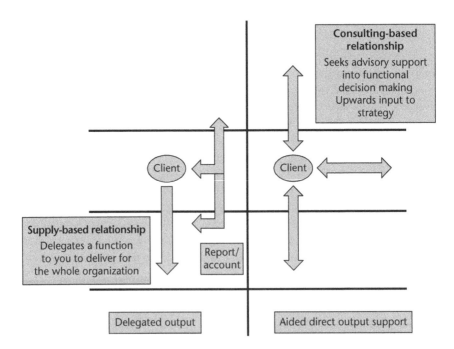

FIGURE 2.2 Engagement structures

TABLE 2.3 Traps in the helping relationship

Traps for the practitioner/helper (after Schein 2009)	Traps for the client (after Schein 2009)
Dispensing wisdom prematurely	Initial mistrust
Meeting defensiveness with pressure	Relief and abdication of responsibility
Taking the problem on too fully and creating dependency	Looking for attention and validation rather than help
Giving support and reassurance rather than help	Resentment and defensiveness
Resisting the helper role	Resisting the client role

Client preferences in accessing help

When approached by a client for help, in addition to absorbing the context, it is also important to listen for the following three key 'meta-variables' as they give key insights into how intervention can best be undertaken and framed in the specific environment:

- the presenting topics that are raised (together with those that are implicit);
- the improvement pathway suggested in the way the client frames the request;
- the client 'orientation' which clarifies the translation phases (Table 1.3) they are likely to be most comfortable with.

The presenting topic

Within the psychosocial consulting arena there are a wide range of potential topic-based requests. These are topics such as strategy, talent and succession, employee well-being, organizational and work design, team building, employee engagement and leadership, employee survey design, assessment and recruitment, managing counter-productive behaviour, diversity and inclusion (D&I), outsourcing, HR function re-design, customer centricity.

If you review the vignettes given in Table 2.1, the requests made rarely match the discipline structure that an academic course of study will use. Different topics often overlap in real client contexts and it is necessary to interpret the client presentation of an issue and make the connection to areas of knowledge, ideally without immediately re-framing the problem to the client. This exploration also allows time for an effective self-check on professional competence, expertise and comfort with the broad area. One of the critical aspects of ethical professional practice at this stage is to pass the work on or decline if the request or need is not in keeping with your assessment of your competence or the ethical obligations on you. Even when it may appear obvious what is required from an approach covering a specific topic (e.g. case three in Table 2.1) in cases such as this, the presenting problem (the need for rehab) can merely be a surface symptom of a much deeper systemic issue. Figure 2.3 gives a brief outline of such an experience from a consulting engagement I conducted on a large construction project.

ROOT CAUSE ASSESSMENT FOR CLIENT ENGAGEMENT

I was asked to help with a safety programme on a large construction site that had seen a dramatic increase in injuries and was at risk of being closed until the cause of the increased injury rate could be identified and resolved. They had already commissioned advice from safety experts and work-flow design and implemented various changes, but the problem had not been resolved.

I asked the Programme Director if I could run a series of focus groups, to explore with the 150 members of the construction team what they thought the issues were, before designing the detailed programme requested. This was viewed as a rather odd request, but I was given permission to do this and listened to two full days of small groups of 20 talk together about issues of unfairness, different pay levels across different groups, not knowing what was going on, working longer hours than they had agreed and a wide range of other concerns and points of tension and frustration. Following the two days' work the injury rate started dropping and within two weeks had returned to the controlled rate required.

The issue was not the injury rate, the issue was the tension associated with felt unfairness, lack of voice and the absence of compassion. The simple creation of space to participate in effective psychosocial micro processing was enough to enable people to self-regulate and self-monitor. So often, asking the right question of the right people is the only intervention required as it allows both a deeper engagement and a simpler resolution.

FIGURE 2.3 A deeper and yet simpler problem

The preferred client improvement pathway

Requests for help do not need to be based on something framed as being 'wrong' or define the existence of a problem. A request can emerge when a supplier contract is up and the client decides to run a market test of supplier options, with a desire to sustain business as usual (BAU) with the best possible supply contract. Requests for help can also be associated with ideas of improvement, development and strategic advantage. The types of 'pathways' I have encountered during my practice can be summarized in the five trajectories in Table 2.4.

During problem elaboration/diagnosis it is helpful to notice the pathway the client is implicitly or explicitly expecting. Any mismatch in the way a practitioner

TABLE 2.4 Client engagement pathways

Type of pathway	Example in Table 2.1
1. BAU → BAU: change in supplier	Case 9
2. Broken → functional: problem	Case 8
3. Cluttered → clean: improvement	Case 16
4. Good → great: innovation	Case 5
5. Broken → great: strategic ambition	Case 13

engages with the request is likely to be considered unhelpful, unless it is a carefully negotiated challenge to the client perception, undertaken for a specific reason.

Client orientation towards the type of help preferred

Different clients and organizational cultures will have different preferences for the type of help they commission. Clients differ in the extent to which they are comfortable talking about things as problems or whether they want to focus on solutions. They vary in whether they are describing a strategic perspective on a topic or a short-term responsive view. Some clients are very comfortable with the idea of solving problems, as would be enabled through approaches such as, for example, Positive Deviance. Other clients are much more comfortable taking a 'strength-based approach' as reflected in Positive Psychology and so would be more open to methods such as Appreciative Inquiry (see methodologies outlined in Chapter 4).

Any specific issue can be presented in a wide variety of different ways and the purpose of using this orientation lens is to tune into this aspect of the client context as it becomes available to you early in the conversation. The four point star diagram in Figure 2.4 summarizes the four potential types of intervention orientation that you may receive.

A client orientation is neither right nor wrong; it is data and is a critical part of the early evidence you need to collect. The orientation preference will be built from an organizationally grounded understanding of what is going on and 'how things get done around here' and it provides further field evidence of 'culture' that needs to be worked with to provide help in the specific context. Table 2.5 outlines in brief the characteristics of these different orientations.

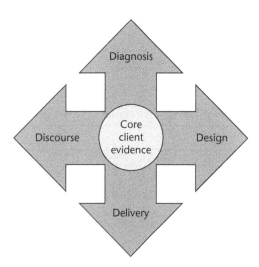

FIGURE 2.4 Client orientation

TABLE 2.5 Descriptions of client orientations

Orientation	Approach to intervention
Diagnosis	To understand the cause of a situation and so to have an indication of what might work to change the organizational situation
Design	To generate a new intervention or project that will make a change to the specified area
Delivery	To manage the implementation of defined 'solution' to generate the required change in organizational practice
Discourse	To enable better conversations and engagement to support collaborative work at any or all levels in an organization

Each orientation encourages a different starting point for dialogue and indicates an important aspect of client expectations. Any practitioner is likely to prefer one of these orientations over the others, but to be able to help, it is important to be able to move fluidly between these different intervention orientations. For example, I have worked in client contexts that are very data hungry and value a diagnostically framed approach. Regularly the challenge in such contexts is to help them move out of analysis and so the help needed is to aid momentum.

By contrast other client organizations have been much more delivery focused in their orientation and the key practitioner skill is enabling a sharing of data and evidence to support action, but without requiring an explicit diagnostic phase. These preferences represent culturally different ways of framing a request for help and guiding the helper on suitability for the context.

To try to bring the idea of client orientation to life, in Table 2.6 I have outlined four different client requests I have been presented with, all of which were connected to the same issue emerging in practice; the psychosocial issues associated with the oppressive design of call centres in 1990s, which all needed broadly the same intervention work but very different client management. The difference in orientation meant the approach developed was subtly different in each case, although the underlying issue was the same.

TABLE 2.6 Requests for help and client orientation

Request for help	Orientation
We don't understand why we have such a high absence rate in our service centre	Diagnosis
We need to come up with a way to improve motivation for our service centre staff to increase productivity	Design
We have bought a customer service training package and need help to implement it	Delivery
Our service centre leadership team doesn't appear to get on as well as we would like and we'd like some team building	Discourse

It must be noted that 'decision making' is not listed as one of the client orientations. The scope for the practitioner to make or influence decisions will be defined by the contract structure agreed as there will be areas that come within the practitioner's discretion. However, the exclusion of decision making as a client orientation is deliberate, because the authority to make decisions is vested via an organization in the context of whatever business structure and legal jurisdiction the organization works within. With this authority there must be accountability and ill-considered consultant actions can decouple this (see Chapter 7: structural source of toxicity and Chapter 8: accountability cluster).

The attempt to abdicate decision making to a third party is one of the mechanisms by which toxic accountability disorders emerge. If there is a sense of abdication of decision making in the client context, it is important to be very wary of engaging with any such requests. There can often be frustration in client exchanges about the nature of recommendations given and the lack of clarity around what it means they should do. These frustrations are inherent to the proper support for suitably authorized decision making. It maybe that the client does need help with formulating a decision, and may seek to be provided with recommendations, but no reasonable request for help will require a practitioner to make that decision for them or tell them exactly what to do.

Conclusion

This chapter has covered how client engagements get presented and activated, the range of work needed to develop this into an effective helping relationship and how client preferences manifest and need to be worked with as the intervention work unfolds.

Intelligent activism inherent in ethical practice is complex and requires respectful and ethical openness to the client context within which the work is to be done, together with highly developed disciplines around self-regulation focused on the obligation to do no harm (see Chapter 5).

It is necessary to approach client engagement in a manner that models the necessary awareness of psychosocial relationships to ensure that any action or intervention from the practitioner is not a source of toxicity for the client organization which runs counter to approaches that codify a single psychosocial 'idea' or 'solution' as the basis for intervention.

References

Bandura, A. (1977) *Social Learning Theory*. New York: General Learning Press.

Cheung-Judge, M. Y. and Holbeche, L. (2011) *Organization Development: A Practitioner's Guide for OD and HR*. London and Philadelphia, PA: Kogan Page.

Jacques, E. (1991) *Requisite Organization*. Arlington, VA: Cason Hall Publishers.

Schein, E. H. (2009) *Helping: How to Offer, Give and Receive Help*. San Francisco, CA: Berrett-Koehler Publishers.

Ulrich, D. (1997) *Human Resources Champions*. Cambridge, MA: Harvard University Press.

3
IDEAS OF INTERVENTION AND CHANGE IN ORGANIZATIONS

Introduction

There are many different ideas of consulting, organizational change and intervention from a wide variety of different perspectives, focused on a wide variety of different presenting issues. This range is outlined in Table 7.1 in Chapter 7 looking at the macro sources of organizational toxicity. The purpose of this chapter is to give three perspectives on this topic as the basis for reflection and to question the idea that there is value in the articulation of a simple consulting or organizational change method. This is structured into the following sections:

- What is wrong with the idea of the consulting cycle?
- What is organizational intervention?
- Change programmes and change platforms: an exploration.

What is wrong with the idea of the consulting cycle?

The consulting cycle (Woods and West 2010) lays out a simplistic set of steps in the client engagement process. The steps given broadly are:

- contracting
- problem diagnosis/identification
- identify options for intervention
- choose solution
- implementation
- evaluate solution.

Based upon my experience of organizational intervention I consider that the simple formulation given in the consulting cycle is problematic, because it is framed as a problem-solving model rather than from the perspective of a helping relationship.

I tried to use these steps in my early years but began to reject them, as they were unhelpful to my understanding both of client relationship and delivery. I consider that the rational, problem-solving-based method statement in this formulation is rooted in the scientific thinking which, as outlined in Chapter 1, is not fully translated for field application.

From the perspective of a mundane jobbing practitioner, I am now confident to say that this model does not work. It felt like a rework of the process steps taught for research work being imposed onto a field context, and I found it unfit for purpose. Most of the work I did (that had the desired client impact) was 'off-piste' as far as this model is concerned. I finally decided it was the model at fault rather than me. I suffered from a lot of mistakes in the field that were quite bruising before I gained the confidence to say this. I have four practical reasons for my view.

'Contracting' is an ongoing piece of work throughout any engagement

Contracting is not a 'stage'. While there will be a point when a formal contract is in place, this does not necessarily define all the delivery requirements of any intervention. The linear nature of the consulting model implies a bounded contract stage with a single authority (rather like that which comes with a research grant) rather than a complex stakeholder environment where changing resource factors (billing, budgets, timescales, etc.) must be managed in real time, alongside delivery. Expectations management, course correction and managing the consequences of change are critical, ongoing contracting skills necessary to ensure that the intervention process is able and seen to adapt to meet the developing need as it unfolds in real time.

There is not always the scope or time for 'diagnosis' as a distinct stage

However, a client has asked for and needs help. The luxury of an extended problem definition stage is not usually available when engaged to help with a real-time 'wicked problem'. If there is enough time for this, you may well have a client environment that needs to move to the action end of the translation phases to detox 'stuck-ness' (an attachment disorder – see Chapter 9). The opportunity for real diagnostic engagement comes as the emerging client–practitioner relationship grows in trust.

Diagnosis therefore needs to be understood as an ongoing and developing aspect of client engagement rather than a step in a process that has to happen before anything else can be done. The danger in seeing this as a stage is either that the proposed diagnostic work is too expensive and too abstract to be commissioned, or at the other extreme a practitioner jumps to a quick diagnostic conclusion to complete the stage and implements interventions that are not helpful or potentially can do harm.

No space for creativity, design, monitoring and course correction

The formulation of the consulting cycle makes no clear provision for the phase of creative design work or the trial and error that is inherent in the move to implementation (see design thinking methods, outlined in Chapter 4). It also does not allow for the stakeholder and coaching work needed to help those in a complex workplace move from the 'intention' stage to 'emergence into action'. Abrahams (2013) has described this as working with behavioural oscillation. Instead there appears to be an implicit assumption that making a decision 'causes' an implementation. Decision and action are not the same.

Our work as practitioners is creative, emotional work, intimately connected with the 'living tissue' of an organization and has the potential to cause unintended harm. It is not merely an act of rationally exploring options to make a decision. Given this, we must allow for monitoring and course correction (as an inherent safety mechanism) to be built in as an integral part of the design process.

Including evaluation as a stage is erroneous

Evaluation is not properly part of a helping relationship with a client but is instead a piece of meta-level knowledge work (see Chapter 1, Table 1.4). The first issue with evaluation is that it does not directly (or even indirectly) help a client, as it is undertaken too late to support the helping exchange with any specific client. The second issue is that to evaluate properly is expensive.

To suggest to a client that they should make such an investment with so little return is ethically questionable. I would suggest that instead a proper and respectful consideration of what is expected from the client funds allocated is necessary. Figure 3.1 gives a 'thought experiment' to illuminate this issue. Measurement in this context needs to be based on benefits tracking with a feed into a course correction framework.

A new model of translation dynamics

In contrast to this simplistic linear model, my experience informed by over 25 years of practice is that practice takes place in a complex set of dynamic translation processes. These dynamics include the movements between different aspects of knowledge translation. These dynamics are illustrated in Figure 3.2 using the icons from Chapter 1, Tables 1.3 and 1.4.

WOULD YOU PAY FOR EVALUATION?

To illustrate, if you as an individual had to pay for surgery and consequent treatment, due to being diagnosed (e.g. with a cancerous tumour), I would predict that as part of this surgery and treatment you would except to get constant individual monitoring of your anaesthesia levels (to mitigate against the risks of a negative outcome from the procedure) and your vital signs to check on your return to health.

I predict your focus would be on ensuring that you were well and remained well – so you would use one single yes/no 'evaluation criterion', and if you were not well, 'evaluation' would not change the outcome for you.

If you survived surgery and treatment you would be unlikely to volunteer to pay again, for an evaluation of what you went through, or how it worked.

If at a national level, a society wanted to evaluate surgical outcomes across different regions that is a whole different discussion and certainly not part of a normal treatment cycle.

If your surgeon wanted to include you in such an evaluation programme you might agree (but you might not and this would be appropriately your decision) but you would not expect to pay for participation. You might even expect a fee for your time.

Suggesting that a client invests in an evaluation of a programme is equivalent to this scenario. We need to be much clearer about the use of measurement and knowledge development in the organizational intervention processes we advocate.

FIGURE 3.1 Evaluation is not part of client engagement

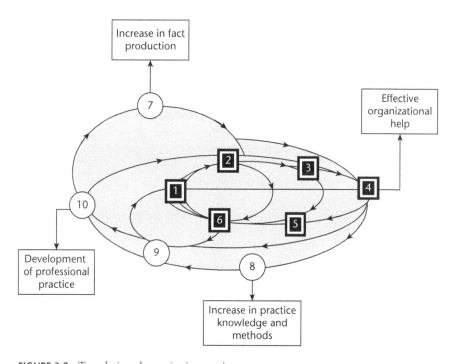

FIGURE 3.2 Translation dynamics in practice

Central to this practice-based dynamic model, is the 'call for help' and that there are four distinct outputs from these dynamics:

1. to provide effective organizational help;
2. to increase practice knowledge and methods;
3. to develop individual professional practice skills;
4. to increase 'fact' production.

Figure 3.2 shows that the dynamics around best practice and knowledge production are distinct from the dynamics of engagement with clients.

The key intersection between 'fact' production and client engagement, I would suggest, is at the insight stage of translation, and these insights might not be directly shared with a client. If they are shared, it can be in a wide variety of ways; it could be through insights being embedded into coaching advisory work or by influencing the way the later stages of work are designed and delivered.

At any point we need to be clear about the purpose of any specific work we are engaged in. In my view only the first of these is an appropriate purpose for a client engagement process and if there is any other intent, we need to be clear that this could bring a potential conflict of interest. Should a client choose to invest in any of the three other purposes listed above, this needs to be treated as a distinct activity with a distinct set of contractual arrangements defined around it.

What is organizational intervention?

The critical issue that underpins the idea of the consulting cycle is that intervention is being proposed that cuts into the living tissue of an organization and so needs to work helpfully with the systemic nature of the commissioning client. Considering the idea of intervention is necessary as it describes a particular intent. Intervention is an important concept as it is widely used in discussing developments in organizations, institutions and the provision of health, social care and education. Dictionary definitions are always a helpful starting point and two are given below:

- Oxford dictionary: 'To come between spaces, places, people and events to change something.'
- Merriam-Webster dictionary: 'To interfere with an outcome or course so as to prevent harm or improve functioning.'

These definitions cover both the process and the intent, and give a very clear indication of what constitutes intervention in organizations:

- The process is active: 'to come between' and hence points to getting into the fabric of the organization to change how it functions; not what it knows, but what it does.
- It is focused on improvement, the intent to 'help'.

The elaborated definition I use for intervention is as follows:

> Intervention in the workplace is theoretically pragmatic, that is, for positive impact, the insights applied are evidence based, the design is focused on improving the psychological environment and there is a commitment to monitored implementation with real-time adjustments as required.
>
> It requires organizing a small-scale disruption, often orchestrating a series of such disruptions, to a dynamic organizational context. The assumption is that small, aligned disruptions work towards improving the conditions, which in turn will enable a positive change in outcomes.
>
> Alignment of disruptions happens through the orchestration of a 'platform' and the wide participation of organizational members. This is manifested through seasonal intervention cycles designed to deliver engagement and rapidly tested prototypes for real-time implementation.

In parallel with the macro level understanding of translation dynamics, there are also micro processes unfolding in intervention, illustrated in Figure 3.3. I describe this as trial and error, but it is much more an experience of the organization giving you continuous subtle feedback about the impact of the intended disruption you are generating and the speed at which you are working.

During my practice I have undertaken organizational intervention from a wide variety of role positions across complex organizations, each of which has required

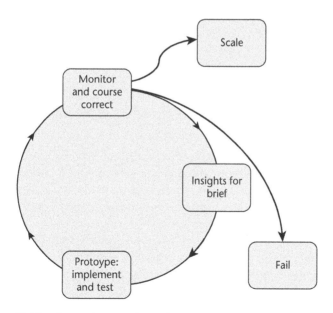

FIGURE 3.3 Trial and error intervention micro processes

ROLE IMPACT ON INTERVENTION STYLE

Consider the following different roles

- Working as a consultant external to an organization running design and development processes that include large and small group facilitation.
- Working as an internal senior leader delivering a new global operating model design and implementation.
- Working as an external organizational effectiveness auditor following reputational exposure, both legal and brand.
- Working as a coach, confidante and adviser (both internally and externally).
- Working as an external supplier, commissioned to deliver specified branding, social media and communication skills training.
- Working as an internal team leader.

Questions for group discussion

- Identify what you consider to be the key responsibilities of each position.
- What impact do you think each different role/position will/should have on how an intervention approach can work?
- What help may be needed to enable an individual in each of these roles to be able to intervene successfully?
- Consider what social science knowledge you already have that may feed into the 'management of self' for each of these roles.

FIGURE 3.4 Discussion: role position and intervention

me to approach the work in a distinctive fashion, but in each the trial and error micro process is an inherent part of the work. The exercise in Figure 3.4 is designed to encourage individual reflection about role position and practice.

Time horizons and intervention work

Time is a critical consideration in thinking about organizational intervention. This is both whether the focus is past or future and (when future) whether it is short term or long term:

- Past focused, which is the work of learning from experience or the approach taken if an audit of a serious malfunction is required. The reason I raise this past orientation in the context of intervention, is where the 'lab'-based ideas of problem solving help. I use this perspective in organizational audit engagements delivering a formal inquiry associated with a serious problem.
- Future focused, which is the work of creating what will be. This is where the idea of intervention sits. Intervention practice requires the capacity to work in real time with uncertainty.

A strategic long-term orientation in a large organization leads to better mid-term organizational performance than a short-term focus (Brauer 2013). However, it is also important to acknowledge the political reality of the focus on short-term viability and accountability in complex organizations. It is critical to recognize that both these time frames are always in operation as intervention is a 'disruption' in the short term designed to have a longer-term impact.

To avoid activating the short-term/long-term dispute I tend to use a different set of terms, to describe the two time frames that we need to work with in organizational intervention:

- Stewardship – for example, the stewardship of the land requires an attention to the conditions that maintain its capacity over the long term to be healthy and productive and hence the intrinsic value of the land and the types of investment required to sustain it as productive beyond immediate needs – without this attention we may have a harvest today but will have no food in the future.
- Seasonality – for example, the process and understanding of planting and harvesting is undertaken on a seasonal basis that needs detailed tending and responsiveness to emerging conditions to ensure that immediate productivity is maximized through the vicissitudes of weather, plague and conflict – without this continuous attention to the present we have no food now.

In the context of intervention in the workplace, stewardship encourages a focus on orchestration and the alignment of organizational change. In parallel a seasonality approach enables action through locally defined intervention priorities of different groups and interests around an organization. This combination is shown in Figure 3.5 later in this chapter.

Change programmes and change platforms: an exploration

In contrast to the psychosocial emphasis being developed in this book, the 'long-term planned change' or Organizational Change Management (OCM) approach, comes from a calculative planning perspective (Czarniawska 2009) with 'scientific management' rhetoric implicitly embedded within it (Pettigrew et al. 2001). Strategic decision making is the future focused long-term decision making that traditionally is undertaken by a small number of senior contributors in an organization. This conventional approach involves specifying a long-term intent, often called 'vision' and then producing a detailed road map to achieve the intent. This is still the dominant convention underpinning suggestions about how to implement the output of strategic decision making, but this convention is slowly changing, in line with the consolidated experience and knowledge indicating its lack of positive impact in complex workplaces. There are various models used, with the eight steps of the Kotter (1995) model probably being the best known and most widely taught.

Failure of planned change programmes

A systematic review of research into the impact of Organizational Change Management (OCM) methods, based on papers published between 1980 and

2010 indicated that there was little evidence of any substantive impact from this work (Barends et al. 2014). Prior to this systematic review many general literature reviews of this activity had also come to the same conclusion and there is a vast academic and practice literature outlining the failures of this long-term planned approach (Kotter 1995). Broadly, estimates of 30 per cent to 90 per cent failure rates for change and innovation programmes are regularly reported, depending upon the scale and complexity of the intended innovation/change, with literature across the many different disciplines in organizational studies describing the same phenomenon (Aiman-Smith and Green 2002; Jacobs et al. 2015).

There is a growing concern in organizational studies both about the accuracy and 'real-life' effectiveness of these abstract models of change, which have been predominantly developed for use in teaching strategy in business schools (Pettigrew 1990). The issues raised in such critiques point to the importance of micro processes for the success of macro initiatives. They also describe the negative consequences of imposing a new set of imagined practices onto existing organizational habits without understanding how micro processes currently function.

To illustrate, in the context of studies of failure in implementing knowledge management systems (KMS), Rowlinson et al. (2010) explore the importance of social memory on the communication and use of knowledge in organizations and question how this is created. They demonstrate that the dominant model of memory used in KMS is that of a 'storage bin', an abstract mental model, which gets embedded into the design and roll-out of KMS. However this model does not match the psychosocial realities of memory and learning, so the developed designs do not fit the psychosocial context and so cannot meet the workplace need. Specifically, the implicit assumption in KMS is that the system needs to be information/data driven and so overlooks the central importance of the distinctly human, subjective experience of remembering through 'episodic memory'; memory that is held and recalled in situ through the grammar of story.

Strategic decision making is always undertaken in the context of risk and uncertainty. It involves working with future unknowns both about the environment and the responses that will be required. 'Well rehearsed role improvisation' and localized prioritization generates better organizational outcomes in responding to uncertainty (Czarniawska 2009). By contrast long-term planned approaches to change are inherently ideologically separate from the need to work with uncertainty, as they assume that a defined set of future organizational change requirements can be fully scoped out by a distinct team of designers and leaders and then imposed onto an organization. While a CEO taking a long-term perspective may be beneficial to the prosperity of an organization, prescribing a detailed and controlled approach over the long term is not. This dominant rhetoric around calculative change ignores the requirements for collaborative job crafting and multi-functional scenario planning when working with uncertainty. Developments in decision science have shifted attention from individual rational control in thinking to the overall cognitive capabilities in an organization, consistent with the approach developed in practice and shared in this text. In parallel there is less attention given to the rational processing of environmental factors (Gavetti 2005) which has led to a much more emergent view of organization strategy (Paroutis et al. 2013) and transformational change (Balogun et al. 2015).

These OCM approaches also assume that with sufficient attention paid to 'people change management' employees will implement the organizational changes as designed. Planned long-term culture change programmes – that is, defining and telling people how they should behave – do not deliver the desired changes. Instead they generate damaging unintended consequences as people make their own meaning (see Chapter 9) and respond to the implied social norms rather than the explicit behavioural statements.

Attention to frames of reference and leadership modelling used in intervention design and delivery is critical. If employees are treated without care or are 'ordered around', then a 'culture' is created where being uncaring and bossy is acceptable and normalized. It is then predictable that service users will experience treatment that is uncaring and bossy. Gilbert et al. (2012) suggest that the belief in exerting behavioural control on others is built on an assumption that organizations are 'green field sites' rather than 'developed sites' that have a deep-seated and profound psychosocial history. The assumption that an organization will move into a pre-defined new state, regardless of the existing organizational norms of behaviour, is not consistent with the reality of the social psychology of groups, the way groups put pressures on behaviour, the realities of intention formation (Ajzen 1991) or the 'nudges' that are increasingly being used in large-scale, small behaviour change (Haynes et al. 2010).

Studies of the impact of implementing culturally dissonant practices on an existing organization show that a mutual adaptation process happens between the current culture and the new intent. This generates an outcome that no one predicted or intended and often that no one wants or likes (Canato et al. 2013). Part of the problem with these conventional approaches is that they attempt to override how things currently work, without understanding how things currently work.

Using the theory of planned behaviour (Ajzen 1991) studies of why people do not behave as they have been told (and even how they think they should) in high stakes contexts demonstrates the importance of managerial attitudes and organizational norms as direct and indirect predictors of safety violation behaviour. Relational factors (group norms, other people's attitudes and behavioural control) were more predictive of violation intent and behaviour than any assessments using safety climate or engagement surveys (Fogerty and Shaw 2010). By contrast, norms based on improvisation have been particularly linked to effective response to unexpected and high stakes (dangerous) events (Rankin et al. 2013).

Evidence of damage from the implementation of this planned approach is manifested in the emergence of unintended and counter-productive consequences (Harris and Ogbonna 2002). These generate business problems around organizational viability through resource waste and lead to the creation of toxic psychological environments. The experience of the failure to implement intended changes and the emergence of unintended consequences leads to clinical depression – 'learned helplessness' (Seligman 1972) and employee withdrawal through both the loss of trust in the organization and their ability to change things (Eriksson 2004). Individual stories of failure become increasingly salient and these experiences then turn into embedded organizational narratives, which reinforce social memories of failed implementation, thereby creating cynicism about the organization's ability to change (Fisher and Howell 2004).

The experience of disconnections between what is said about change and what actually happens causes confusion and conflict. Jacobs et al. (2015) suggest that 'implementation climate' is the critical factor in change effectiveness. They demonstrate that this is created through the provision of extensive support, with managers and staff engaging together setting expectations. This issue was outlined in the early research on change failure, which pointed to the impact of a behavioural disconnect between the stated intent in the contents of a change programme and the actions of those leading implementation (Evans 1974). The disconnect leads to experiences of stress, with employees protectively withdrawing attention from the innovation (Leonardi 2009). The reality of 'fronting this disconnect' also creates stressful challenges for managers both in maintaining a clear sense of self in role and communicating a coherent shared sense of direction (Spicer 2011).

Repeating, systemically embedded political practices are central to how organizational strategy, decision making and implementation processes actually unfold. Miller et al. (2008) provide research evidence that shows that finance and marketing departments (and sometimes the main operational part of the business) are always invited to strategic discussion, but input is rarely sought from other functions. To accept the long-term planned model is to accept the absence of attention to the power, politics and influencing factors inherent in organizations (Pettigrew 1990). It has been suggested that we need to readjust our models of change to accommodate the robust evidence we now have about how these strategic and psychosocial processes operate (Wilson et al. 2010).

Change platforms

The dynamic impact of the psychosocial need to sustain belonging, contributing and meaning (see Chapters 6 and 9) in organizations has led to a search for different ideas about how to enable effective change. Katzenback et al. (2012) suggest that instead of using these imposed long-term planned approaches to change, we should use an approach that starts by 'appreciating a culture not attacking it' and so advocates a strength-based approach to enabling change (see Chapter 4).

The dynamic nature of 'sense making' (Weick 1990) together with the deliberate use of dialogic approaches has been shown to be more successful at enabling change that sticks (Bate et al. 2000). The use of small psychosocially focused interventions also seems to be infectious. For example, those connected to participants in a coaching intervention also demonstrated improvements in well-being suggesting a more nuanced approach is needed in designing interventions in complex adaptive systems (O'Connor and Cavanagh 2013). This recognition of psychosocial contagion is supported in the recent exploration of the impact of rudeness in social systems (Foulk and Woolum 2015).

Another example of a psychosocially focused emergent approach to change has been built into the Theory 'U' model (Senge et al. 2005). This privileges the work of sense making and 'co-creating the future', through deliberate attention to key psychosocial micro processes; judgement, cynicism and fear.

The adoption of the idea of a 'change platform' is linked to the increased use of 'social movement' techniques (Klandermans 1984; Oliver and Marwell 1992), because these activate people who have an explicit choice about whether to participate or not and increasingly this is the reality in complex workplaces. These ideas work from the 'Big Task – Small Ask' concept, which invites participation in making a big difference to a problem (Big Task) by lots of people each making a small contribution (Small Ask).

The quality of support and communication experienced by staff across an organization is predictive of the extent to which employees will support and advocate change and of overall organizational resilience (Shin et al. 2012). This is linked to the positive impact of participation covered earlier (Linna et al. 2011). Participative approaches generate far less cynicism and learned helplessness than do long-term planned programmes. It is suggested that this is because distributed sense making is enabled about the paradoxical requirements and outcomes, so participation transforms the organizational logic about change across the workplace (Jay 2013).

In contrast to the narratives of 'learned helplessness' (Seligman 1972) built from experiences of long-term planned organizational change, I have found that these alternatives enable a sense of effectiveness through doing 'our bit' to make our workplace better. The study of relational micro processes suggests that small changes by one person can impact the entire system (Kowch 2013). Central to the change platform formulation is the concept of 'distributed leadership' (Buchanan et al. 2007). In contrast to the idea of an individual in a senior role, distributed leadership describes the situation where many people across an organization are involved in activities which together increase 'organizational leadership capability' (Leslie and Canwell 2010).

Buchanan et al. (2007) described this as 'no-one is particularly in charge' and further that 'ambiguous, fluid and migratory' responsibilities are enabled. This makes our work with accountability and authority in organizations complex. Smets et al. (2012) give evidence of the shifts in the operation of a whole workplace from subtle improvisation in the day-to-day practices of individuals and teams. When exploring how change impact is sustained in organizations, a comparison of directive and participative leadership on long-term and short-term outcomes indicated that directive leadership was extremely effective in ensuring short-term activities were completed, but that the gains from this tended to decline over time. A participative leadership style was slower to generate evidence of change, but the performance gains were sustained over the long term (Lorinkova et al. 2013).

Participate (see Figure 3.3 for more details of this)

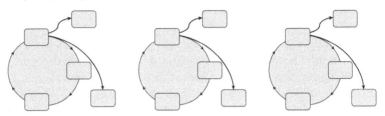

Repeating 90 day (seasonal) cycles of localized intervention

Orchestrate

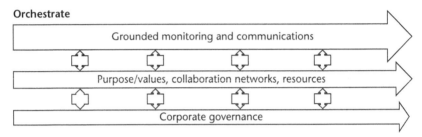

FIGURE 3.5 Orchestration/participation model of intervention

I have used these ideas in large-scale organizational intervention and change and work with two broad design protocols:

- *Orchestration:* Change is supported and enabled not planned. Support is provided through three foundations:
    - o   minimal and aligned corporate governance;
    - o   clarity about purpose, collaboration networks and resources;
    - o   communications and grounded monitoring for double-loop organizational learning.

- *Participation:* This can include local scope for improvisation, facilitated large and small group work and cross-boundary initiatives (employees, customers and other interested parties) to engage in locally driven initiatives for change.

These aspects of practice around complex adaptive change, illustrated in Figure 3.5, generate impact from the repeating cycle of intervention operating across the system in response to localized needs and priorities coordinated through symbolic communication practices rather than acts of control.

Conclusion

In this chapter I have covered the problems with the current idea of the consulting cycle, the work of intervention and how models of change are becoming more dynamic and less calculative. The complexity this generates requires a greater understanding of psychosocial micro processes and how they are supported and denatured. In turn this creates a greater need for practitioners with the capabilities for intelligent activism to mitigate organizational toxicity.

References

Abrahams, F. (2013) *Designing Thriving Organizations*. Vienna: EODF. http://www.tavinsti tute.org/projects/just-exploring-dilemmas-choices-organizational-design.

Aiman-Smith, L. and Green, S. G. (2002) Implementing new manufacturing technology: The related effects of technology characteristics and user learning activities. *Academy of Management Journal* 45(2): 421–430.

Ajzen, I. (1991) The theory of planned behavior. *Organizational Behavior and Human Decision Processes* 50: 179–211.

Balogun, J., Hope Hailey, V. and Cleaver, I. (2015) *Landing Transformational Change: Closing the Gap between Theory and Practice*. London: CIPD 7101.

Barends, E., Janssen, B., ten Have, W. et al. (2014) Effects of change interventions: What kind of evidence do we really have? *Journal of Applied Behavioral Science* 50(1): 5–27.

Bate, P., Khan, R. and Pye, A. (2000) Towards a culturally sensitive approach to organization structuring: Where organization design meets organizational development. *Organization Science* 11(2): 197–211.

Brauer, M. F. (2013) The effects of short-term and long-term oriented managerial behavior on medium-term financial performance: Longitudinal evidence from Europe. *Journal of Business Economics and Management* 14(2): 386–402.

Buchanan, D. A., Addicott, R., Fitzgerald, L. et al. (2007) Nobody in charge: Distributed change agency in healthcare. *Human Relations* 60(7): 1065–1090.

Canato, A., Ravasi, D. and Phillips, N. (2013) Coerced practice implementation in cases of low cultural fit: Cultural change and practice adaptation during the implementation of Six Sigma at 3m. *Academy of Management Journal* 56(6): 1724–1753.

Czarniawska, B. (2009) *Organizing in the Face of Risk and Threat*. Cheltenham: Edward Elgar.

Eriksson, C. B. (2004) The effects of change programs on employees' emotions. *Personnel Review* 33(1): 110–126.

Evans, M. G. (1974) Failures in OD programs: What went wrong? *Business Horizons* 17(2): 18–22.

Fisher, S. L. and Howell, A. W. (2004) Beyond user acceptance: An examination of employee reactions to information technology systems. *Human Resource Management* 43(2/3): 243–258.

Fogerty, G. J. and Shaw, A. (2010) Safety climate and the theory of planned behavior: Towards the prediction of unsafe behavior. *Accident Analysis and Prevention* 42(5): 1455–1459.

Foulk, T. and Woolum, A. (2015) Catching rudeness is like catching a cold: The contagion effect of low intensity negative behaviors. *Journal of Applied Psychology*. Epub ahead of print 20 June 2015. DOI:10. 1037 apl0000037.

Gavetti, G. (2005) Cognition and hierarchy: Rethinking the micro foundations of capabilities development. *Organization Science* 16(6): 599–617.

Gilbert, C., Eyring, M. and Foster, R. (2012) Two routes to resilience. *Harvard Business Review* 90(12): 65–67.

Harris, L. C. and Ogbonna, E. (2002) The unintended consequences of culture interventions: A study of unexpected outcomes. *British Journal of Management* 13(1): 31–49.

Haynes, L., Service, O., Goldacre, B. et al. (2010) Test, learn, adapt: Developing public policy with randomised controlled trials. http://www.behaviouralinsights.co.uk.

Jacobs, S. R., Weiner, B. J., Reeve, B. B. et al. (2015) Determining the predictors of innovation implementation in healthcare: A quantitative analysis of implementation effectiveness. *BMC Health Services Research* 15(1): 142–164.

Jay, J. (2013) Navigating paradox as a mechanism of change and innovation in hybrid organizations. *Academy of Management Journal* 56(1): 137–159.

Katzenback, J., Steffen, I. and Kronley, C. (2012) Culture change that sticks. *Harvard Business Review* 90(7/8): 110–117.

Klandermans, B. (1984) Mobilization and participation: Social-psychological expansions of resource mobilization theory. *American Sociologist* 49(5): 583–600.

Kotter, J. P. (1995) Leading change: Why transformation efforts fail. *Harvard Business Review* 73(2): 59–67.

Kowch, E. G. (2013) Conceptualising the essential qualities of complex adaptive leadership: Networks that organize. *International Journal of Complexity in Leadership and Management* 2(3): 162–184.

Leonardi, P. M. (2009) Why do people reject new technologies and stymie organizational changes of which they are in favor? Exploring misalignments between social interactions and materiality. *Human Communication Research* 35(3): 407–441.

Leslie, K. and Canwell, A. (2010) Leadership at all levels: Leading public sector organisations in an age of austerity. *European Management Journal* 28(4): 297–305.

Linna, A., Väänänen, A., Elovainio, M. et al. (2011) Effect of participative intervention on organisational justice perceptions: A quasi-experimental study on Finnish public sector employees. *International Journal of Human Resource Management* 22(3): 706–721.

Lorinkova, N. M., Pearsall, M. J. and Sims Jr, H. P. (2013) Examining the differential longitudinal performance of directive versus empowering leadership in teams. *Academy of Management Journal* 56(2): 573–596.

Miller, S., Hickson, D. J. and Wilson, D. C. (2008) From strategy to action: Involvement and influence in top level decisions. *Long Range Planning* 41(6): 606–628.

O'Connor, S. and Cavanagh, M. (2013) The coaching ripple effect: The effects of developmental coaching on wellbeing across organisational networks. *Psychology of Wellbeing* 3(2): 1–23.

Oliver, P. E. and Marwell, G. (1992) Mobilizing technologies for collective action. In A. Morris and C. Mueller (eds) *Frontiers of Social Movement Theory*. New Haven, CT: Yale University Press.

Paroutis, S., Heracleous, L. and Angwin, D. (2013) *Practicing Strategy: Text and Cases.* London: SAGE.

Pettigrew, A. M. (1990) Longitudinal field research on change: Theory and practice. *Organization Science* 1(3): 267–292.

Pettigrew, A. M., Woodman, R. W. and Cameron, K. S. (2001) Studying organizational change and development: Challenges for future research. *Academy of Management Journal* 44(4): 697–713.

Rankin, A., Dahlback, N. and Lundberg, J. (2013) A case study of factor influencing role improvisation in crisis response teams. *Cognition Technology and Work* 15(1): 79–93.

Rowlinson, M., Booth, C., Clark, P. et al. (2010) Social remembering and organizational memory. *Organizational Studies* 31(1): 69–87.

Seligman, M. E. P. (1972) Learned helplessness. *Annual Review of Medicine* 23(1): 407–412.

Senge, P., Scharmer, O., Jaworski, J. et al. (2005) *Presence: Exploring Profound Change in People, Organisations and Society.* London: Nicholas Brealey.

Shin, J., Taylor, M. S. and Seo, M. Y. (2012) Resources for change: The relationships of organizational inducements and psychological resilience to employees' attitudes and behaviors toward organizational change. *Academy of Management Journal* 55(3): 727–748.

Smets, M., Morris, T. and Greenwood, R. (2012) From practice to field: A multilevel model of practice-driven institutional change. *Academy of Management Journal* 55(4): 877–904.

Spicer, D. (2011) Changing culture: A case study of a merger using cognitive mapping. *Journal of Change Management* 11(2): 245–264.

Weick, K. E. (1990) Technology as equivoque: Sense-making in new technologies. In P. S. Goodman and L. S. Sproull (eds) *Technology and Organizations*. San Francisco, CA: Jossey-Bass.

Wilson, D. C., Branicki, L., Sullivan-Taylor, B. et al. (2010) Extreme events, organizations and the politics of strategic decision-making. *Accounting, Auditing and Accountability Journal* 23(5): 699–721.

Woods, S. A. and West, M. A. (2010) *The Psychology of Work and Organizations*. Australia: South-Western Cengage Learning.

4

EVIDENCE AND INTERVENTION METHODS AS TOOLS FOR PRACTICE

Introduction

I have been using 'evidence-based' approaches to organizational practice in complex workplaces for over 25 years and have used a wide range of sources of evidence and methodologies to support practice. The appropriate evidence to use is very much dependent upon the expressed client need (see Chapter 2) and I will make the assessment about whether localized and emerging evidence or external evidence (or a combination of these) is required. The most important consideration for intervention practice is to have a breadth of methodologies and lenses to use and a rich understanding of the evidence available and how to use it, as requisite diversity in source and approach is essential to be able to act intelligently across settings and issues. Table 4.1 gives an outline of the different sources of relevant evidence for psychosocial intervention.

The methodologies

To explore how evidence can be used in field settings, and how this is fundamentally different from the use of evidence in lab contexts, I explore five methodologies in this chapter:

- evidence-based practice;
- positive deviance;
- design thinking;
- large group methods and dialogic organization development (OD);
- Appreciative Inquiry.

There are many other process descriptions and lenses that are available for organizing data and evidence from field settings and it is beyond the scope of this text to cover them all.

TABLE 4.1 Evidence sources in practice

Immediate and evolving evidence			*Delayed and fixed evidence*		
Emerging events and talk in context	Recorded events/video from context	Tracked data stored in context – e.g. HR analytics	Media reports of emerging management trends	Codified best practice Professional publications	Academic peer reviewed papers
Practitioner experience and authentic intuition	Visual and physical artefacts/photographs	Codified perceptions from context – e.g. previous client reports	Chatham House rules practice discussions	Continuing Professional Development events	
Stakeholder comments	Collated perceptions/opinions from people in the client context	Stories/jokes/myths that live in the client context			
Field specific					*Abstracted from field*

There are several unifying features of all of the psychosocial methodologies I have chosen for this review. They are all built upon the idea of a short-term intervention for a long-term benefit and they all explicitly use evidence. They share the intent to intervene in how people make sense of the organization they are in and so all use discursive practices to enable change. Each can bring a range of different lenses to the work, so for example a design thinking project could be focused on an organizational structural issue and so the Galbraith star (see Stanford 2004) model could be integrated into the insight process. Alternatively, a dialogic process could be focused on major strategic change in the context of considerable fear for the future and could make use of the Scharma (2009) Theory U model and practice in its design to explicitly address emotional processes.

These methodologies differ in the way they require you to conceptualize the role of the practitioner, the way they approach problems, the evidence they give primacy to, the stages of knowledge translation they support (see Chapter 1, Table 1.3) and how to work with a client. Table 4.2 gives an overview of these chosen methodologies and the purposes for which I would consider using them.

TABLE 4.2 Presented methodologies and their uses

Methodological approach	Examples of what I would use each methodology for
Evidence-based practice	Organizational audit and 'past-focused' inquiry-based engagements Psycho-legal engagement with workplace clients White paper requests on a specific topic
Positive deviance	Resolving intractable operational problems in organizations, particularly those that have to work with external targets and so need measurement savvy built up in an organization
Design thinking	Applied to intervention work when any engagement requires a design (i.e. most of them) Facilitation work with groups in organizations for generating new ideas To enable the development of innovation practices in organizations
Large group methods (including Dialogic OD)	For facilitated co-creation work in large (and small) groups to address complex strategic and operational challenges Large and small group facilitated events that need to process systemic difficulty in a way that does not disable action To build communities of practice (which can be enabled virtually) To break silo boundaries in complex organizations As skills training in management development Can also be used therapeutically but this is outside my area of competence
Appreciative Inquiry (also includes ideas from Positive Psychology)	To generate optimistic future-focused intention statements Workplace improvements for teams, organizations or communities that find a 'problem frame' unhelpful

Each method is addressed in overview in this chapter, but there is slightly more attention given to evidence-based practice (EBP) than to the others. This is because EBP is gaining increasing profile as the (only) appropriate way to do psychosocial practice in organizations, to the point where it could almost be described as fashionable. This means it is legitimately placed to accept the critique that its advocates direct at other 'fads and fashions' (Rousseau 2006) of practice.

Being able to use all of these approaches fluidly gives the intelligent activist a repertoire for managing intervention, without being locked into a single set of assumptions from a specific method.

Evidence-based practice (EBP)

EBP describes itself as being about 'making decisions through the conscientious, explicit, and judicious use of four sources of information: practitioner expertise and judgment, evidence from the local context, a critical evaluation of the best available research evidence, and the perspectives of those people who might be affected by the decision' (Barends et al. 2014) and is described as a series of practice steps outlined in Table 4.3. This table also gives my analysis of the issues with each of these steps.

Critique of EBP

I am both an advocate of the use of evidence in practice and am concerned about the current approach described by EBP, as it is currently formulated as a lab export. It states that it is intended for use in the field, but has not yet had the necessary modifications/translations for full field application. EBP has been influenced by evidence-based medicine (Guyatt et al. 1992), which sought to challenge how medics worked with scientific output. There were two distinct concerns underpinning this articulation of evidence-based medicine:

- medics did not apply much scientific evidence in their practice;
- a lot of medical scientific evidence was of poor quality and not relevant for practice.

The estimate was that only 10 per cent of medical scientific evidence was both relevant and of high enough quality to be considered useful. This same 10 per cent figure has been given for academic management and psychosocial evidence (Guest and Zijlstra 2012). The proposed solution formulated as evidence-based medicine was that medical practitioners needed to become much more active in critically reviewing the evidence available to them, a solution which has also been adopted by those advocating EBP for the workplace. I have conceptual issues with this:

Disconnection between the root cause and the proposed solution

Although the problem stated is about the quality and relevance of academic output, the proposed solution does not advocate attention to the academic production

TABLE 4.3 Evidence-based practice steps and practice critique

Stage in EBP (see CEBMa website)	Key practice challenge to this formulation
Asking: by translating a practical issue into an answerable question	The tension between the desire for a 'tight' problem and the messiness of the field reality of wicked problems
Acquiring: by systematically retrieving the best available evidence	If using academic ideas of evidence selection this excludes written practice evidence and there are also questions about where to place the boundaries around 'evidence'. The sheer volume of evidence in any field context is overwhelming
Appraising: by critically reviewing the evidence for validity and relevance	Who gets to say what is valid and relevant in any specific context is impacted by power and biases in operation in the client context. Is it realistic to expect a practitioner to 'mark the homework' of academics? With the issues about replication (Open Science Collaboration 2015) and evidence from studies of CBT that what works in practice changes with time (Johnsen and Friborg 2015) such a review is complex and could potentially exclude all academic knowledge for these reasons
Aggregating: by weighing and synthesising the sources of evidence	Processing evidence in field settings and deciding what it means is a contested political process, and there are no agreed protocols for 'weighing'
Applying: by using the evidence in the decision-making process	Using evidence to make a decision is not application for those who work in a field setting. A decision is a 'theoretical' step, whereas putting this into practice is where 'reality bites'
Assessing: by reference to the outcome of the decision taken	As decisions do not generate tangible outcomes, assessment in the manner suggested is not a realistic proposition as there are many variables that impact outcome in addition to the 'decision'

process. Instead it advocates a change to the way practitioners and managers use lab output. It would be more straightforward to argue that because most of the evidence obtained from research was irrelevant and of poor quality, practitioners and managers should limit their use of this evidence.

In addition, it has been observed in the education of graduate students that the narrowing of a problem to engage in this EBP approach is ill-suited to many types of problem statements that the senior manager MBA students frame (Salipante and Smith 2012). In the interests of letting the 'field' speak for itself about this issue the following comments from a Linkedin discussion about EBP are shared in Figure 4.1.

As Haslam (2014) indicates, psychosocial intervention is always political because it involves social identity management and the EBP attempt to change the practices of those outside the academy is inevitably going to activate intense personal reactions across this boundary.

FIELD COMMENTARY ABOUT THE IDEAS IN EVIDENCE-BASED MANAGEMENT

'It is still very hard for practical people to know how reliable and salient research truly is . . . many people intuitively sense these problems with hard evidence and so throw the baby out with the bathwater'.

'Subjective values held by individuals play a key part in decision making'.

'Surely a hunch is based on evidence, it's just not collated and presented but based on experience'.

'Sometimes it helps not to over-analyse – speed matters more'.

'When you look at critically appraising the evidence, what of all the competing lines of evidence clinches the argument?'

'It can generate a bias towards research-based, analytical, reproducible approaches that focus on and favour what is measurable and we've seen the damage this has done'.

'We need evidence on how best to use evidence'.

FIGURE 4.1 Field perceptions of evidence-based practice

The implicit assumption that thinking/decision making lead to change

The implicit assumption that cognition leads to change in outcome is not sustainable. People actively try to shield themselves from information that causes psychological discomfort (Karlsson et al. 2009) and people do not change their minds when given new information.

It is helpful, if potentially a little contentious, to illustrate the fallacy in assuming thought is sufficient for a change in outcome, by considering another contemporary and popular idea; the field of 'positive thinking', as this also has an underpinning assumption that thought underpins what happens in the world. Positive thinking is used to describe the belief that how you think about something will have a material impact on the outcome you experience. Specifically this idea claims that if you think positively you will have better outcomes than if you think negatively. The evidence, from studies of health outcomes, quite clearly indicates that it is more complicated than this (Oettingen 2014). Positive thinking combined with purposeful action does generate the best outcomes. However, it is not the positive thinking that causes this (as positive thinking on its own leads to worse outcomes than realistic, sceptical or pessimistic thinking alone or realistic thinking and purposeful action together). Central to this impact on positive outcomes is taking action and how cognition underpins the approach to action.

In addition, the assumption about decision making appears to have come from the experiences of decision making in the academy. In this context, decision making is based on collegium principles rather than operating as an executive hierarchy (Chapter 8, Table 8.2). These different social structures lead to a substantial difference in how authority, accountability and decision making work. The EBP formulation gives no attention to the practical realities of decision making in an executive hierarchy. There is also no reference to how you access 'decision makers' or how you identify who participates in decision making. These tend to be formalized or autonomous in a collegium but are fluid and distributed in executive hierarchies.

In addition, there are insights from decision science of relevance (see Chapter 7, cognitive sources). Hogarth (1981) indicates that within complex organizations, judgements are made over time in changing circumstances, so investing too much consideration in any one decision is not the best use of time and effort available. Bandura (1991) observes that purposive organizational activity requires more than applying cognitive operations to existing knowledge to generate solutions, because emotional self-regulation is so important in the functioning of decision making. This leaves me with a question: why would decision makers invest in such a complex and elaborate thinking process?

It is in the practical exchanges in action where a large proportion of the evidence from the psychosocial sciences has potentially the biggest contribution to make to the functioning of our workplaces and this needs to be explicit in methods aimed at intervening.

The formulation needs to engage with the complexities of taking action, as specifically EBP has not addressed how translation works or what to do when 'reality bites back'.

Challenging this emerging EBP fashion using practice know-how

Instead of offering an academic critique of this method, I consider that it is more helpful to provide a diagnosis of the situation from an ethical practice perspective as this has the benefit of raising the same concerns, while also showing how ethical practice works.

I would suggest that EBP is a delivery-driven (see Chapter 2, Table 2.5) response to a knowledge translation phase one wicked problem (see Chapter 1, Table 1.3) centred on the question: 'Why doesn't our research work have the impact it should?' It is noticeable that in this situation the 'client' problem has actually been articulated as a solution (which is a very common client inversion, probably used to manage the anxieties associated with uncertainty [Menzies Lyth 1960]). As with most complex problems, how this solution has been implemented mirrors many of the Organizational Change Management (OCM) assumptions; namely that you can define a solution without inviting participation from those whose behaviour you wish to change, that you can tell others how to operate and that showing people the evidence will make them see the error of their ways and change what they do. These assumptions are widely evidenced to be ineffective (see Chapter 3) and inconsistent with the psychosocial evidence at our disposal.

In engaging with this client, my first questions would be ethical/political ones (Hodgkinson 2012): 'Whose interests are supported by this proposed solution (an assumed change in managers'/practitioners' relationship with evidence)?' Equally importantly, I would ask 'Who loses from this approach?' Linked with this, I would also raise another ethical concern: that the stated need for a systematic literature review in each decision-making exercise would put extra demand on managers and practitioners without clear evidence of any benefits. Based on the psychosocial evidence we have, increasing demand is a psychosocial hazard and a direct cause of stress from work (see Chapter 6).

To move on from these challenges, I would then encourage problem elaboration, exploring all possible causes, field explanations and previous attempts to improve the situation. For example, I could ask the 'client' to consider the suggestion that the lack of impact is due to a lag between current concern in workplaces and the mechanisms around publication (see Chapter 11, case two). I might also then point to the fact that very little of the research undertaken is disseminated from within the academy, suggesting that what is available as published material is inherently biased (Schmucker et al. 2014). This also would lead to further questions about the impact on the academy from toxicity due to measurement and regulation (see Chapter 7, symbolic sources).

I would then consider reframing the approach (Chapter 7, anchoring bias) by drawing attention to how much evidence the target group already uses day to day. I would outline my experience of experts, managers and leaders employed in organizations using financial data, HR analytics, stakeholder mapping and management, programme monitoring, market research data, scenario planning data and environment scanning as evidence used to govern the viability, sustainability and safety of complex organizations. I would re-frame the assumption to indicate that complex organizations are already evidence hungry and data intelligent and so would be unlikely to respond well to be told they are deficient. I would also introduce the schematic types of evidence (see Table 4.1) that I use as a practitioner to clarify the realities of 'drinking from a hose' (my favourite corporate description of coming up to speed with available evidence when taking on any new workplace responsibility).

I would suggest that although common cultural themes can be identified across organizations, each organization has a unique culture and distinct ways of operating (Knowles and Reddy 2003) so it may be ambitious to aim to provide generic guidance on working with evidence. With this I would clarify that organizations are 'driven by thinking and feeling inhabitants, often as reliant on inspiration and skillful management of emotion and intuition as on calculating cognition' (Hodgkinson and Healey 2011: 1510–1511). I would also draw attention to the research, which indicates that evidence pulled into coherent story structures is the preferred form of presentation to support complex decision making (Pennington and Hastie 1986).

As the final part of this diagnostic review of EBP, I would suggest that there has been substantial investment in intervention methods for complex organizations, and that these have already been field tested using the four types of evidence specified in EBP: practitioner expertise and judgement; evidence from the local context; a critical evaluation of the best available research evidence; and the perspectives of those people who might be affected by the decision. I would suggest that these existing practices, described in the remainder of this chapter (together with the communities of practice and publication that have developed around them) provide a substantial source of evidence both to engage with the underpinning problem about the relevance of academic work and also to design a better solution for client engagement than is currently articulated in EBP.

Positive deviance

Positive deviance is a method that has been developed from work in Community Development and is centred on the power of social mobilization to solve problems *within a setting*. The use of the term 'positive deviance' is used to express the assumption that a 'positively deviant' person or practice already exists somewhere in any system (and this needs to be found) and this existing practice needs testing, improving and sharing. The core story, told within this 'community of practice', links to the issue of child malnutrition in a community in Vietnam. Work focused on the use of existing intelligence within the community to find what worked well and to encourage the change in widespread practices that led to a 74 per cent reduction in child malnutrition: '[p]ositive deviance is the observation that in most settings a few at risk individuals follow uncommon, beneficial practices and consequently experience better outcomes than their neighbors who share similar risks' (Marsh et al. 2004: 1177).

The hunt for positive deviance begins with the 'flip' (Singh forthcoming). The 'flip' refers to the explicit process of the re-framing of the general problem. The question stopped being: 'What can we do to solve the problem of child malnutrition in this Vietnam village?' Instead this became: 'Which children in this Vietnam village are not suffering from malnutrition and why?' The use of the flip question led to the 'discovery' of two parental practices that ensured their children were not malnourished. One was the addition of small freshwater prawns from the paddy fields to the children's rice and the other was spreading the same amount of food over two meals rather than one. Sharing and scaling this positive deviance was a substantial and demanding piece of localized evidence-rich communication, mobilizing all community members through active work sharing the locally relevant data around child weight and height.

The basic principles articulated are that:

- Communities/organizations/groups already have their own solutions.
- They are self-organizing regardless of what 'structure' exists in writing.
- They have the capacity to solve agreed problems sustainably if they are permitted to do so.
- Intelligence is distributed among all rather than located in 'decision makers'.
- The key challenge is to activate this distributed intelligence.

Finally, positive deviance is about doing not thinking. Sternin et al. (1999) suggest that it is easier to act your way into a new way of thinking than think your way into a new way of acting. Since the adoption of this approach in community development in the 1970s it has been increasingly applied to intractable organizational problems, of which the most compelling is the significant reduction in MRSA levels in hospitals (Marsh et al. 2004).

Being an expert non-expert: the steps in positive deviance

An illustration of a positive deviance programme is given in Figure 4.2. Practitioners undertaking a positive deviance programme need to adopt a more tentative approach, compared to conventional ways of working with organizations. This is because it requires the explicit activation of relationship trust rather than knowledge or position trust that comes from importing specific content-based expertise. Working in this way draws on know-how about the functioning of micro and macro processes in organizations outlined in Chapters 7 and 8 and the self-reflective capacity to work sensitively in intervention. The steps are:

- Invitation is based on the establishment of trusted relationships, which is a substantial piece of work in its own right.
- Help the organization to define its problem, which may involve providing simple skills coaching and sometimes didactic input to build inquiry and measuring skills.
- Help the organization build its team to hunt the positive deviance practices existing in the system and create locally defined ways of measuring their impact.
- Facilitate the discussions to define what to do with this evidence.
- Support the initial implementation, monitoring and reporting.
- Broker the scale up and extension of work through developing skills in social mobilization.

The limitations of positive deviance centre on its strength; it is grounded in what is already in existence. This is in contrast to the next method outlined, the techniques in design thinking which are focused practices for creating something new.

Design thinking

Underpinning the idea of design is an expressed need for something that is not yet in existence. This activates the uncertain work of creativity and hence draws attention to the 'fog of uncertainty' required for design. This triggers what is intrinsically vulnerable in us (Farrands 2013). Design rationality or design thinking (Simon 1969) explores the heuristics involved in design, with methods and mechanisms deliberately chosen to activate 'taken for granted' expert ways of knowing to generate insights for new and untested contexts. Integral is an assumption that practice is built from different ways of knowing rather than from directly applying facts codified in science (Waks 2001). Design is intrinsic to all practice and yet is very rarely taught or explicated in the methods that have been developed out of psychosocial academic frames of working with knowledge and evidence. There has been consideration of context and research in relation to design explored by Denyer et al. (2008).

UK-BASED POSITIVE DEVIANCE PROJECT

With thanks to Jane Lewis, CEO of Hidden Insights, for sharing her work (see Lewis 2009).

The project objective for this positive deviance programme in a social services organization, agreed with the organization managers, was to engage people in increasing the proportion of properly completed and closed care records, and throughput of referrals. It was made clear that the project had to be completed without changes to the IT system and that the team and systems had already been through a 'lean' programme which had not solved the efficiency problems.

A volunteer project team was established made up of representatives from across the service, with all levels including administrators and team leaders represented. The Deputy Manager of the whole service was engaged to monitor progress. The role of the team was:

- to work with their colleagues to define their problems in their own terms;
- to carry out observation and enquiry exercises to find out if there were positive deviants and what they did;
- to facilitate team meetings to share discovery and agree action;
- to design ways of spreading what was learned.

By collecting data, they were able to 'bust' some myths about how long record keeping and administration took. They highlighted that missing care records slowed things down. They discovered a number of existing 'positive deviance' practices that helped to speed up record keeping, which, while bending the official procedure, were still safe. These were shared with teams and, based on the experience of actual improvement, other ideas started to emerge:

- Time saving of between 1 and 2.5 hours per person per week which equated to between £50,000 and £110,400 a year, for a team of 60 social workers.
- Time saving for Referrals Management team of 5–30 minutes for each referral.
- Time saving for social workers of between 5 per cent and 30 per cent of a day in dealing with incoming phone calls.
- Increased flexibility enabling a higher level of referrals to be dealt with in spite of a flu epidemic among the teams.
- Streamlining the process, which reduced waiting times for Council tenants.

In addition, there were qualitative improvements in work. The team members all became much more comfortable using data and saw them as their friend. They said that there was now a more positive way to challenge each other. This led to people feeling more able to contribute to improvements, regardless of status, and front line opinions were seen as important. Practically, they produced clearer instructions, drafted by users, for completing care records and reported being able to make better use of time and so experienced less frustration and hassle.

The time that was liberated was used to implement other improvements and updates. The data collected by those providing the services also revealed that the system itself was still very cumbersome, so it was agreed, based on their data, to revisit the computer system design.

FIGURE 4.2 Positive deviance in practice

The current use of the design thinking methods are available in material and examples are given on the UK Design Council website (http://www.designcoun cil.org.uk) and via the Warwick Business School/Design Council Partnership. The focus is on 'design leadership' using evidence-based *insights* from behavioural science and elsewhere as the key to addressing complex organizational problems. In contrast to the formulation of EBP, knowledge alone is not considered sufficient, but is used in the service of an intuitive and creative process to develop something new, rather than to make decisions with the certainty associated with knowing what has worked (or not) in the past.

The design thinking steps

For the purposes of this text, I have pulled together a simplified account of the steps in the design thinking approach.

Clarify the design challenge, which is an articulation of a need with an assumption that there are multiple possible ideas and approaches, all of which can meet this need, there is no one answer, there are many. *For this text, we could articulate that the creation of psychological environments without toxicity is a significant contemporary 'design challenge'.*

Enabling insight which is an elaboration using many sources of insight as they can come from every type of evidence listed in Table 4.1 and there is a range of approaches used to access material that can support the insight process, but there is no requirement to work systematically. The purpose is the activation of insight to feed authentic intuition, not the confirmation of factual certainty about the status of past knowledge. What design thinking makes clear is that the formulation stage exists to generate 'insights' rather than answers. The purpose is to craft possible ways in which the design challenge could be met through a range of different creative ideas.

Prototyping is the fail fast approach, to test ideas that have emerged from the insight process. Rapid prototyping allows the rapid discarding of undesirable, unviable and dysfunctional ideas – they are enabled to fail fast with limited invest- ment. Inherent in this is that the clarity about which ideas are viable comes from action and not thought. This is in stark contrast to the practices where the solution focus is to fix on a logical 'answer' too quickly and then commit large pilot and possible full-scale investment without rapid stress testing. In addition to the fail fast option, the process of iteration is applied to those ideas that appear to work. This is a second stage stress test that either acts as a second point of discard or enables the refinement of an idea into an elegant design that meets the requirements of the design challenge. It is once an idea has been through this fail process that scaling up can be considered.

Innovation: the implementation of the design scaled up to address the design challenge across a complex context is then viewed as a distinct piece of creative and messy practice work of continuously shaping the solution to the environment, whereby both environment and design are tested against each other. In complex organizations this is regularly an exercise of large group and participative methods to encourage systemic prototyping in situ, using various different large group methods.

How design thinking helps with choosing evidence in practice

To frame the client work I do in practice, I have found the simple structure shown in Figure 4.3 to be extremely helpful in keeping true to the intent of a design challenge or intervention. This simple model of 'why', 'what', 'how' gives us a helpful rule of thumb. At each stage of the knowledge translation process it is very easy to find people working at cross-purposes. Clarifying whether why, what or how (or all three) are active at any stage is extremely helpful. This is a heuristic device and which I have applied to a range of in practice issues.

In using this, we can understand that the EBP formulation about evidence is very much centred on 'what' as the facts are privileged above the political. This can encourage a move to define a problem too quickly, with the potential to reduce attention to the evidence about 'why'. By contrast with the focus of positive deviance, a method very grounded in evidence, is animated by 'why'.

The approaches developed in design thinking are more focused on the movement between these steps. The design challenge articulates the approaches that

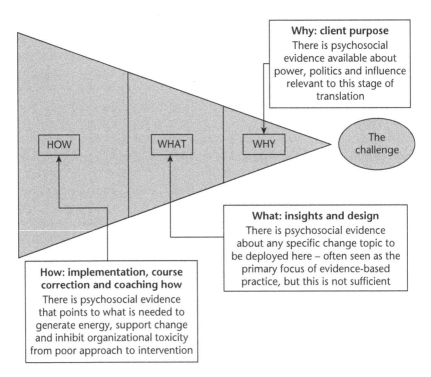

FIGURE 4.3 Design thinking and what evidence is used for

can aid the movement from 'why' into 'what'. Innovation in turn represents the movement from 'what' into 'how'. The next section on dialogic and large group methods is developed from a clear understanding of the importance of evidence about 'how' intervention is undertaken to ensure that there is integrity with 'why' and 'what'.

From my perspective, as ethical practitioners we are obligated to use the best evidence available across all these aspects of intervention. It is not enough that we have knowledge, but we must *use our knowledge* to guide us. Put simply, this means we have to 'walk the psychosocial talk'. For example, asserting that participation is the right way to do something and delivering this as a didactic message to a client disconnects 'walk' and 'talk'. Extending this example, because we now do understand that participation is good for health, presenting an autonomously developed expert-based review of literature, without political awareness, into a client context that disconfirms client perceptions may state what we know, but *does not do what we know*.

Large group and dialogic methods for co-creation

Participation works so it is increasingly used by organizations to build relationships and new workplace practices (Ind et al. 2013; Neilsen et al. 2014). A core concept that underpins the workplace intervention practice of large group methods is that of 'co-creation'; the idea that we design and implement together. Co-creation underpins large group or Whole Scale™ (Tolchinsky 2012) approaches that are based on the assumption that the 'wisdom is in the system' akin to the orientation in positive deviance, but in this context this is applied for future-focused co-design rather than scaling what is already happening in the system. This approach underpins the methods described as Appreciative Inquiry (AI) outlined in the next section. There are other large group approaches such as World Café (Brown with Isaacs 2005) and Open Space (Owen 2008), which extend the focus of large group dialogue beyond the employment boundaries of a workplace. Lewis (2011) provides illustration of these approaches.

This work of co-creation relies on talk or 'conversation' (Shaw 2002) which has developed into a large field of practice known as Dialogic OD (organization development). This has recently gained increasing attention due to the lowered investment and greater impact of these more human approaches to change:

> By working with the self-organizing, emergent qualities of human communities, Dialogic OD works around the obstacles that make controlled, orderly change difficult in complex situations and side steps the problems of resistance to change and unintended consequences that often accompany attempts to implement solutions. Surfacing and creating generative images, however, is easier said than done.
>
> *(Bushe 2013: 17)*

Talk as our key technology for change

Key to the work undertaken in facilitating and developing dialogic capabilities in organizations is the intent to work with what is described as the 'centre of a conversation', rather than its edges (Isaacs 1999). Bohm (1996) suggests that these points of overlap are the source of creative 'thinking together'. These ideas represent a practical development in our understanding of how to work with 'talk' as one of the primary technologies for change in the workplace. This investment in talk technology is evidenced in the following emerging organizational practices:

- The Whole Scale™ (Tolchinsky 2012) approach with later articulation of AI (Cooperrider et al. 2001) and other large group approaches such as the World Café (Brown with Isaacs 2005) or Open Space Technology (Owen 2008).
- The specific development of dialogic approaches to organization development (Isaacs 1999; Bushe 2013).
- The growing use of coaching in the workplace, which started as a dyadic approach but has recently extended to team-based approaches (Hawkins 2014) enables social support and the benefits of a critical friend.
- The development of individual dialogue skills, to improve the functioning of critical psychosocial micro processes outlined in Chapter 8, and which deploy much of what we are learning about social influence into skill building approaches (Rozenthuler 2012).

Figure 4.4 gives an illustration of 'talk technology' in action in organizational intervention.

Regardless of how much we 'know', if we try to implement this knowledge using established didactic methods, we will merely replicate the existing issues we have with organizational toxicity. It is critical that we recognize what the evidence suggests about *how* we should act.

USING DESIGN AND DIALOGUE METHODS TO REDRESS PERFORMANCE MANAGEMENT TOXICITY (ALSO SEE CHAPTER 10)

The contextual pattern that was emerging – internal insights:

- 'My manager doesn't actually know what I do, she works in a completely different place from me.'
- 'My manager doesn't do objective setting with me, but he does tell me when what I've done isn't good enough.'
- 'My manager knows that only a few people can get good results and she has her favourites so I'm destined for a bad mark.'
- 'I don't use the 360 feedback to assess my team, cos people just nominate their friends.'

- 'Why am I forced to assess my team based on a simple five point scale? I've selected them for their different strengths, I can't justify my decision to them cos I don't believe in it.'
- 'They tell me I should collaborate with the rest of the team, but why should I? I'm getting good marks and they're the competition.'
- 'Yes we set objectives last year, but everything has changed now – and I'm still held accountable for things we don't need and I couldn't possibly have done.'
- 'These objectives makes no sense, I can't do anything that I can show has a direct impact on sales, but they have been told to use this as an objective.'
- 'Why do we waste all our time collecting 360 degree feedback when all that counts is the impression my manager has of me?'
- 'It's just a very horrid way of letting people know their face doesn't fit . . . it looks objective but it is completely unfair.'

The design challenge was a re-framed inquiry – from 'how should we do performance management?' to 'how do we all get our work aligned?'

The dialogue-based prototype trialled: 'Time to Talk'

This involved a three-month process of 1–1 sessions scheduled monthly between each staff member and their manager, having a conversation. The focus of the dialogue was on the person, their aspirations, what is going on at work, what they would like their manager to know. All evaluative components were removed from this process. All parties were encouraged to adapt the approach and refine as they thought necessary.

The key iteration was based upon some managers expressing concerns that they did not know what they were required to do. To respond, some impromptu development input, focused on building dialogue and interpersonal skills, was offered. This involved a two-hour seminar run at the relevant workplaces and was widely taken up. The content and approach were both much more highly rated than previous 'training' that had involved a taught required process over a full day removed from the day to day.

The prototype feedback indicated that:

- Despite the monthly time invested with each person, the report was that this took less time than in a standard performance management process but with much more tangible impact on alignment and commitment.
- Supervisors/managers reported that they had a better idea of what was going on and how their people would approach issues.
- Emerging issues were shared and problems resolved, rather than people backing off from points of concern, which had been a problem previously.
- The information flow around operational work was real time and allowed managers to support and intervene when necessary.
- There was much more camaraderie and better team-work, together with improved perceptions of organizational fairness.

Following the prototype, the approach was taken into a full organizational review to explore how this 'Time to Talk' approach could be scaled across different departments.

FIGURE 4.4 Design with dialogue through 'Time to Talk'

A key challenge for Dialogic OD methods can enable us to co-create a pathway out of the denatured functioning of the micro processes (see Chapter 8) in toxic organizations. The issue for Dialogic OD centres on the impact of accountability/authority on what can be talked about and how what is talked about impacts how people are treated, which can lead to silence. Without attention to the potential impact of authoritarian power (the accountability disorders – see Chapter 12) it is problematic to claim that dialogue is an option. In such toxic contexts, talk is more likely centred on position taking, debate and negotiation than on the creative process covered in expositions of dialogic methods.

Appreciative inquiry (AI)

AI both sits within the framework of large group methods outlined above, and describes a very specific framework for large group conversations. An illustrative example of the use of Appreciative Inquiry in large group conversations is given in Figure 4.5. Appreciative inquiry (AI) (Cooperrider et al. 2001) now involves four simple steps that are described as the 4D model:

- discover
- dream
- design
- destiny.

It operationalizes how organizational change conversations need to be enabled based upon the evidence. This is an illustration of 'knowing how' instead of 'knowing what'. This approach is animated by an ethical concern with the

---

APPRECIATING AFRICA

With thanks to Sarah Owusu and Judith Okonkwo for sharing their work and Africa 2.0 for allowing us to use this illustration.

Every year, the Africa 2.0 community comes together to create plans and ignite action that drives the transformation of the African continent. In 2013, we met in the African Union Building in Addis Ababa, Ethiopia – a space where many problems have been tackled, challenges analysed and issues addressed. But this group came together in a different spirit – celebratory, hopeful and purposeful – to build a business plan for Africa. To set the scene for the workshops to come, we devised an opening session for a group of 40 participants who arrived the day before the event.

In the context of so much challenge (from big humanitarian crises to the small inhibiting every day struggles) and a perpetuating narrative about Africa that is primarily negative and disempowered, how do you create and sustain a constructive space?

This was to be a free space; to set some principles for working together, to bring a positive and solution-focused perspective, to impart tools that participants could bring to future work in their own countries, across Africa and beyond.

The session plan we designed was intentionally focused on the best of Africa and grounded in powerful existing African traditions. The three core parts were:

- *To assess what makes a leader and describe what your own leadership style is by developing a personal Oriki*: Oriki is a type of praise poetry seen among the Yoruba people of West Africa. It is aspirational, focusing on an individual's contribution or purpose. We used this powerful intervention to create meaningful connections among participants and celebrate the strength, potential and purpose they bring to the movement (Okonkwo 2010).
- *To use the Discover, Dream, Design, Destiny (4D) model to start catalysing ideas*: the 4D model was the focus of a 90 minute group working session that generated blue-skies ideas and opportunities to leverage that were taken into the pure planning workshops that followed.
- *To use their insights on leadership and on Africa's existing strength (gleaned from the 4D working session) to co-create a set of ground rules that would guide their way of working together in the days ahead.*

Through this process the group was immediately in possession of a set of nine ground rules that emerged from the conversations – most memorable was: 'We are uniquely African in everything we do'.

A long-term impact of the 4D intervention was the emergence of a key theme: the idea of UNITY across our continent, despite our DIVERSITY. This kernel of an idea has now been transformed into a social movement and social media campaign called WeAre1ne, focused on building solidarity and unity across all of Africa and creating a new, empowered narrative for the continent: a true illustration of the appreciative approach. This approach seems inherently aligned with African cultures and using it, in a culturally relevant way, is key to effective mobilization of movements and transformation on the continent.

Consultants: Sarah Owusu (session design, facilitation) and Judith Okonkwo (Oriki leadership and coaching tool, facilitation).

About Africa 2.0: Africa 2.0 is a pan-African Civil Society organization, established in 2010, and well on its way towards the vision of being a catalyst for accelerated and sustainable growth on the African continent. Its 600+ members, from across Africa and the Diaspora, are visionary leaders in their own right and together they make up an unstoppable community dedicated to the transformation of Africa. To find out more visit: www.africa2point0.org; https://www.facebook.com/pages/We-Are-1ne-Global/1592072901012567.

FIGURE 4.5 Appreciating Africa

importance of strength-based perceptions, for generating optimism (Sharot 2012) linked to the research on the importance of social identity, such as the stress buffering enabled by positive social identity (Ketturat et al. 2015 and see Chapter 8) and the dysfunction caused by negative feedback (see Chapter 10).

Positive psychology

Underpinning this AI formulation is the importance of appreciation in the human capacity to contribute and engage with work, which has been integrated under the ideas of positive psychology (Lewis 2011). Central figures in the growth of positive psychology are Csikszentmihalyi (2002), Seligman (2006), Cameron (2008), Linley et al. (2010) and Lewis (2011).

It must be noted that this is a distinct field from positive thinking mentioned earlier in this chapter, although they are often presented together. Positive psychology re-frames (see Chapter 7, framing bias) the problem-based approach in much of organizational psychology by asking questions that are characterized as 'strength based' and so generates a different frame for inquiry. Rather like the 'flip' in positive deviance engagements, the fundamental intellectual underpinning for positive psychology is a re-frame from research methods. This makes sense because the consequences of the 'problem' or 'weakness'-based approach when applied to managing people at work are clearly illustrated in Chapter 10, which explores why performance management does not work.

Positive psychology has made a clear contribution to ideas about flourishing at work and the development of associated methods, but when we consider organizational toxicity, it has not yet engaged with the requirements needed for an intervention pathway away from toxicity to repair the denatured functioning that manifests. Kashdan and Biswas-Diener (2014) outline the importance of feeling bad in productive endeavour and Sharot (2012) indicates the importance of optimism being fed in moderation to ensure it is not a bias that gets out of control and leads to erasure of significant negative signals in the environment.

A key concern in practice is how a strengths-based orientation can manage the risk of increasing cynicism in a distressed complex organization, subject to significant macro sources of toxicity in its structure and in the symbolic ways it treats people.

Conclusion

This chapter has outlined the need for and availability of a diversity of methods for intervention. The approaches presented balance inquiry with creativity and I would suggest that the claim that one technique can be used across all contexts must be treated with scepticism. Having an awareness of the wide range of sources of evidence and skills in a diversity of methodological approaches for intervention is critical for ethical practice. In keeping with the design thinking principles, we need to be able to articulate why we are using any particular method for any particular client need, and what the evidence we are accessing is for, rather than repeating a single set of process steps unthinkingly in all eventualities. In my experience, each client engagement ends up with a bespoke method built out of different aspects of the available diversity of models, only some of which have been presented in this chapter.

References

Bandura, A. (1991) Social cognitive theory of self-regulation. *Organizational Behavior and Human Decision Processes* 50: 248–287.

Barends, E., Rousseau, D. and Briner, R. (2014) *Evidence Based Practice: The Basic Principles*. Booklet. Netherlands: CEBMA. http://www.cebma.org.

Bohm, D. (1996) *On Dialogue*. London: Routledge.

Brown, J. with Isaacs, D. (2005) *World Café: Shaping Our Future through Conversations that Matter*. San Francisco, CA: Berrett-Koehler.

Bushe, G. R. (2013) Dialogic OD: A theory of practice. *OD Practitioner* 45(1): 11–17.

Cameron, K. S. (2008) *Positive Leadership: Strategies for Extraordinary Performance*. San Francisco, CA: Berrett-Koehler.

Cooperrider, D., Sorenson Jr, P. F., Yaeaer, T. F. et al. (eds) (2001) *Appreciative Inquiry: An Emerging Direction for Organizational Development*. Champaign, IL: Stipes.

Csikszentmihalyi, M. (2002) *Flow: The Classic Work on How To Achieve Happiness*. London: Rider.

Denyer, D., Tranfield, D. and Ernst van Aken, J. (2008) Developing design propositions through research synthesis. *Organization Studies* 29(3): 393–413.

Farrands, R. (2013) *Design Rationality: Working with Donald Schon*. Vienna: EODF.

Guest, D. E. and Zijlstra, F. R. H. (2012) Academic perceptions of the research evidence base in work and organizational psychology: A European perspective. *Journal Occupational and Organizational Psychology* 85(4): 542–555.

Guyatt, G., Cairns, J., Churchill, D. et al. (1992) Evidence-based medicine: A new approach to teaching the practice of medicine. *Journal of the American Medical Association* 268(17): 2420–2425.

Haslam, S. A. (2014) Making good theory practical: Five lessons for an applied Social Identity approach to challenges of organizational, health and clinical psychology. *British Journal of Social Psychology* 53(1): 1–20.

Hawkins, P. (ed) (2014) *Leadership Team Coaching in Practice: Developing High Performance Teams*. UK: Kogan Page.

Hodgkinson, G. P. (2012) The politics of evidence-based decision making. In D. M. Rousseau (ed.) *Oxford Handbook of Evidence Based Management*. Oxford: Oxford University Press. http://www.cebma.org/articles/.

Hodgkinson, G. P. and Healey, M. P. (2011) Psychological foundations of dynamic capabilities: Reflexion and reflection in strategic management. *Strategic Management Journal* 32(13): 1500–1516.

Hogarth, R. (1981) Beyond discrete biases: Functional and dysfunction aspects of judgment heuristics. *Psychological Bulletin* 90(2): 197–217.

Ind, N., Iglesias, O. and Schultz, M. (2013) Building brands together: Emergence and outcomes of co-creation. *California Management Review* 55(3): 5–26.

Issacs, W. (1999) *Dialogue and the Art of Thinking Together*. New York: Currency Doubleday.

Johnsen, T. and Friborg, O. (2015) The effects of cognitive behavioral therapy as an anti-depressive treatment is falling: A meta-analysis. *Psychological Bulletin* 141(4): 747–768.

Karlsson, N., Loewenstein, G. and Seppi, D. (2009) The ostrich effect: Selective attention to information. *Journal of Risk and Uncertainty* 38: 95–115.

Kashdan, T. and Biswas-Diener, R. (2014) *The Upside of Your Dark Side*. New York: Penguin.

Ketturat, C., Frisch, J. U., Ullrich, J. et al. (2015) Disaggregating within- and between-person effects of social identification on subjective and endocrinological stress reactions in a real life stress situation. *Personality and Social Psychology Bulletin* 18 November. Online before print. DOI: 10.1177/0146167215616804.

Knowles, M. C. and Reddy, P. (2003) Variations in organisational culture. *Australian Journal of Psychology* 55: 134–134.

Lewis, J. (2009) Positive deviance: A case study in finding and harnessing the wisdom of organizational communities. *Business Information Review* 26(4): 282–287.

Lewis, S. (2011) *Positive Psychology at Work: How Positive Leadership and Appreciative Inquiry Create Inspiring Organizations*. Oxford: Wiley-Blackwell.

Linley, P. A., Harrington, S. A. and Garcea, N. (eds) (2010) *Oxford Handbook of Positive Psychology*. Oxford: OUP.

Marsh, D. R., Schroeder, D. G., Dearden, K. A. et al. (2004) The power of positive deviance. *British Medical Journal* 329: 1177–1179.

Menzies Lyth, I. (1960) Social systems as a defence against anxiety. *Human Relations* 13: 95–121.

Neilsen, K., Abildgaard, J. S. and Daniels, K. (2014) Putting context into organizational intervention design: Using tailored questionnaires to measure initiatives for worker well-being. *Human Relations* 67(12): 1537–1560.

Oettingen, G. (2014) *Rethinking Positive Thinking: Inside the New Science of Motivation*. New York: Penguin Random House.

Okonkwo, J. (2010) Coaching for leadership using myths and stories: An African perspective. In J. Passmore (ed.) *Leadership in Coaching: Working with Leaders To Develop Elite Performance*. London: Kogan Page.

Open Science Collaboration (2015) Estimating the reproducibility of psychological science. *Science* 349(6251) [online].

Owen, H. (2008) *Open Space Technology: A Users Guide*. San Francisco, CA: Berrett-Koehler.

Pennington, N. and Hastie, R. (1986) Evidence evaluation in complex decision-making. *Journal of Personality and Social Psychology* 51(2): 242–258.

Rousseau, D. M. (2006) Is there such a thing as evidence-based management? *Academy of Management Review* 31(2): 256–269.

Rozenthuler S (2012) *Life-Changing Conversations*. London: Watkins.

Salipante, P. and Smith, A. (2012) From the 3 Rs to the 4 Rs: Toward doctoral education that encourages evidence-based management through problem-focused research. In D. M. Rousseau (ed.) *Oxford Handbook of Evidence Based Management*. Oxford: Oxford University Press.

Scharma, C. O. (2009) *Theory U: Leading from the Future as It Emerges*. San Francisco, CA: Berrett-Koehler.

Schmucker, C., Schell, L. K., Portalupi, S. et al. (2014) Extent of non-publication in cohorts of studies approved by research ethics committees or included in trial registries. *PLoS One* 9(12):e114023. DOI:10. 1371/journal.pone.0114023.

Seligman, M. (2006) *Learned Optimism: How to Change Your Mind and Your Life*. New York: Vintage.

Sharot, T. (2012) *The Optimism Bias*. London: Constable and Robinson.

Shaw P (2002) *Changing Conversations in Organisations: A Complexity Approach to Change*. Oxon: Routledge.

Simon, H. (1969) *The Sciences of the Artificial*. Cambridge: MIT Press.

Singh, A. (forthcoming) *The Flip: The Positive Deviance Approach to Solve Complex Social Problems*. Asia: SAGE.

Stanford, N. (2004) *Organization Design: Engaging with Change*. Oxon: Routledge.

Sternin, M., Sternin, J. and Marsh, D. (1999) Scaling up a poverty alleviation and nutrition program in Viet Nam. In T. Marchione (ed.) *Scaling Up, Scaling Down: Capacities for Overcoming Malnutrition in Developing Countries*. Amsterdam: Gordon and Breach.

Tolchinsky, P. (2012) *Engaging the Whole System in Design*. Birmingham: European Organizational Design Forum (EODF).

Waks, L. J. (2001) Donald Schon's philosophy of design and design education. *International Journal of Technology and Design Education* 11: 37–51.

5

ETHICAL ISSUES IN PRACTICE

Introduction

Work undertaken in complex organizational contexts is quite distinct from the research or individual client contract relationships that many of the current ethics statements in psychosocial professions address. I would suggest we do not yet have a clear codified statement of ethical behaviour for complex contexts. Ethical practice in complex organizations is not about getting the 'right answer', instead it is about sustaining a justifiable approach, in all the circumstances, that you monitor and change if necessary, being fully mindful of ethical, stakeholder and practical pressures and challenges. There is no 'moral high ground', merely choices about more or less moral acts. This chapter seeks to give some practical guidelines for approaching intervention choices ethically.

Capabilities for ethical organizational practice

Chapter 1, Table 1.2 outlined nine practice capabilities. These are used in Table 5.1 as the framework to explore the types of ethical dilemmas I have faced in 30 years of professional practice. Managing these ethical dilemmas is not straightforward and I would never claim to have 'got them right'. They are continuing, real and live issues that are animated by the power and political issues of working with the realities of the psychosocial context in the workplace and my own sense of what I can and cannot tolerate.

To practise ethically is to be continually aware of these issues, of the day-to-day judgements involved (even when we are not necessarily aware we are making a decision) and of the need to engage in the meta-process of ethical consideration alongside all practice. For any practitioner intervening in the workplace, the inherent system complexity brings conflicts of interest and legal constraints into play far more extensively than working with a single client in a therapeutic relationship.

TABLE 5.1 Practice capabilities and ethical dilemmas

1. Engaging with wicked problems.

    - Accepting the client authority to define the help needed and their right to articulate the problem (they have authority over the issue) without you as a practitioner giving up your right to hold a distinct view.
    - Managing the uncertainty that comes from needing to use bespoke approaches to ensure the context is properly considered.
    - Keeping questions such as 'what constitutes helping, who am I helping?' as a continual reference point.
    - Using the psychosocial knowledge base to inform how practice is approached, not merely what is done (and managing the possible tensions between these two uses of evidence).

2. Accessing and using a wide range of evidence from multiple sources.

    - Understanding the importance of contextual (client) evidence and knowledge and how to access and use this evidence.
    - Ensuring evidence from all sources is collected, deployed and stored ethically – specifically considering whose confidentiality must be respected and how this is managed?
    - Understanding the difference between authentic intuition (10,000 flying hours) and opinion, and how to work with this distinction in self and others.
    - Interacting respectfully with other disciplines and understanding the wide range of different interests and ethical drivers.
    - Managing the professional limits of competence – the 'I don't know what to do for the best' scenario.

3. Confidentiality and contracting in the client relationship.

    - Being clear about what the client is asking, what you are committing to, what you are ethically able and prepared to do.
    - Acknowledging client confidentiality covers commercial sensitivity and competitive advantage reasons, not just the obligations around personal data.
    - Managing the tensions around professional obligation to disseminate given the complex confidentiality obligations.
    - Contracting effectively with all parties, with specific reference to the complexity of relationships in organizations.
    - Informed consent for employee participants and requirements to follow reasonable instructions in the employment contract.
    - Being explicit (e.g. in coaching which often has three-way contracts) about when and how can you ethically disclose an individual's 'data' to an organizational level paying client.
    - Monitoring for unintended impacts on the organization and being aware of when to withdraw from a specific practice engagement.

4. Diagnosis of client problems for intervention formulation.

    - Documenting how the wide range of evidence is pulled together and how assessments of relevance are made to ensure transparency in your professional decision making.

(continued)

TABLE 5.1 *(continued)*

- Balancing the need to demonstrate caring and confidence with appropriate caveats on certainty about assessments around what you recommend should be done.
- Articulating responsibilities for addressing any toxic manifestations you become aware of and being clear about your reasons for ceasing to support a client with toxic organizational issues.
- Articulating when an external disclosure may be required about concerns emerging from evidence collected internally and how any such process will be handled ethically with your client.

5. Using elaboration and synthesis in the processing of evidence.

- Being clear about how considerations of inclusion must impact your professional practice. Enabling voice and participation is clearly evidenced as a psychosocial need in the workplace.
- Managing the politics of involvement, including considerations of how voice will be enabled for different stakeholders.
- Managing the process of 'drinking from the corporate hose' – there is always more evidence embedded in a complex organization than can be handled.
- Articulating the relevance of external evidence in producing a context-relevant formulation of the issue.
- Deciding when to close down the collection of wide ranging evidence.
- Delivering a context relevant impact or 'business case' which includes clarity about whose 'synthesis of problem evidence' you are supporting and why.

6. Designing interventions.

- Activating the 'do no harm' ethic fully when designing interventions.
- Working with an understanding of the 'not invented here' process in the approach to design.
- Using client resources responsibly, enabling resource constraint and prototyping to ensure that impact is understood before large funds are invested.
- Understanding what informed consent means for the client when engaged in a 'fail fast' design prototyping process.
- Being prepared to give up ideas that don't work – resisting 'strategic persistence.
- Managing what 'measurement' does to the psychosocial realities of a client organization in the decisions around the prototypes used.

7. Monitor emergence and course correction.

- Engaging with what real-time monitoring looks like and not falling back on long-term research methods – we are 'cutting into living tissue' we cannot wait for months to know if it is working (knowing the difference between monitoring and evaluating).
- Managing the ethics of 'measurement' around multi-measures for pattern recognition, understanding the use of proxies and the possible harms from single targets linked to the behaviour it 'nudges' in complex systems.
- Engaging with how to enable pattern recognition by those in governance roles from the careful design of 'benefits tracking' protocols.

- Balancing the client impact from investment in intervention with the benefits that accrue from spend on measurement.
- Being able to say 'the intervention I implemented is not having the intended impact and stop it'.
- Enabling necessary course correction by having change mechanisms designed into the work.

8. Deploy knowledge through practice.

- Managing the self and enabling reflective space, for example through supervision to enable ongoing fitness to practise awareness and to manage own biases.
- Having a wide range of 'know-how' approaches available to match the specific client context productively, so grounding action in psychosocial knowledge.
- Role-modelling how to work productively to create psychological safety.
- Being inclusive in the use of knowledge and evidence in action.
- Balancing gaining acknowledgement for the help to build professional awareness with building client confidence in its abilities to improve (i.e. managing the dependency issue).
- Committing to Continuing Professional Development (CPD).
- Using the 'sin-eater' phenomenon to good effect (this is the process where someone comes to 'the village' and carries all the bad feeling out with them when they go – can convert to scapegoating which is a damaging attack rather than a service).

9. Focus on impact in context.

- Acknowledging issues of power, voice, globalization and colonization in the relationship with knowledge.
- Bringing clarity about the difference between methods from the lab and those suitable for the field.
- Being aware that knowing a 'fact' does not mean this 'fact' will 'help' in any specific context.
- Considering issues of harm and help as the underpinning driver of ethical practice.

You will work with many individuals, to all of whom you have some level of ethical responsibility, and who may be in conflict with each other and possibly also with you. In addition there will be a wide variety of professional perspectives, all of which have their own distinct interests and imperatives. For example when working in a complex workplace you will come across a wide range of different professional codes, contracts, legislative frameworks and business ethics imperatives. Figure 5.1 gives an illustration of such complexities. These can be contradictory and variably emphasize the primacy of different interests in different ways.

Ethical themes in organizational intervention

The ethical themes that I have found to been particularly critical to consider for organizational practice are:

- helping and harm;
- authority/accountability and power/knowledge;
- confidentiality and contracting in complex workplaces;
- self-regulation and supervision.

Helping and harm

When the purpose of work is knowledge production, ethics is focused on the validity of knowledge collection and output, ensuring we minimize the harm done to create it. Ethical questions for research therefore focus on approaches to avoid harm to research participants, while ensuring that the processes around creating knowledge are robust, reliable and valid.

When we move into the 'field' or client context the ethical questions are different and involve much wider interpretations of impact rather than taking a single

---

CASE ILLUSTRATION OF ETHICAL PRACTICE COMPLEXITIES

In my early years of working as an organizational psychologist, I was responsible for the review, design, implementation and consequent functioning of new team structures across Europe, Middle East and Africa (EMEA).

These were to be set up following the transition of staff and virement of contracts from one large organization into another. I was employed by the acquiring organization, working in the UK with an EMEA remit, reporting to a US-based divisional Executive Vice President. Managing this work required me to give attention to contract law across different jurisdictions and also to the statutory provision of the Acquired Rights Directive (European law).

I was a newly Chartered Psychologist in the UK at the time, covered by the Charter and Statutes of the British Psychological Society (BPS) which meant that I had chosen to be guided by the relevant code of ethics (this was before the Health and Care Professions Council (HCPC) regulatory framework came in). The complexity of my workplace practice situation meant that the BPS ethics guidance available, primarily designed to cover research practice and therapeutic interventions, did not fully engage with the process of ethical decision making for my practice in this complex organization.

The 'client' was an individual who had the authority vested from the organization to commission my work. In addition to providing 'help to the client' in my professional capacity, I was an employee in UK jurisdiction with all the contractual obligations this brings, but working for someone in a different employment jurisdiction, so with a different set of expectations from the employment relationship. The 'client' was therefore also *one* of my bosses as the complexity of reporting relationships in large matrix global companies regularly means there are at least two if not three 'bosses' at any one stage at work.

To be effective in my work also required me to work with a multitude of different individuals and it was not clear whether my exchanges with each individual would be covered by the client confidentiality provisions outlined in the British Psychological Society (BPS) ethics guidelines.

Effective delivery of my responsibilities also required me to work collaboratively with a range of different functions and professions. In designing and leading a new global team structure and operating model, I was working with a variety of professional interests all of which were critical to the effectiveness of the organization and had a different ethical orientation:

- The sales and marketing team were concerned that this work met customer expectations and would lead to customer reference-ability for future sales.
- The HR function, which comprised a team working across EMEA so was covered by various different qualification protocols and legislative frameworks, was focused on documenting transparent methods of transfer to support business viability, while managing the legal risk to the organization.
- Each manager (me included) in the business had an obligation under the employment contract to follow all reasonable instructions and to work in the best interest of the business.
- The professional psychology codes give primacy to client confidentiality, informed consent and the well-being of the individuals involved in this process.
- The legal team was focused upon adherence to ensuring the lawful process in each different jurisdiction (and there were many) was followed. This involved a risk assessment of the consultation and contract issues.
- Each trade union in each different country was concerned with the rights of/ benefits to its individual members and the adherence to sustaining the existing contract conditions required under the various regulations.
- The overall business ethics framework was focused upon reputation, compliance across jurisdictions and mitigating against any potential harm done to reputation from what was reported externally.

Discussion topics for group work

1. Discuss how each of these different professional interests can engage ethically with others and how the ethical boundaries can be managed.
2. Consider how the psychosocial evidence we have about psychological safety and well-being at work could influence how we think about the ethical issues in this case.
3. What do you consider to be the ethical and practice lessons to be taken from this for those starting out as a newly qualified practitioner?

FIGURE 5.1   Discussion: working ethically in complex organizations

focus on the 'costs' of fact production. A focus on helping with knowledge raises many questions:

- How does the ethics of knowing and helping line up?
- Which one takes precedence at any time?
- When does the drive to 'know' undermine the capacity to help?
- What does confidentiality mean in the context of a client engagement and what knowledge can be shared with whom?
- What about informed consent – if you let a client know that you are doing knowledge work rather than helping work, would they commission you? Should they commission you?

The helping relationship assumed in the majority of ethics codes is the 1–1 therapeutic relationship. However realities of the complex workplace bring different helping dynamics and hence different ethical concerns. The work of Schein (2009: 4–5) on 'helping' outlines the array of 'helping relationships' that co-exist in complex workplaces:

- 'The computer expert walking you through the steps to fix a computer problem'.
- 'The operating-room nurse handing the surgeon the right instrument just in time'.
- 'The executive coach advising a manager on how to handle subordinates'.
- 'The boss advising subordinates how to do their job better'.
- 'The caregiver ministering to a sick person'.
- 'The consultant trying to improve the functioning of an organization'.

Intervening, as well as being part of a helping relationship in itself, may well impact other helping relationships in the workplace, and this requires ongoing consideration. For me intelligent activism is constantly governed by a reflective awareness of the potential for helping and harm in all of the encounters required. This has to address both the ethical imperatives from what we know and the potential for harm. The balance of helping and knowing can be explored by considering the case illustration in Figure 5.2.

Authority/accountability and power/knowledge

Intervention is never neutral but undertaken in a complex political and power-laden context. There is authority, power and knowledge residing in the client context and authority, power and knowledge claimed in the consultant context. This dynamic is again slightly different from therapeutic contexts as the power balance in organizational intervention sits more in the client hands than in those of the practitioner (which is another differentiating factor not fully addressed in the ethics codes currently available to guide professional practice). This complex client relationship brings with it two ethical questions:

- How do we work with the client authority/accountability and power/knowledge?
- How do we work with our own authority/accountability and power/knowledge?

Clients hold authority/accountability vested through organizational position and reinforced with purchasing power. The obligation of any client purchaser (whether accessing internal or external services) is to commission and access help and intervention in the best interests of the whole organizational 'body'. This represents a complex array of stakeholder contexts, external interests and governance procedures activated as part of being a large complex employment organization.

HOW TO HELP USING KNOWLEDGE IN A FIELD CONTEXT

I was asked for help from a client concerned about what they considered to be the failures of their recruitment process, which was manifesting as high overall turnover and particularly of ethnic minority recruits and women.

There were high demands in the environment and managers only prepared to give cursory attention to the job definition and the recruitment process in the context of myriad other pressing obligations and considerations.

The person commissioning the work in the client organization was new to the role and wanted to make their mark through introducing 'scientific approaches to recruitment'. A constrained budget was available to spend in the next three months with a business case required as output to enable further investment in organizational changes. This budget was a special dispensation to the new incumbent because the organization had tried to change their recruitment practices before without success.

Professionally, the standard view is that testing in the workplace has produced more reliable outcomes than using interview assessments alone. However I was vaguely aware of long-established research that contradicted this conventional view and indicated that while some tests may differentiate on capability, they have no predictive power in determining how well someone will do a job (Blinkhorn and Johnson 1990) and that this held particularly for personality testing. Further I was aware of emerging evidence that many ability tests have cultural biases built in (Aguinis et al. 2010) and the client issue appeared to be one of inclusion.

The ethical dilemma for me in this situation was how did I manage the conflicting knowledge I had about testing with the evidence from the client context to feed into a 'helping relationship', working within the tight timescales which meant there was no time for any of the specific systematic review approaches to be completed.

To work through issues of helping and harm in knowledge driven consulting engagements discuss the following questions.

- How might you engage with this request?
- What considerations other than recruitment may be relevant?
- What are the opportunities to help the organization?

  - Your paying client?
  - The employees of the organization?
  - Those applying for work?

- What may be the conflicts you need to manage in ensuring that these three groups are all 'helped'?
- What are the risks of harm: to the organization? To the individual client purchaser? To the existing employees of the organization? To those applying for work?
- What might be the challenges for an ethical practitioner in engaging with these risks?
- How could each of the different sets of codes – employment contract, customer delivery, psychological, legal, HR risk and reputation/business ethics – play out differently in this situation?

This scenario is a composite from various client engagements that I have been involved in.

FIGURE 5.2 Discussion: balancing the ethics of helping and knowing

The purchasing relationship and the contract associated with it, makes explicit the importance of the client definition of what is problematic and the types of intervention considered suitable. While a focus on helping would certainly encourage working with this presenting formulation, this is not the only consideration in ethical practice. We also need to consider when it is appropriate to challenge their presentation and the best way to do this. This requires working carefully in the middle ground (which also requires an understanding of contractual framework and course correction protocols in place) accepting the presenting formulation as the necessary starting point to help, while also being prepared to challenge the client in the interests of both the organization and its wider social impacts. This is a significant political question as shown in Figure 5.3.

In addition, ethical issues linked to client authority require understanding the complex stakeholder and regulatory processes that exist in and around large complex workplaces which are beyond the scope of this text, but touched upon in the case given earlier in Figure 5.1.

Practitioners' authority/power/knowledge comes through evidence and expertise, often linked to working for a reputable firm. The ethical issues associated

---

CLIENT AUTHORITY/ACCOUNTABILITY: COMMISSIONING FOR GOOD OR ILL?

There have been serious concerns about the way the substantial psychological evidence base has been used for development in two contexts that bring this ethical dilemma to life.

One is the support that has been available for the design of interrogation techniques for Guantanamo Bay (https://www.psychologytoday.com/blog/dangerous-ideas/201504/the-apa-and-guantanamo-actions-not-words) (APA report Hoffman 2015).

The other is the use of selection approaches for reality TV shows like 'Big Brother' in the UK, which are deployed to ensure that the viewer gets an entertaining and voyeuristic experience (http://www.independent.co.uk/news/media/psychologists-in-trouble-for-big-brother-711122.html).

In each there is the 'client' request for help and the professional has provided this help based upon the best available external evidence. There will be employment relationships and contracts for services in place. So far this work has been considered acceptable in the relevant jurisdictions since to the best of my knowledge there have been no prosecutions, despite public scrutiny and profession censure.

Both of these examples use the authority of scientifically based professional knowledge to help a client. However, there have been ethical challenges.

In group discussion consider the following:

- What forms of client authority are involved in activating this work?
- What are the considerations at play here considering all of the different sets of ethical codes that may apply?
- What are your personal ethical reactions to these areas of work?

FIGURE 5.3 Discussion: client authority and professional limits

with the content of this knowledge and the privileges embedded in it can be overlooked and this is not acceptable for intelligent activism. This expertise comes from a balance of authentic intuition that comes through experience and the use of the 'knowledge gems' generated from the lab. When we select which insights, evidence and 'knowledge' to use and how to use them, we have an obligation to understand and if necessary question how this knowledge was created; not at the level of the individual paper but centred on the institutional processes around knowledge production.

Most of our 'lab' gems have been produced from the implicit assumption that there is objective generalizable knowledge, considered 'true' regardless of context. The core assumption is that there are 'essential' and stable properties of entities, whether those entities are rocks, viruses, fruit, individuals, teams or organizations. Given the cultural and experiential diversity across our world, these assumptions could be described as colonizing when not confined to use as a parameter to enable work in the lab but instead taken directly to the field.

This way of knowing 'works' by putting clear boundaries around 'things' to enable the 'thing' to be investigated. Good lab practice involves testing hypotheses by designing research studies or experiments that actively control and filter out extraneous variables to the point where these essential properties or facts can become clear. An example of this orientation to knowledge, applied to psychosocial practice is illustrated in the following: 'organizational psychology can inform on how to increase desirable behaviours [. . .] Desirable behaviors align with organizational interests while undesirable behaviors do not' (Davey 2011: 467).

The critical ethical questions raised by this quote are: 'who gets to say which behaviours are desirable and why?' 'Whose "organizational interests" get privileged and whose views are silenced in defining "desirability" or "interests"?'

When coupled with the existence of client authority, this orientation has the capacity to work to reinforce a set of inherently oppressive assumptions that in turn works to disempower marginal groups and interests by limiting the rights to speak, to know and to act, to a small select group and so are in themselves implicated in organizational toxicity. Nichterlein (2015) explores further these implications for practice.

Such science creates 'subjects' and does not make explicit where the authority to do this comes from. Applying this outside the 'lab' normalizes the right of one group to have such 'authority' over another. This is not merely in the relatively constrained employment contract associated with managing the work of another, but in the much more extreme situation of having a 'higher claim' to assertions of 'truth': '[i]t is an unfortunate misunderstanding (a legacy of rationalism) to think that truth can only be "the truth" universal; that truth is that which is repeatable and constant rather than that which is fleeting' (Bakhtin 1993: 37). My ethical concern is that this unchecked leads to colonization of the field and the eradication of the emergent. Accepting and working with field emergence is central to engaging ethically with wicked problems, beautifully illustrated in *Ordinary Affects* (Stewart 2007), which offers an emergent anthropological account of how social reality takes shape and the extent to which emotion dominates the trajectories of experience.

This said, choosing not to use the knowledge generated from this orientation must also give us pause, because there are potential harms from ignoring the contents. This work has generated insights that can be used to give voice to those with less power and also gives us insights into many of the mechanisms of organizational toxicity. However, the method (the means) that produced these insights constitutes a serious source of such organizational toxicity in itself if allowed outside these very tightly controlled domains. My view is that when working as an intelligent activist, we should use these products judiciously, with great care around how they are deployed and we must ask the following ethical questions of our practice:

- Does what we know stand up to scrutiny for use in this environment?
- What context (and what sample) was used to generate this 'fact'?
- Who benefits or loses from the proposed work based on this 'fact'?
- What may be the unintended consequences of deploying this knowledge in this situation?
- What is the financial/reputation justification for using this knowledge? Who pays? Who gains? Who loses?
- What implicit assumptions am I imposing on others in using this knowledge?
- What scope do those with less power have to disagree or opt out of this process?
- How does what we know align with the hard won legal and other regulatory constraints on the organization?

An alternative to this 'entities and properties approach' is critical theory, which is concerned with mechanisms and systems of power. Critical thinking can provide an excellent framework for effective supervision and reflective practice and so work to help the intelligent activist deconstruct the power relationships in their work, as organizations, social systems and power structures are the 'subjects' in this critical practice.

However, I consider that the use of critical theory also needs to come with a health warning, as it generates a power structure that subordinates the 'human' to the 'word'. From my point of view, and as a 'lapsed' member of the secular project that I was born into, there is a paradoxically religious quality to the form of authority it activates. There seems to be a desire to find a 'moral high ground' immune from the politics of power, but with no acknowledgement that any idea of 'high ground' always comes at the expense of others. The sense of detachment this creates can manifest in experiences of powerlessness, hopelessness and the inability to act for fear of being in the wrong.

Intelligent activism is the choice to live and work within a contested power structure with awareness and intent to change, rather than operating from this 'safe' distance:

When women choose to unite to challenge white supremacy, a profound revolution of value will take place. Love of justice will be expressed by changing thought and action. Visionary feminist thinkers have already shown everyone that we can be disloyal to the dominator culture, that we can indeed build bonds of solidarity that help us heal from traumatic wounds caused by racist assault as well as the traumas of sexist and classist oppression. When the world truly listens to the voices of women who have and are daily working to decolonize our minds, who live in the joy of that transformation, we can all walk the path to greater liberation, to solidarity.

(hooks 2013: 57)

Intelligent activism cannot work from the disembodied space generated by 'lab' thinking, but instead needs to embrace a messy and muddled commitment to work towards a life that is worth living. We need to know that the words used in any organizational setting are inherently mutable and that we can use the power of the word for impact and compassion not distance.

In contrast to these issues with 'knowledge production', the emerging 'lower status' approaches within 'know-how' (practice) implicitly recognize the tension between means and ends. This is evidenced in the increasing advocacy of 'co-creation' approaches in the workplace. These approaches are explicitly designed to relinquish authority and control over what is produced and also what 'it' must mean to everybody. These approaches have emerged in response to the practical recognition that participation mitigates toxic workplaces, coupled with the practical wisdom that knowing how we take the fact into the field must not mirror the method that was used to create it.

Confidentiality and contracting in complex workplaces

Confidentiality and contracting are closely connected considerations in organizational practice, which are undertaken within various legal and regulatory structures. They are often either codified in contract or active in the implied nature of other contracts. In addition, clients very often have substantial power in access to this regulatory environment and can impose considerations of confidentiality through contractual provision. There are three themes that need consideration under this heading:

- the complex nature of confidentiality requirements;
- the awareness of the legal realities of contracts;
- the need to manage change and emergence in contracted work.

Confidentiality is a distinctive issue in the helping relationship with a complex workplace as it does not involve one individual, but includes a corporate body and relationships and exchanges with many individuals. The organizational requirements around confidentiality bring considerations of competitive advantage and what this means for the ownership of the work undertaken. This can lead to a tension between professional obligations to disseminate and contractual obligations to the client and need to be clearly articulated and managed. For suppliers who provide services such as employee surveys to commercial organizations, part of this tension can be managed via contracts whereby the data-set is the property of the supplier, but such data cannot be published in a form that identifies the individual client. The supplier can use this data for generating norm bases to outline general principles, and to answer queries against the data-set from the client. However, they are usually not contractually allowed to disclose either the client or a client-identified publication of survey findings. The advantage to the client organization from this arrangement is that it provides a mechanism that guarantees the individual confidentiality they are obligated to provide to their employees, while protecting the commercial sensitivity inherent in the data.

The confidentiality structure around survey is an exemplar to work through the ethical considerations and potential conflicts between commercially sensitive data and professional obligations to disseminate knowledge. Managing such tensions in practice is not straightforward and contributes to a scarcity of detailed published material from practitioners. It may be assumed that there is no substantial practice knowledge developed, but this is not the case. The lack of published material is often due to the obligation to honour complex confidentiality clauses in corporate contexts and these ethical and legal considerations are fully active in the production of this text. There are completely different confidentiality obligations in 'lab work' managed in line with the ethics mechanisms in place, as science focuses upon the impact on each individual 'subject'. There is no mutual understanding of these obligations between the lab and field context, which has been a major issue for me when brokering 'science' research access into commercial contexts.

In addition to these corporate complexities, there are also equivalent obligations to each individual involved in the intervention process, due to the codes imposed on practitioners together with the ethic of 'do no harm'. As the work is being paid for by the client organization, and the data collected in work time, the confidentiality obligations due to the individual are complex. A key confidentiality requirement is to contain the frustrations that will inevitably be expressed in the process of intervention, so creating a safe space for voice and modelling the necessary psychosocial micro processes that mitigate toxicity. This impacts what gets recorded and how it gets reported. It is crucial to resist the temptation to collude with the paying client about the problems associated with this normal frustration or be drawn into gossip about what unfolds in this process.

There is also the need to manage conflicts between organizational and individual interest such as that in the three-way contract for business coaching where the organization pays and the individual participates. It is important to spell out the confidentiality provisions you will apply. My approach is to guarantee confidentiality to the individual about what is said in a session but that the assessments I make can be shared, if I consider it to be in the best interests of both parties. In audit and inquiry engagements and the associated formal interviews and group discussions, it is critical to make it clear what will not be shared, what can be shared and what you have a professional obligation to share (linked to the prevention of harm to others). This also requires attention to obligations around commercially sensitive information that is disclosed to you and your need to be clear about your contractual obligations in this regard.

The awareness of the legal realities of contracts and regulatory context is important, as there is always an implied contract, whether or not it is in writing if money is to be exchanged. There can of course be some uncertainty about whether or not money is to be exchanged and this is a critical part of any client discussion. At which stage of the engagement a contract exists, and how precise this needs to be, is dependent on circumstance. It does not need to be a complex written version to have legal impact. As there can be considerable relationship or tender activity before there is any commitment to payment this is not a straightforward matter as there will be intellectual property issues that are beyond the scope of this text.

The practical matters that need attention include the obligations to ensure you are entitled to work in the relevant jurisdictions, that you hold indemnity and liability insurance and that you are mindful of your duty of care to self and others under any Health and Safety legislation in the relevant jurisdiction. It is also important to make yourself aware of the various employment protections and equality provisions offered through localized statute.

In addition, as a practitioner using a particular knowledge set the contractual assumption will be that you bring expertise. The obligation to use this effectively, recognize when something is outside your specific expertise and to keep expertise up to date will be part of the implied terms of any agreement around work that you will do, regardless of whether this is written down.

There is literature in work psychology focused on the idea of the psychological contract (Rousseau 1995), which can inform this, but I find the idea of implied contract terms articulated in law more helpful in ethical practice as it brings an indication of the regulations, duties and obligations that impact practice. In the UK this is expressed in the idea of 'mutual trust and confidence' which can be helpfully informed through a consideration of psychosocial factors that need attention in mitigating organizational toxicity.

Finally under this heading, there is also the ethical and professional issue of when it is in the public interest to override contractual obligations (therefore lawful) and disclose an issue. The details of managing such a consideration as a practitioner are beyond the bounds of this text book, but whistleblowing is a growing concern in working in complex organizations, particularly those that are manifesting some of the more troubling and toxic manifestations, as explored in Chapter 12.

The contract can change – just because there is an agreement in place does not mean that there can be no change in the work to be done. Research that I did in the construction industry, early in my career, when I was studying the impact of contract and contract variation indicated that the best financial outcomes came from a moderate level of contract variation. It is a research insight that I have used throughout my practice career. There are two key dynamics I would draw your attention to:

- The need for mechanisms of course correction to keep the work focused on 'purpose'; the 'why' of the design thinking model (see Chapter 4).
- The potential for misunderstandings and conflict in ideas and expectations.

Course correction is often in the best interests of the organization and needs to be actively designed into the work to happen effectively. There are a multitude of ways to establish protocols around this should it be necessary. It needs to build in careful time lines and benefits tracking around what you will do, when you report, how you report and how you authorize and account for change. A failure to enable and manage this process can result in the workplace suffering from practitioner-introduced toxicity both because of the damage done through strategic persistence (see Chapter 7) and the potential for conflicts around perceptions of success, failure and delivery.

The psychosocial realities outlined elsewhere in this text mean that there is a large scope for misunderstanding in expectations around agreements made and the work done. A critical skill for the practitioner is expectation management, which requires the constant attention to the perceptions of the work held by all interested parties. It is important to understand what their concerns may be and how these may unfold through the work. How a practitioner self-regulates in this reality is one of the major ways in which we can role model the practices needed to mitigate toxicity. Fundamentally it requires an acceptance that as a practitioner you are in the system and everything you do has symbolic impact.

Self-regulation and supervision in practice

To be an ethical practitioner, asking the self-referent question 'Am I competent to do this work?' and committing to regular Continuing Professional Development (CPD) is necessary, yet not sufficient evidence of self-regulation. We must also be aware of how the use of 'self' can be part of the helping relationship. This brings with it questions about what support must be in place for you as a practitioner to be able to work effectively. As psychosocial practitioners, we work in the context not merely on the context. As all our actions are in effect, system interventions, each needs to be ethically driven if we are to be effective 'intelligent activists'; 'so manage the tension between presenting, which is putting on a face, and action' (Bakhtin, 1993: 54).

The five concepts I use in self-regulating my practice are:

- working as a 'boundary object';
- setting the tone;
- steering recognition;
- personal risk-taking through role modelling 'authenticity';
- governing the self.

Working as a 'boundary object'

This is a critical skill in enabling diverse groups to work collaboratively and central to the work of effective knowledge translation across silos, professions and different organizations. Holding this space skilfully enables a practitioner to 'disrupt' toxic organizational functioning. This work involves containing the difference between 'inside' and 'outside' in the face of strong and ubiquitous group process. Working in this way requires constant attention to the possibility of the practitioner 'going native' (O'Reilly 2009). This is an anthropological term used to describe the stage when an individual becomes so identified with a group that she or he can no longer 'see' what is going on in that group.

Instead it is necessary to work explicitly as a boundary object containing any of our anxieties about belonging, so new insights, understanding and creativity can flow. To be able to do this work well requires a clear understanding of how participation, belonging needs and scapegoating processes operate in the specific workplace context. This knowledge needs to inform how we enable participation and benign psychosocial interaction. The work of intervention often leads to initial expressions of dissatisfaction, frustration and lack of trust from people in the organization, directed at the practitioner as the 'vehicle' of the organization. Containing this well and not taking it personally is critical both to demonstrate the safety of speaking up and to ensure that you do not get expelled from the system.

Setting the tone

To have serious impact, we need to take ethical responsibility to work with mood and tone. Working from embodied self-awareness rather than working from the power of abstraction opens the space for play, lightness and compassion. Humour in such circumstances is a serious business, and there is substantial evidence of the positive impact on productivity, creativity, innovation and well-being that comes from enabling this freer psychological state. A consideration for activating 'play', which emerges from activation of the compassionate system (Gilbert 2009 and see Chapter 6), is the use of story and metaphor in the work of intervening (Chapter 9). Doing this may not represent the knowledge you bring in a manner that the knowledge producer would recognize, but it is critical for ideas to have impact. It is really hard to care or play from the position of expert, particularly when there has been a source of distress in a system. Tone is increasingly being identified as one of the critical aspects of 'leadership' and as a consultant the conscious ability to impact the tone is a critical part of the ethical skill set to remove toxicity from complex workplaces.

Steering recognition

Intervention helps by subtly impacting the workplace conditions to change possible outcomes. Any intervention itself may not necessarily generate the tangible outcome desired, but instead it creates the conditions where those within a work-place generate the desired outcomes for themselves. Effective interventions disrupt by enabling people to feel safer to speak up, to work with those they do not know, to be more open to learning new things and to relax and access their imagination to come up with new ideas. When intervention 'works', it will be relatively invis-ible, because those that fully participate in these toxicity-disrupting processes will rightfully take ownership of the impact. The challenge for an ethical practitioner is to be able to articulate this work clearly so that recognition is shared appropriately. The intent is not to claim all the credit, which is disrespectful, undermines the work of others and will be toxic in consequence, or to become so invisible that the importance of our practices in enabling this shift is missed. On many occasions I have come across attempts to 'prove' intervention works by focusing on the out-come or by claiming too much credit. An ethical approach needs to claim enough credit to ensure that the improvement work will continue without underplaying the importance of what the client has done.

Personal risk-taking through role modelling 'authenticity'

This is a crucial skill set when working with systems in distress. There is some con-sideration of the idea of authenticity and the extent to which this is a justification for just saying what you think without filters in any given situation; a perspec-tive which has been characterized as 'true to self'. To be clear, this is not what I mean by authenticity but instead I prefer the adaptive model of authenticity (Ibarra 2015). 'Authenticity' involves owning the personal authority of being present, being vulnerable and taking the personal risk necessary for truth telling and unde-fended inquiry. If the practitioner cannot do this, they cannot intervene in toxic systems, they can only maintain the status quo. Using authenticity and presence is critical in allowing the things that must be said to be aired safely, to enable creativ-ity and to generate the confidence that things can be better.

Governing the 'self'

This requires a conscious use of the processes involved in setting the tone, tak-ing appropriate personal risks, diagnosing and managing discourse with a range of people and having the capacity to operate in real time, combining two 'selves': the self that knows itself and the other that just acts (Bakhtin 1993).

Bringing distinctive specific expertise (compared with shared expertise) can lead to feelings of ostracism (Jones and Kelly 2013). Developing and delivering a process for a particular context, trusting the process of intervention, relying on the people participating to create the output, all while sustaining the 'boundary object' posi-tion, makes ethical intervention practice uncomfortable, lonely and very skillful work. In my view it is critical to acknowledge that the full belonging, contribut-ing and meaning-making needs of the practitioner (whether as a consultant or a manager) will not be met through doing such work. In many other practices there is a requirement for supervision, coaching or the space for reflection. Psychosocial intervention in the workplace does not yet have a clear or accepted reflective practice requirement. Comparing this situation with the education of medics is helpful as there is increasing attention to the purpose of supervision in their practice not merely being about gaining knowledge, but much more importantly developing this client centred helping ethic (Bombeke et al. 2010). This need must be addressed for anyone doing substantial work with toxicity in complex systems. The growth of coaching style relationships is a potential part of the solution to this issue, but is generally more available for those working as managers or 'tempered radicals' (Meyerson and Scully 1995) in the context. For those working externally to an organization, a key ethical question centres on how to put in place the support processes needed to sustain fitness to practice. The work of Schon (1983) on reflective practice and professional expertise is helpful in this context.

Conclusion

In this chapter I have raised the key areas for ethical consideration when intervening in complex systems: helping and harm; authority; confidentiality; and self-regulation. This has also outlined the ethical capabilities needed for practice.

Further reading

The two following articles are not referenced in the text but help in exploring the complexities of large organizations and the ethical issues endemic within them, that practitioners need to navigate.

Linstead, S. (2013) Organizational bystanding: Whistleblowing, watching the work go by or aiding and abetting. *M@n@gement* 16(5): 680–696.
Shadnam, M. and Lawrence, T. B. (2011) Understanding widespread misconduct in organizations: An institutional theory of moral collapse. *Business Ethics Quarterly* 21(3): 379–407.

References

Aguinis, H., Culpepper, S. A. and Pierce, C. A. (2010) Revival of test bias research in preemployment testing. *Journal of Applied Psychology* 95(4): 648–680.
Bakhtin, M. M. (1993) *Towards a Philosophy of the Act*. Austin, TX: University of Texas Press.
Blinkhorn, S. and Johnson, C. (1990) The insignificance of personality testing. *Nature* 348(6303): 671–672.
Bombeke, K., Symons, L., Debaene, L. et al. (2010) Help I'm losing my patient centeredness! Experiences of medical students and their teachers. *Medical Education* 44(7): 662–673.
Davey, G. (ed.) (2011) *Applied Psychology*. Chichester: BPS Blackwell.
Gilbert, P. (2009) *The Compassionate Mind*. London: Constable and Robinson.
Hoffman, D. H. (2015) Report to the Special Committee of the Board of Directors of the American Psychological Association. http://www.apa.org/independent-review/APA-FINAL-Report-7.2.15.pdf.

hooks, b. (2013) *Writing beyond Race: Living Theory and Practice*. New York: Routledge.

Ibarra, H. (2015) Adaptive authenticity: The authenticity paradox. *Harvard Business Review* January/February [online].

Jones, E. E. and Kelly, J. (2013) The psychological costs of knowledge specialization in groups: Unique expertise leaves you out of the loop. *Organizational Behaviour and Human Decision Processes* 121(2): 174–182.

Meyerson, D. and Scully M. (1995) Tempered radicalism and the politics of ambivalence and change. *Organization Science* 6(6): 585–600.

Nichterlein, M. (2015) https://www.psychologytoday.com/blog/post-clinical/201512/deleuze-and-stupid-psychology.

O'Reilly, K. (2009) *Key Concepts in Ethnography*. London: SAGE.

Rousseau, D. M. (1995) *Psychological Contracts in Organizations: Understanding Written and Unwritten Agreements*. Los Angeles, CA: SAGE.

Schein, E. H. (2009) *Helping: How to Offer, Give and Receive Help*. San Francisco, CA: Berrett-Koehler.

Schon, D. (1983) *The Reflective Practitioner: How Professionals Think in Action*. New York: Basic Books.

Stewart, K. (2007) *Ordinary Affects*. Durham, NC: Duke University Press.

PART II

Building an integrated model of organizational toxicity

The chapters included in this part of the text build an integrated model of organizational toxicity, based upon empirical work from a wide variety of disciplines.

Chapter 6 provides a review of the current literature relevant to organizational toxicity. It produces a new formulation of organizational toxicity, based on the idea of the 'toxic dose', and presents a multi-level model of the processes that make workplaces psychosocially toxic. It builds upon the increasing emphasis in the literature on the affective revolution and the recognized connections between micro and macro levels in organizational function.

Chapter 7 gives an overview of the structural, cognitive, behavioural and symbolic macro environmental sources of toxicity and how these lead to toxicity. This chapter outlines the literature that informs these considerations in practice.

Chapter 8 introduces four psychosocial clusters – accountability, compassion, appreciation and growth – which represent the relationship processes that can mitigate toxicity on a day-to-day basis but which can be denatured at certain toxic dose levels.

6

WHAT WE KNOW ABOUT ORGANIZATIONAL TOXICITY

Introduction

There are many accounts outlining the evidence of toxic outcomes in complex organizations; financial services are 'designed' to enhance the value of money through managed and shared risk and there are many examples of how they have worked effectively to make money worthless. Health services are established to cure disease and yet contemporary high profile media stories talk of how they cause harm. These popular accounts of such organizational problems tend to offer simplistic assertions of solution advocating 'culture change' or 'better leadership'. As Chapter 3 indicates there is now comprehensive evidence that the planned approach to organizational change via dictate does not create the change desired. Further Chapter 3 outlines the subtle, time consuming and resource demanding work with the current realities in each workplace, necessary to enable change in functioning.

Understanding the causes of organizational toxicity is critical for ethical intervention and requires us to translate social science knowledge into psychosocial interventions to address these serious problems. To be able to do this 'translation' effectively we need a formulation of how organizations can become toxic, and determine what the blocks, barriers and constraints are on effective system function.

There has been increasing attention to the connections between the macro and micro levels in organizations (Martell et al. 2012; Bogenhold 2013; Greve 2013). This chapter presents a model of organizational toxicity integrating macro–micro factors. What a psychosocial perspective on organizational toxicity allows us to identify is how micro processes in the workplace interact with macro sources of toxicity to cause these outcomes. What this indicates is critical for intervention; it is that we need to work at both of these levels in parallel, as outlined in the orchestrate/participate model. Just focusing upon the macro can build up higher doses of toxins in the system. Just focusing upon the micro 'blames the individual' for things that no one of us alone can control and so increases levels of cynicism and fear. The material for this exploration of organizational toxicity is presented in two sections:

- An integrated understanding of organizational toxicity using the early formulation of the idea of toxicity.
- A review of the existing social science literature relevant to concerns with organizational toxicity.

Towards an integrated understanding of organizational toxicity

To build an integrated model of toxicity my chosen starting point is the original concept of toxicity: '[e]verything is poison and there is poison in everything: only the dose makes it toxic' (attributed to Paracelsus 1493–1541). Paracelsus is also of interest to psychology as he is widely recognized as being the first philosopher/theorist to ascribe psychological causes for illness, which he described as 'diseases of the imaginal'.

The toxic dose

This formulation introduces the concept of the 'toxic dose'. It does not assume a simple cause and effect phenomenon based on whether an agent is poisonous, but instead assumes that there is a threshold concentration at which any 'agent' has a qualitatively different impact than it does at lower concentrations. Toxic effects are not felt until certain levels of exposure are reached and the working assumption is that any agent could potentially reach a toxic level. Figure 6.1 offers an illustration of how dose differentially impacts outcome in the human body.

What this insight allows us to consider is that when we talk of organizational toxicity, we are not discussing alien factors, but instead must consider those things

---

TOXIC DOSE IN THE PHYSICAL WORLD

A good example is botulism which occurs everywhere, usually without negative impact and can be used in certain doses without a problem, as evidenced in the use of botox treatment, but:

- at increased doses it will lead to the respiratory system beginning to function in a different way;
- removing the poison does not stop the toxic impact because the organism has started to function differently;
- this can lead to the death of the person.

FIGURE 6.1 Botulism and the toxic dose

found in the normal everyday in organizations, that become problematic for psychosocial functioning when they have reached a specific level or 'dosage'.

Toxicity is caused by interaction

More recent definitions of toxicity, for example quoted in the OECD Glossary, provide us with an insight into the current understanding of this term: '[t]oxicity is the ability of a substance to *cause* poisonous effects resulting in severe biological harm or death after exposure to, or contamination with, that substance' (emphasis added). This indicates that the contemporary onus places the attention on the negative outcomes, but with a clear reference to the internal processes expressed into the concept of 'cause'. While attention to negative outcomes clarifies the existence of a contemporary problem, it does not provide us with the necessary insights to intervene effectively.

Paracelsus' original formulation of toxicity suggested that the production of toxins is the consequence of a dynamic process between an external 'poisonous' agent and the biological (natural) processes within a living entity. When the dose of the external agent is sufficient, the external agent and the internal processes of the living entity work together, via the 'denaturing' of a normal function, to produce poisonous effects. It is these effects that can consequently lead to the living entity's damage or destruction. Considering this early formulation allows us to ask a series of questions, explicitly chosen to support approaches to intervention.

I consider that it is essential to bring to the foreground this idea of a *toxic process as an interaction* to be able to effectively understand organizational function and dysfunction, as it is the organizational interaction with the potentially poisonous agent which offers the focus for intervention design. To illustrate, the idea of competitiveness in the context of the current design of performance management gives a helpful insight into this process. Moderate levels of competitiveness can be productive, playful, benign and engaging, however Chapter 10, which examines performance management and how it makes workplaces toxic, illustrates the profound negative impacts of social comparison and gaming behaviour when the context places too much competition into an environment that relies on collaboration.

To enable this we need to consider the contribution of each of the following aspects of the interaction characterized in Table 6.1.

What the literature tells us about organizational toxicity

The idea of organizational toxicity is not new and there is literature across the social sciences of relevance. Organizational psychology has been addressing the human experience of work since the early 1900s (Hollway 1991). Recently, the study of stress at work has been a significant aspect of this. The most well-established work from this field has been the contribution to understanding the factors that contribute to workplace stress (e.g. Cooper and Payne 1978; Cox 1978; NIOSH 1999).

TABLE 6.1 The organization toxicity dynamic

1. We need to know:	2. So that we can:
a. What is potentially 'poisonous' to large complex workplaces? b. What doses of any agent are critical to disrupt organization (environment) functioning and so lead to toxin production? c. What psychosocial micro processes get denatured by this toxic process in the workplace? d. How toxicity manifests as a system problem and how do these problems develop?	a. Know how to decrease the likelihood of the toxic interaction (improve organization environmental resistance) b. Know how we might stop 'normal' psychosocial interactions from reaching toxic dose levels (prevent organizational toxicity) c. Know how to mitigate the toxic impact once it has started (define what interventions work)

The chosen starting point for this review is the formulation of 'stress' as a workplace problem that gained practical attention in the 1980s and 1990s.

Overview of the stress agenda and epidemiology

Any literature search will give an indication of how widespread the stress idea of human problems at work has become. The initial attention to this topic was intra-individual (i.e. what were the characteristics within an individual that meant they were more or less likely than others to get stressed). The significant step in this work was the shift to studying the environmental causes for this manifest problem (Cox et al. 2000). This was an important shift as it moved the 'blame' for the dysfunction from the individual to the workplace psychological environment, recognizing that solutions lay in the organization not the individual victim. There are various models of the relationship between the individual and the environment and the way this interaction causes a stress reaction. These include the Job Demand–Control model (Karasek 1979), the Effort–Reward Imbalance model (Siegrist 1996) and the Job-Strain model (Karasek and Theorell 1990).

Central to this early work has been the distillation of research from psychology and other social sciences into a statement of those factors at play in a workplace environment that are implicated in a heightened experience of stress at work. It also clarifies those aspects of work that must form part of an approach to Health at Work risk management in the workplace. The most commonly used set of 'psychosocial hazards' identified has been articulated in the work of the Health and Safety Executive (HSE) in the UK (see Figure 6.2). Psychosocial hazards are the factors in an environment that cause individuals to experience stress.

My experience is that these HSE-defined hazards only include the factors that have been shown to damage individuals. They do not extend to the full set of

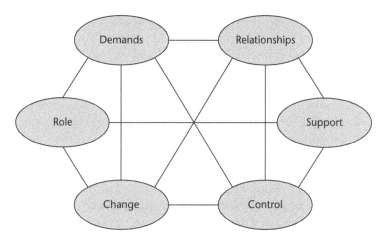

FIGURE 6.2   Psychosocial hazards in the workplace (HSE)

'agents' that can denature an organization so is a necessary but not sufficient account of potential workplace toxins. A fuller account of various organizational causes of stress at work is given in Leka and Jain (2010) in a World Health Organization publication. In addition, it is important to note that organizational toxicity is manifested in more ways than just the stress reaction. The macro sources of toxicity are explored in Chapter 7 together with the psychosocial processes that are implicated in the toxic reaction.

A global problem

LaMontagne et al. (2008) argue that the consequence of these out of control psychosocial hazards in the workplace is a catastrophic public health problem distributed widely across the world. There is consistent evidence that high job demands, low control and effort–reward imbalance are risk factors for mental and physical health problems causing strain on public spending due to the need for increased expenditure on public healthcare (Leka and Jain 2010).

Stress caused by psychosocial hazards in the workplace has been identified as a significant issue across all geographies, not just the European contexts that initiated this extension to Health and Safety at Work provision. Mukhalipi (2014) outlines the need for an approach to managing stress across the wide range of occupations relevant to the growth of the African economy. In China, workers reporting high job demands and low job control or high efforts and low rewards had elevated risks of job dissatisfaction, psychosomatic complaints and depressive symptoms (Yu et al. 2008). Studies of stress from Taiwan indicated that employees with high demand jobs had workers who perceived high stress at work (Yeh et al. 2009). Furthermore this tended to be connected to being employed under 'pay for per-formance' schemes. In support of the issues raised here, Chapter 10 outlines the cross-cultural and negative impact of our poorly designed performance management processes.

The OECD describes mental ill health from work as a global crisis. It estimates that mental ill health costs each economy at least 3.5–4 per cent of Gross Domestic Product (GDP) of which approximately half is work related and the impact from work is increasing. Table 6.2 offers a quick calculation of the estimated annual costs from mental ill health across a randomly selected range of economies using the figures from the trading economics website. Of this 4 per cent it is estimated that problems caused by the workplace constitute a minimum of 50 per cent of the cost.

Consequently, the notion of psychosocial hazards has been built into global approaches to understanding and mitigating mental ill health from work. Example organizations are SafeWork Australia, the European Agency for Safety and Health at Work (EASHW), the International Labour Organization (ILO) as well as the World Health Organization (WHO).

There are a multitude of workplace questionnaires and indicators available to assess these psychosocial hazards with 35 national systems identified across 20 different countries and four multi-country systems, specifically from the EU. In various jurisdictions the use of these has been added to the Health and Safety at Work legislative framework, as a policy response to attempt to address the scale of the problem (Leka and Jain 2010).

Stress is not only a psychological issue but is directly and causally linked to physical morbidity. In laboratory-based investigations adrenaline and cortisol were seen to rise consistently in response to stress and this elevation is likely to impact heart health (Pollard 1997). For example, results of a Finnish large-scale longitudinal study indicated that workers reporting job strain were 2.2 times more likely to experience cardiovascular mortality, compared to their colleagues that did not report job strain (Kivimäki et al. 2002). It appears that stress at work is implicated in heart disease, bronchitis and musculoskeletal disorders (Leka and Jain 2010).

TABLE 6.2 GDP and mental ill health costs across global economies

Country	GDP (2013 US$ billion pa)	4% (min. mental health costs in US$ billion pa)	Workplace caused costs US$ (billion pa)
Japan	4,901.00	196.04	98.00
Brazil	2,245.67	89.83	44.90
S. Africa	350.63	14.03	7.00
China	9,240.27	369.61	184.80
USA	16,768.10	670.72	335.40
Nigeria	552.64	22.11	11.00
France	2,734.95	109.40	54.70
India	1,876.80	75.07	37.50
UK	2,522.26	100.89	50.50
Italy	2,071.31	82.85	41.40

Knowledge about the stress problem has not stopped the stress problem

While we now have clear consolidated knowledge about these mechanisms and the associated economic, social and personal costs, we have not yet seen sufficient change in workplace practices. The ongoing assessment of outcomes shows that the level of mental ill health due to workplace dysfunction is increasing (see OECD website material) with little evidence of the changes in organizational practice that could lead to improvement. There is a growing body of knowledge that is exploring the factors that can mitigate stress and mental ill health in the workplace (Bakker and Demerouti 2007; Ketturat et al. 2015) and a recognition of different levels of intervention (Biron et al. 2012; Joyce et al. 2015). The organizational approach to stress at work that I have seen in practice has tended to be to invested in 'bolt on' risk management approaches to mitigate legal exposure and to outsource employee assistance. Any web-search of 'Employee Assistance Programmes' (EAPs) will indicate the growth of this service provision across geographies. It appears that it will be increasingly necessary for legislative and 'force'-based interventions to be taken to address the issue.

Based upon the outline of knowledge translation (Chapter 1, Table 1.3) I would suggest that one important factor in this current lack of substantive impact on this problem is that our emphasis to date has been predominantly to establish a specific knowledge base within an existing legal framework. I would argue that this substantial work has taken us to the point equivalent to the stage of the Costa Rican confirmation of the antibiotic effect of penicillium (see Chapter 1, Table 1.1). This evidence base has recently been codified, in the UK, into Guidelines from the National Institute for Clinical Excellence (NICE 2015) focused on workplace policies and management practices for the health of the workforce.

We now need to invest in much more robust translation processes around design and implementation. Knowledge alone cannot lead to the requisite changes in organizational practice. Figure 6.3 provides an illustration of the problems with knowledge as intervention. The psychosocial hazard knowledge base has determined what is problematic. It has also led to the production of a defined and measureable set of factors in a workplace that calibrate the costs of this issue at national and international levels. However, there has been less attention to the ways in which emerging workplace processes lead to particular experiences, how these then lead to the toxic outcomes reported and how we can intervene. This lack of 'practical' knowledge means those responsible within the impacted workplaces have little understanding of what else can be done about this health crisis, other than purchase services that mitigate their legal risk.

We have an epidemiological picture of the scale of the problem, because each hazard has been researched for its impact, but as yet this body of knowledge does not provide sufficient insight into how to think about aetiology (cause) or to intervene into the reality of dynamic workplaces. Instead we have clear evidence that the problems are getting worse. A recent study commissioned by the EASHW

DEPLOYING KNOWLEDGE?

I found that when I used to present the evidence from the stress research within organizations, I was confronted with a 'so what?' response. By contrast, when I moved to using a more dialogic approach (Chapter 3) to my practice to explore, for example, 'how are support and control enabled in the workplace?' or 'what is getting in the way?' I found that the issues that needed attention started emerging.

Generally, I have found that raising the concept of stress in such situations tends to get in the way of meaningful conversations. My experience has been that it works to emphasize a large, abstract and unsolvable problem (a wicked problem) instead of attending to the options for improvement in the specific situation. My assessment is that this experience of an unsolvable problem works to lower perceived control for the client. Too much focus on the big problem reduces felt control and so could be considered a psychosocial hazard.

We could suggest that 'our science' needs to learn from itself to inform the 'how' of practice. The growing preference for approaches like Positive Psychology and Appreciative Inquiry (see Chapter 4) would suggest these 'positive' approaches address the 'how' of intervention in a way that actively enhances the perceptions of control and social support. In working in this way it reduces the psychosocial hazards introduced by intervention. In the context of concerns with organizational toxicity it probably brings a lower risk of toxicity compared with other more explicitly evidence-based practices.

With reference to the distinction between 'lab' and 'field' outlined in Chapter 1, the important consideration this topic draws to our attention is how the need for perceived control to manage psychosocial hazards is managed differently across the two domains. Within the 'lab' control is exercised through a particular relationship with closing down a problem and then applying 'experimental methods'.

This approach to problem definition is not viable in intervention into real-time activity in a 'field' context. In contrast, the existence of the 'wicked problem' is accepted in the field and the point of control is action, defining what can be done and creating space for trial, error and adjustment; 'experimentation' by another name. The attempt to use 'lab' authority in the 'field' context is an ethical issue and considered in Chapter 4.

'The content of our science is better used to guide us in the how of practice, and is less helpful when directly shared with clients.' Discuss.

FIGURE 6.3 Discussion: knowledge as a psychosocial hazard

indicates that the annual cost to Europe from work-related depression alone is €617 billion (Hassard et al. 2014).

Blame the victim revisited

Unfortunately our ideas about solving the problem appear to have again located the problem in the individual (so blaming the individual for the damage done to them by their normal reactions to systemic factors that are outside their control). The key approach is helping people cope with increasing levels of organizational toxicity through teaching individual skills like mindfulness. There is evidence that, for example, Acceptance and Commitment Therapy (ACT) style training in workplaces can positively impact individual responses and productivity (Flaxman and Bond 2010) and within organizations I have had first hand experience of the positive impact on individuals from the various approaches to intervention used. However, I do have concerns with the predominant focus on individual resilience as the solution, rather than focusing on the toxic organization as the cause of the problem:

- It blames the victim by implying that somehow the reason you are finding things difficult is a failure in your ability to cope, rather than acknowledging how damaging the environment is.
- Approaches such as mindfulness, in effect, focus on actively developing individual psychological skills to enable disengagement from the damaging context and consequently from the activity of collaboration. We could suggest that developing these psychological skills could run counter to our collective needs for collaborative contribution.

Psychological safety and toxicity at work

The entry in the Organizational Studies encyclopaedia offers the following definition:

> Organizational toxicity is the widespread, intense, energy-sapping, negative emotion that disconnects people from their jobs, coworkers, and organizations. Painful emotions that are inevitably part of organizational life become toxic when others respond to them in harmful and destructive ways. Organizational toxicity has pervasive negative effects, undermining individuals' confidence, hope, and self-esteem and damaging their morale and performance, both at work and outside.
>
> *(Maitlis 2008)*

Developments in behavioural science are providing insights that indicate in situ workplace micro processes have a profound impact on the toxicity of organizations and these will be considered in a bit more detail in Chapter 7 on cognitive sources of toxicity. In recognition of the evidence from the study of stress at work coupled with the relative lack of organizational impact, psychological and social science research since the 1990s has been more focused on understanding the psychosocial micro processes in organizations that emerge in the affective and relational day-to-day aspects of working life. This has been described as an 'affective revolution' in how workplaces are studied, where emotions (feelings) and their impacts are no longer invisible or subordinated to the role of cognition (thinking) at work.

Keifer and Barclay (2012: 603) suggest that how emotions are experienced is a critical factor in toxicity: '[p]ainful emotions, arising from events such as unexpected and disruptive changes and difficult interactions with bosses, colleagues, and customers, are ever-present in organizations'. As Frost (2003) has noted, such pain is not in itself toxic but becomes so in the face of others' 'harsh, insensitive, or indifferent responses to it'. Negative emotional events are described as toxic because of the heavy use of psychological resources needed to manage them, which then cannot be directed at work. This has been explored in a study of 'toxic decision processes'. Maitlis and Ozcelik (2004) describe the interactions between 'decision makers' and other people and the activation of emotions such as anxiety, fear, shame, anger and embarrassment. They suggest these are suppressed leading to volatility and the emergence of a 'danger zone' in an organization, which is spread by emotional contagion and means no one speaks of the contested matters. It is now recognized that work cannot rely merely on thinking because emotional self-regulation is critical to the effective functioning of psychosocial systems (Bandura 1991).

Keifer and Barclay (2012) examined psychologically recurring, disconnecting and draining experiences and found that behavioural interventions from supportive managers and peers in the moment could help prevent mental ill health in the longer term. Their work also demonstrated that the ways in which experiences were processed were related to attitudes towards the organization, performance and helping (compassionate) behaviours in general. Other studies have indicated that supervisor support around issues of job insecurity mediated the negative impacts on performance from this insecurity, pointing to the positive impact that helping relationships have on organizational performance (Schreurs et al. 2012).

Dollard and Bakker (2010) suggested that psychological safety is the logical site for work stress intervention and the attempts to identify the micro processes implicated in toxic or productive outcomes are covered in the study of blocks to psychological safety at work. Dollard et al. (2012) demonstrated that organizational contextual factors are the origins of the work stress process and the necessary focus for intervention.

Psychological safety is directly related to team outcome (Edmondson 1999; Edmondson and Lei 2014). Perceptions of psychological safety also appear to explain why some people are more engaged at work, better able to share information, better able to extend themselves in their roles and are more innovative than others (Baer and Frese 2003; Premeaux and Bedeian 2003; Tjosvold et al. 2004; Tucker et al. 2007). Acceptable levels of psychological safety in the workplace make people more likely to notice issues and speak up (Leroy et al. 2012). A significant factor implicated in the negative impact on organizational effectiveness from low psychological safety is 'voice'. If psychological safety is high employees speak well of their employer and speak up about problems. The impact of low psychological safety in an organization or team is silence, withdrawal and suspicion (Liang et al. 2012) explored in more detail in the case on whistleblowing in Chapter 12.

Psychological safety and learning is higher in groups with a sense of mastery and autonomy in the area of group work, than for those given either a performance goal or no goal instructions (Ashauer and Macan 2013) indicating the importance of participative goal setting. The effect of psychological safety on project performance is found to be indirect and mediated through team turnover so the type and continuity of working relationships is a significant factor (Chandrasekaran and

Mishra 2012). There is also substantial evidence that such 'good workplaces' are critical to well-being (NICE 2015) and the ability to work well in difficult situations (Haslam et al. 2006).

It is not surprising, given the wide range of relational and emotional factors involved that in any workplace, the experience of psychological safety tends to vary widely between teams and functions within a single organization. One team can be operating in a way that is experienced as psychologically safe, and the next team has a completely different experience. Predictors of low psychological safety at work are: deficiencies in work design and role ambiguity (Salin and Hoel 2011; Clegg et al. 2014); a compromised sense of social identity (Haslam 2014); high demands together with deficiencies in leadership behaviour; and evidence of tolerance for bullying (Einarsen et al. 2011; Hershcovis and Rafferty 2012). A history of 'organizational trauma' described as survivor syndrome (Baruch and Hind 1999) is also predictive of low psychological safety across a whole organization. Such traumatic events include repeated re-structuring, large-scale redundancy initiatives and public reputation damage with media or regulatory shaming (Kaham 2006).

The human threat response

Overall the body of work considering psychological safety and toxicity is rooted in the emotional experience of people, how this plays out at work and how the features of the workplace mitigate or exacerbate these experiences. Inherent in this is a concern about the 'emotional to biological' impact of a psychosocial threat. As this book is focused upon the use of psychosocial knowledge for intervention in the workplace, only a very brief outline of this work is provided. However, there are interesting explorations of how these integrated bio-psychosocial processes impact both micro processes such as relating, decision making and behaviour and also the macro outcomes such as the collapse of the stock market in 2008 (Coates 2012).

The experience of threats of reprisal and the perceived probability of unfair treatment has a serious negative impact on the ability of people to participate in work because these perceptions lead to stereotypical thinking and withdrawal (Sternberg 1999). These experiences generate perceptions that the organization is dangerous, unfair and set in its ways. In such working contexts people will 'keep their heads down', 'keep their mouths shut' and 'turn a blind eye' (Heffernan 2011).

To understand how this sense of threat impacts us, there has been recent interest in the neuropsychology underpinning our potential responses to situations. This is focused on the interplay of what is described as the 'old instinctual brain' and the 'new compassionate brain' (Gilbert 2009). Gilbert's work very helpfully outlines three identified response mechanisms that are always active and that environmental conditions trigger. He has used this model of different 'affect regulation responses' to build compassion and self-compassion through therapeutic exchanges. This clearly also has relevance for the understanding of the relational and emotional realities of work.

The threat system

The suggested purpose of this system is to alert us to danger. This mechanism gets the priority focus of attention. This response runs through the amygdala, which processes these alerts quickly. Cortisol is one of the key brain communicators for this messaging and is responsible for the sustained levels of stress and anxiety from workplace psychosocial hazards. Many of the problems in workplace design could be construed as due to the unintended consequence of activating a sense of psychosocial threat, which keeps us locked in this threat response. The economic models of behaviour that concentrate on gain as the key driver are completely contradicted by the primacy that our internal processing gives to the avoidance of threat. This suggests that we need to challenge all the economically driven designs used in the workplace as misguided and misinformed.

The thrive system

The suggested purpose of this system is to support resource seeking to enable us to prosper. As mentioned above, despite the assumption in most economic theory that this is the primary drive in humans, it is subordinate to the threat system. The frustration associated with not achieving what is desired activates the threat response. Dopamine produces the good feelings associated with this and also the feeling of loss when dopamine levels drop after achievement.

The compassionate system

The suggested purpose of this system is contentment and is also integral to being able to relate to and nurture others, both of which are implicated in the capacity to experience social and psychological safety and to work collaboratively. Two brain communicators are relevant here. Endorphins appear to generate the sense of calm and oxytocin the sense of safety. It is interesting to note that the telling of stories appears to increase our oxytocin levels and when our oxytocin levels are increased we tend to behave well. Gilbert (2009) argues that the sense of interconnectedness operating from this system gives is critical to being able to live and work collaboratively.

Injustice and the human threat response

Fundamentally 'we have an inborn desire to be treated well because we are psychologically programmed to believe our lives are dependent on it and we cannot but help react to mistreatment. We have a low threshold for indignity and unacknowledged feelings of shame for being mistreated lie at the heart of all human conflict' (Hicks 2011: 6–7). Being mistreated feels unfair: it feels shameful. A critical component therefore of achieving psychological safety at work is to understand how treatment and events are filtered through the 'fairness' lens (Rupp et al. 2014).

A longitudinal study of employees and fairness across different work contexts indicated that working in a low justice workplace predicted the onset of clinical depression (Grynderup et al. 2013). Another study demonstrated that how people perceive their treatment by others at work impacts a person's loyalty to their employer, the likelihood of bullying and the onset of negative mental health experiences (Otto and Mamatoglu 2015). The studies of organizational justice have outlined four different parts of this complex dynamic (Greenberg and Colquitt 2005) each of which work individually and together to create and sustain workplace justice perceptions. Figure 6.4 outlines the factors that have been assessed in coming to any fairness evaluation.

Accepting the importance of the emotions and relationships in creating psychological safety, means the behavioural integrity of each manager is centrally implicated in a team's experience of the workplace and their capacity to focus on their tasks (Leroy et al. 2012). This is consistent with the finding that middle manager capability is the most significant variable in overall organizational performance (see Chapter 10). Having individuals on the team who have above average emotional perception and emotional self-regulation improves member perceptions of psychological safety (Harper and White 2013). Figure 6.5 uses Frost's (2003, 2004) model of toxic transgressions to explore experiences of toxic behaviour.

Individual leadership traits have been identified as critical here (Hogan and Hogan 2001; Furnham and Taylor 2004), most specifically the impact of sub-clinical manifestations of narcissism and psychopathy evidenced in a very small proportion of senior leaders (Babiak and Hare 2006). While this cannot be ignored as part of the whole pattern, and is clearly evident in many of the contexts I have

---

WORKING WITH THE COMPLEXITY OF FAIRNESS PERCEPTIONS

Distributive justice: the extent to which differential outcomes are perceived as fair.
Procedural justice: the extent to which processes are perceived as fair in themselves and also whether they are equally applied across different groups and situations.
Interactional justice: the extent to which the day-to-day treatment of people by people in the workplace is considered fair.
Informational justice: the extent to which availability of information about what is going on and how decisions are made in the workplace are considered fair.

Discussion

Discuss the different types of justice and how they may manifest in an organization and what might lead to felt unfairness in each.
　　Discuss how fairness in one may lead to unfairness in another.
　　Then consider the announcement of performance-related pay awards in an organization and consider how these different justice dynamics get activated and how such announcements may best be managed.

FIGURE 6.4 Discussion: dynamics of workplace justice perceptions

---

EXPLORING 'DESTRUCTIVE BEHAVIOUR': THE EYE OF THE BEHOLDER

Based upon the work of Frost (2003, 2004) who described emotional transgressions at work and formulated the idea of the '7 deadly "Ins"'.

The '7 deadly "Ins"'	Reflection
<ul><li>Intention</li><li>Incompetence</li><li>Infidelity</li><li>Insensitivity</li><li>Intrusion</li><li>Inevitability</li><li>Institution</li></ul>	Consider your experiences at work or in organizations. Pull out those that could be categorized under each of the '7 deadly "Ins"' headings.

Use your reflections to work on the following three exercises

Exercise 1
Where did the experience come from?
How did it make you feel?
How did you react?
Where did you get support?

Exercise 2
Think of a time you may have done something that impacted someone else, which could be characterized by one of these headings?
How did the other person react to you?
What did you do about their reaction?
What did you learn from the experience?

Exercise 3
What ideas do you have for working as an ethical practitioner to address these interactions effectively both for the individual and the organization?

FIGURE 6.5 Discussion: behavioural transgressions at work

worked in, I consider it is unlikely that this specific factor is the predominant cause of organizational toxicity. By contrast, my experience suggests that dysfunctional systems create the space for counter-productive styles of operating among otherwise benign people.

While suggesting individual trait theory was insufficient to explain toxicity, Judge et al. (2009) suggested that it is much more important to consider how these individual differences get mitigated or reinforced in dynamic organizations. They indicate that the system interaction between factors involved must be considered and outlined three interacting aspects of workplaces described as the 'toxic triangle':

- destructive leaders
- susceptible followers
- conducive environments.

However, this explanation is again predicated upon the assumption that a 'destructive leader' is necessary for toxic manifestation in the workplace. By way of contrast, I would suggest that we must consider how workplace environments create the conditions where good people do bad things (Heffernan 2011), rather than attempting to find individual scapegoats for the systemic dysfunction. To illustrate, the following are types of situations I have observed during my practice that point to the more subtle psychosocial processes at work:

- Why did a very kind and compassionate manager avoid a subordinate to whom she had just given a low performance rating (Hicks 2011)?
- Why did a conscientious and committed nurse walk past a patient in pain and distress (Gardiner and Chater 2013)?

Assessment of what is described as 'toxic' leadership behaviour is not straightforward, but very much linked with the position of the observer. Out-groups see aggressive leader behaviour as more negative than in-groups. Also, in-groups consider any attack on an internal member of the team as more toxic than the same behaviour directed at an outsider (Pelletier 2012). In considering how victims of abusive treatment at work are selected, there are two key predictors, the supervisor perception of deep level dissimilarity coupled with perceptions of subordinate performance (Tepper et al. 2011). This does not locate the 'problem' in the leadership traits but instead in the leader's perception of differences in identity, their relationship with in-group and out-group dynamics and consequent ideas about performance (see Chapters 8 and 10). We are aware that assessments of subordinate performance are subject to profound biases, particularly linked to issues of gender and race.

Public health promotion strategies have suggested, based on this emerging picture, that responses to workplace well-being should also address organizational justice as a specific preventative dimension, in addition to the earlier work on psychosocial hazards.

The key type of organizational intervention that leads to increased levels of perceived justice in organizations across these different dimensions is the use of participative methods in day-to-day workplace activity (Linna et al. 2011; Van den Heuvel et al. 2015). There is evidence that directive leadership produces quick results but that these are not sustained and over a few months the productive benefits of the slower starting participative leadership become clear (Lorinkova et al. 2013). We can develop people to improve psychological safety in the workplace through investment in time for self-regulation, providing space for helping behaviour, increasing inquiry skills and making participation a reality. Making participation a reality means, not merely that people are consulted, but that changes are enabled and created through their participation – it enables real-time collaboration. Participative approaches work as they increase individual control and enhance perceptions of support and so would be predicted to reduce psychosocial hazards at work.

Macro acts, micro impacts and macro consequences: the toxic dynamic

There has been considerable attention to the importance of these emotional reactions for organizational effectiveness and individual health (Donaldson-Feilder et al. 2008; NICE 2015). However, there remains a disconnect between a recognition of the importance of these micro processes in shaping effective psychological environments and understanding how the macro level factors in workplaces impact these micro processes for good or ill.

To be able to provide helpful knowledge translation for complex and distressed organizational environments requires a thorough yet subtle understanding of the social psychology of the workplace. It requires recognition of the way in which our different approaches to relating and perceiving have a profound impact on the working environment we create together.

This means that we need to have a clear picture of the connections between the macro or 'strategic' approaches to organization, the relational micro processes and the 'organizational symptoms' we might see, that are together implicated in the creation of counter-productive workplace environments. Understanding the connection between macro and micro levels in organizations is gaining increasing importance (Greve 2013). This is illustrated in Chapter 10 and is evidenced in the suggestion that intangible and relational reward is more impactful on performance than performance-related pay systems (CIPD 2015). Figure 6.6 offers an exercise to explore the interplay of the micro and the macro. Neilsen (2013) suggests line manager behaviour is critical in hindering or supporting strategic intent and suggests the need for complementary micro processes interventions alongside 'focal' business critical changes. In the study of austerity on public sector work behaviour it was demonstrated that the way in which the micro and macro work together is impacted by the way in which purpose and other factors operate at the psychosocial level. Difficult organizational environments have been demonstrated to lead to customer complaints due to equity adjustments in employee behaviour. In the context of the public sector it appears that employees take a very different approach, filling in the gaps caused by austerity (Conway et al. 2014), until they burn out from the demands.

Existing organizational approaches to intervention, such as culture change, change management or organizational design, have tended to privileged the macro (and managerialist) approach to change over a consideration of the psychosocial micro process. However, as outlined in Chapter 3, these planned approaches to change rarely achieve the business benefits or objectives they were designed to achieve and cause damage to people.

The integrated model of organizational toxicity

The approach to organizational toxicity developed for this book aims to provide a new formulation of the connections between individual micro processes and

---

MACRO–MICRO CONNECTIONS IN ORGANIZATIONAL INTERVENTION

As a metaphor to help think through the difference between macro and micro processes as applied to organizations, the following is an illustration of the difference as applied to the human body. If an individual presents with a raised temperature, a macro level analysis would lead us to put the person in a cold bath – in extreme circumstances this is the immediate action required. A micro approach would be to assess what is going on in the cells of the individual to see what has caused this raised temperature and possibly treat with time or an antibiotic. The micro understanding both helps identify the cause in the individual situation and also can feed into a further macro level approach, once the infection has been identified, as it enables a focused public health communication and/or inoculation process.

Consider one of two scenarios

1. The need to reduce the numbers of injuries and improve the rehabilitation of those with back problems in a job involving heavy lifting.
2. The need to reduce the levels of bullying in an organization.

- Consider what risks an organization may be trying to manage through focusing on your chosen issue.
- Consider what a 'macro' organizational change response to this problem could be and what the benefits of such an approach could be.
- Consider what the relevant 'micro' psychosocial processes linked to your chosen issue might be and the potential consequences on these from the macro tactics you have identified.

In groups, discuss the similarities and points of disconnect between the macro and micro level tactics and how understanding these could impact how we approach organizational intervention.

FIGURE 6.6 Discussion: macro/micro levels in intervention

system macro level manifestations in the workplace. This integrated model is illustrated in Figure 6.7. The inner arrows outline those macro factors that are regularly the sources of toxicity in a workplace. These are positioned within the ring of psychosocial micro processes as these micro processes can both mitigate the worst impacts of macro factors but also become denatured in toxic dose conditions and begin to operate in a different fashion. Chapter 7 outlines the macro sources and Chapter 8 the psychosocial micro processes listed in this model.

These two different levels of organizational thinking, feeling and activity can and often do operate relatively independently in organizational contexts. Very often this disconnect leads to embedded organizational stories told at the micro level that create a psychosocial reality inconsistent with many of the abstractions desired when giving attention to these macro factors. There is a considerable managerialist literature that will point to the micro processes (often called behaviours) as being the problem to be solved. In parallel there is a substantial

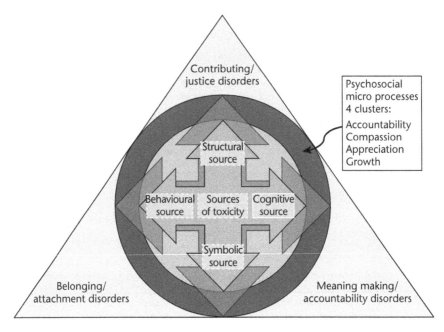

FIGURE 6.7 Integrated model of organizational toxicity

literature on power and resistance which points to the macro intentions as being the problem. Both literatures have their point, but they are inherently partial because each assumes a moral divide between one being in the right and one being in the wrong: in practice it is altogether more complicated than that and this disconnect in itself is also another profound source of toxicity.

The outer triangle of this model refers to the workplace psychosocial environment as it is experienced day-to-day. I have developed three broad diagnostic frames (contributing, belonging, meaning) for assessing the environment, together with a set of regular patterns of toxic disorder (justice disorders, attachment disorders, accountability disorders) that I have experienced in practice. These diagnostic frames are outlined in Chapter 9 and Chapters 10, 11 and 12 give case illustrations of working with patterns of toxicity in the workplace.

Conclusion

This chapter has outlined the current available psychosocial knowledge relevant to the manifestation of organizational toxicity and presented an integrated formulation of the macro sources of toxicity, the micro processes that both mitigate and are impacted and the diagnostic themes that emerge from their interaction. It suggests that we need to move from a focus on developing what we know to attending to later stages of knowledge translation to mitigate toxicity.

References

Ashauer, S. A. and Macan, T. (2013) How can leaders foster team learning? Effects of leader-assigned mastery and performance goals and psychological safety. *Journal of Psychology* 147(6): 541–561.

Babiak, P. and Hare, R. D. (2006) *Snakes in Suits: When Psychopaths Go to Work*. New York: Regan Books.

Baer, M. and Frese, M. (2003) Innovation is not enough: Climates for initiative and psychological safety, process innovations, and firm performance. *Journal of Organizational Behavior* 24(1): 45–68.

Bakker, A. B. and Demerouti, E. (2007) The job demands–resources model: State of the art. *Journal of Managerial Psychology* 22(3): 309–328.

Bandura, A. (1991) Social cognitive theory of self-regulation. *Organizational Behavior and Human Decision Processes* 50: 248–287.

Baruch, Y. and Hind, P. (1999) Perpetual motion in organizations: Effective management and the impact of the new psychological contract on 'survivor syndrome'. *European Journal of Work and Organizational Psychology* 8(2): 295–306.

Biron, C., Karanika-Murray, M. and Cooper C. (2012) *Improving Organizational Interventions for Stress and Wellbeing: Addressing Process and Context*. London and New York: Routledge.

Bogenhold, D. (2013) Social network analysis and the sociology of economics: Filling a blind spot with the idea of social embeddedness. *American Journal of Economics and Sociology* 72(2): 293–318.

Chandrasekaran, A. and Mishra, A. (2012) Task design, team context, and psychological safety: An empirical analysis of R&D projects in high technology organizations. *Production and Operations Management* 21(6): 977–996.

CIPD (2015) Show me the money: The behavioural science of reward. Research report. http://www.cipd.co.uk/hr-resources/research/show-money-behavioural-science-reward.aspx.

Clegg, C. W., Bolton, L., Offut, R. et al. (2014) Work design for compassionate care and patient safety. In L. Tate, E. Donaldson-Feilder, K. Teoh et al. (eds) *Implementing Culture Change within the NHS: Contributions from Occupational Psychology*. London: British Psychological Society.

Coates, J. (2012) *The Hour between Dog and Wolf: Risk Taking Gut Feelings and the Biology of Boom and Bust*. London: Harper Collins.

Conway, N., Keifer, T., Hartley, J. et al. (2014) Doing more with less: Employee reactions to psychological contract breach via target similarity of spillover during public sector organizational change. *British Journal of Management* 25(4): 737–754.

Cooper, C. L. and Payne, R. (eds) (1978) *Stress at Work*. Chichester: Wiley.

Cox, T. (1978) *Stress*. London: Macmillan.

Cox, T., Griffiths A. and Rial Gonzalez, E. (2000) *Research on Work-Related Stress*. European Agency for Safety and Health at Work. Luxembourg: Office for Official Publications of the European Communities.

Dollard, M. F. and Bakker, A. B. (2010) Psychosocial safety climate as a precursor to conducive work environments, psychological health problems, and employee engagement. *Journal of Occupational and Organisational Psychology* 83(3): 579–599.

Dollard, M., Opie, T., Lenthall, S. et al. (2012) Psychosocial safety climate as an antecedent of work characteristics and psychological strain: A multilevel model. *Work and Stress* 26(4): 385–404.

Donaldson-Feilder, E., Yarker, J. and Lewis, R. (2008) Line management competence: The key to reducing stress at work. *Strategic HR Review* 7(2): 11–16.

Edmondson, A. (1999) Psychological safety and learning behaviour in work teams. *Administrative Science Quarterly* 44(2): 350–383.

Edmondson, A. and Lei, Z. (2014) Psychological safety: The history, renaissance, and future of an interpersonal construct. *Annual Review of Organizational Psychology and Organizational Behavior* 1: 23–43.

Einarsen, S., Hoel, H., Zapf, D. et al. (eds) (2011) *Bullying and Harassment in the Workplace.* Florida: CRC Press, Taylor and Francis.

Flaxman, P. E. and Bond, F. W. (2010) Acceptance and commitment training: Promoting psychological flexibility in the workplace. In R. A. Baer (ed.) *Assessing Mindfulness and Acceptance Processes in Clients: Illuminating the Theory and Practice of Change.* Oakland, CA: New Harbinger.

Frost, P. J. (2003) *Toxic Emotions at Work: How Compassionate Managers Handle Pain and Conflict.* Boston, MA: Harvard Business School Press.

Frost, P. J. (2004) Handling toxic emotions: New challenges for leaders and their organizations. *Organizational Dynamics* 33(2): 111–129.

Furnham, A. and Taylor, J. (2004) *The Dark Side of Behavior at Work: Understanding and Avoiding Employees Leaving, Thieving and Deceiving.* Basingstoke: Palgrave Macmillan.

Gardiner, E. and Chater, N. (2013) Guarding against collective failures. *Nursing Management* 20(2): 11.

Gilbert, P. (2009) *The Compassionate Mind.* London: Constable and Robinson.

Greenberg, G. and Colquitt, J. A. (2005) *Handbook of Organizational Justice.* New Jersey: Lawrence Erlbaum Associates.

Greve, H. R. (2013) Microfoundations of management: Behavioral strategies and levels of rationality in organizational action. *Academy of Management Perspectives* 27(2): 103–119.

Grynderup, M. B., Mors, O., Hansen, A. M. et al. (2013) Work-unit measures of organisational justice and risk of depression: A 2-year cohort study. *Occupational and Environmental Medicine* 70(6): 380–385.

Harper, S. R. and White, C. D. (2013) The impact of member emotional intelligence on psychological safety in work teams. *Journal of Behavioral and Applied Management* 15(1): 2–10.

Haslam, S. A. (2014) Making good theory practical: Five lessons for an applied social identity approach to challenges of organizational, health and clinical psychology. *British Journal of Social Psychology* 53(1): 1–20.

Haslam, S. A., Ryan, M. K., Postmes, T. et al. (2006) Sticking to our guns: Social identity as a basis for the maintenance of commitment to faltering organizational projects. *Journal of Organizational Behaviour* 27(5): 607–628.

Hassard, J., Teoh, K., Cox, T. et al. (2014) *Calculating the Cost of Work-Related Stress and Psychosocial Risk.* European Agency for Safety and Health at Work (EU-OSHA). Luxembourg: Publications Office of the European Union.

Heffernan, M. (2011) *Wilful Blindness: Why We Ignore the Obvious at Our Peril.* London: Simon and Schuster.

Hershcovis, M. S. and Rafferty, A. (2012) Predicting abusive supervision. In J. Houdmont, S. Leka and R. Sinclair (eds) *Contemporary Occupational Health Psychology: Global Perspectives on Research and Practice*, vol. 2. Chichester: Wiley-Blackwell.

Hicks, D. (2011) *Dignity: The Essential Role It Plays in Resolving Conflict.* New Haven, CT: Yale University Press.

Hogan, R. and Hogan, J. (2001) Assessing leadership: A view from the dark side. *International Journal of Selection and Assessment* 9(1/2): 40–51.

Hollway, W. (1991) *Work Psychology and Organizational Behaviour: Managing the Individual at Work.* London: SAGE.

Joyce, S., Modini, M., Christensen, H. et al. (2015) Workplace interventions for common mental disorders: A systematic meta-review. *Psychological Medicine*. Epub ahead of print 1 December 2015.

Judge, T., Piccolo, R. F. and Kosalka, T. (2009) The bright and dark sides of leader traits: A review and theoretical extension of the leader trait paradigm. *The Leadership Quarterly* 20(6): 855–875.

Kaham, D. M. (2006) What's really wrong with shaming sanctions. *Texas Law Review* 84: 2075–2103.

Karasek, R. A. (1979) Job demands, job decision latitude and mental strain: Implications for job redesign. *Administrative Science Quarterly* 24(2): 285–308.

Karasek, R. A. and Theorell, T. (1990) *Healthy Work, Stress, Productivity and the Reconstruction of Working Life*. New York: Basic Books.

Keifer, T. and Barclay, L. J. (2012) Understanding the mediating role of toxic emotional experiences in the relationship between negative emotions and adverse outcomes. *Journal of Occupational and Organizational Psychology* 85(4): 600–625.

Ketturat, C., Frisch, J. U., Ullrich, J. et al. (2015) Disaggregating within- and between-person effects of social identification on subjective and endocrinological stress reactions in a real life stress situation. *Personality and Social Psychology Bulletin*. Epub ahead of print 18 November 18 2015. DOI: 10.1177/0146167215616804.

Kivimäki, M., Leino-Arjas, P., Luukkonen, R. et al. (2002) Work stress and risk of cardiovascular mortality: Prospective cohort study of industrial employees. *British Medical Journal* 325(7369): 857.

LaMontagne, A. D., Keegel, T., Vallance, D. et al. (2008) Job strain: Attributable depression in a sample of working Australians – assessing the contribution to health inequalities. *BMC Public Health* 8: 181.

Leka, S. and Jain, A. (2010) *Health Impact of Psychosocial Hazards at Work: An Overview*. Nottingham: World Health Organization (WHO) and Institute of Work Health and Organizations, University of Nottingham.

Leroy, H., Frederik, A., Anseel, F. et al. (2012) Behavioral integrity for safety, priority of safety, psychological safety, and patient safety: A team-level study. *Journal of Applied Psychology* 97(6): 1273–1281.

Liang, J. C., Farh, C. and Farh, J.-L. (2012) Psychological antecedents of promotive and prohibitive voice: A two-wave examination. *Academy of Management Journal* 55(1): 71–73.

Linna, A., Väänänen, A., Elovainio, E. et al. (2011) Effect of participative intervention on organisational justice perceptions: A quasi-experimental study on Finnish public sector employees *International Journal of Human Resource Management* 22(3): 706–721.

Lorinkova, N. M., Pearsall, M. J. and Sims Jr, H. P. (2013) Examining the differential longitudinal performance of directive versus empowering leadership in teams. *Academy of Management Journal* 56(2): 573–596.

Maitlis, S. (2008) Organizational toxicity. In S. R. Clegg and J. R. Bailey (eds) *International Encyclopedia of Organization Studies*. London: SAGE. http://knowledge.sagepub.com/view/organization/n409.xml.

Maitlis, S. and Ozcelik, H. (2004) Toxic decision processes: A study of emotion and organizational decision making. *Organization Science* 15(4): 375–393.

Martell, R. F., Emrich, V. and Robison-Cox, J. (2012) From bias to exclusion: A multi-level emergent theory of gender segregation in organizations. *Research in Organizational Behavior* 32: 137–162.

Mukhalipi, A. (2014) Managing stress. *African Newsletter on Occupational Health and Safety* 24(1): 7–9. http://www.ttl.fi/AfricanNewsletter.

Neilsen, K. (2013) How can we make organizational interventions work? Employees and line managers as actively crafting interventions. *Human Relations* 66(8): 1029–1050.

NICE (2015) Workplace policy and management practices to improve the health and well-being of employees. http://www.nice.org.uk/guidance/ng13.

NIOSH (1999) *Stress at Work.* Publication no. 99–101. Cincinnati, OH: National Institute for Occupational Safety and Health.

OECD http://stats.oecd.org/glossary/detail.asp?ID=2734.

OECD http://www.oecd.org/health/mental-health-and-work.htm.

Otto, K. and Mamatoglu, N. (2015) Why does interactional justice promote organizational loyalty, job performance, and prevent mental impairment? The role of social support and social stressors. *Journal of Psychology* 149(2): 193–218.

Paracelsus (1493–1541) https://en.wikipedia.org/wiki/The_dose_makes_the_poison.

Pelletier, K. (2012) Perceptions of and reactions to leader toxicity: Do leader–follower relationships and identification with victim matter? *Leadership Quarterly* 23(3): 412–424.

Pollard, T. M. (1997) Physiological consequences of everyday psychosocial stress. *Collegium Antropologicum* 21(1): 17–28.

Premeaux, S. and Bedeian, A. (2003) Breaking the silence: The moderating effects of self-monitoring in predicting speaking up in the workplace. *Journal of Management Studies* 40(6): 1537–1562.

Rupp, D. E., Shao, R., Jones, K. S. et al. (2014) The utility of a multifoci approach to the study of organizational justice: A meta-analytic investigation of normative rule, moral accountability, bandwidth fidelity and social exchange. *Organizational Behaviour and Human Decision Processes* 123(2): 159–185.

Salin, D. and Hoel, H. (2011) Organisational causes of workplace bullying. In S. Einarsen, H. Hoel, D. Zapf et al. (eds) *Bullying and Harassment in the Workplace.* Florida: CRC Press, Taylor and Francis.

Schreurs, B. H. J., Van Emmerik, H., Günter, H. et al. (2012) A weekly diary study on the buffering role of social support in the relationship between job insecurity and employee performance. *Human Resource Management* 51(2): 259–279.

Siegrist, J. (1996) Adverse health effects of high-effort/low-reward conditions. *Journal of Occupational Health Psychology* 1(1): 27–41.

Sternberg, R. J. (ed.) (1999) *Handbook of Creativity.* Cambridge: Cambridge University Press.

Tepper, B. J., Moss, S. E. and Duffy, M. K. (2011) Predictors of abusive supervision: Supervisor perceptions of deep-level dissimilarity, relationship conflict, and subordinate performance. *Academy of Management Journal* 54(2): 279–294.

Tjosvold, D., Yu, Z. and Hui, C. (2004) Team learning from mistakes: The contribution of cooperative goals and problem-solving. *Journal of Management Studies* 41(7): 1223–1245.

Tucker, A., Nembhard, I. and Edmondson, A. (2007) Implementing new practices: An empirical study of organizational learning in hospital intensive care units. *Management Science* 53(6): 894–907.

Van den Heuvel, M., Demerouti, E. and Peeters, M. C. W. (2015) The job crafting intervention: Effects of job resources, self-efficacy and affective well-being. *Journal of Occupational and Organisational Psychology* 88(3): 511–532.

Yeh, W.-Y., Cheng, Y. and Chen, C. J. (2009) Social patterns of pay systems and their associations with psychosocial job characteristics and burnout among paid employees in Taiwan. *Social Science & Medicine* 68(8): 1407–1415.

Yu, S., Gu, G., Zhou, W. et al. (2008) Psychosocial work environment and well-being: A cross-sectional study at a thermal power plant in China. *Journal of Occupational Health* 50(2): 155–162.

7

THE MACRO SOURCES OF TOXICITY IN ORGANIZATIONS

Introduction

This chapter is concerned with elaborating the central aspect of the integrated model of organizational toxicity presented in Chapter 6, Figure 6.7. It considers the macro sources that sit at the centre of this model, each of which can poison an organization. For ease I have divided these sources of toxicity into the following four categories:

- structural sources of toxicity;
- cognitive sources of toxicity;
- behavioural sources of toxicity;
- symbolic sources of toxicity.

Structural sources of toxicity

The impact of the way we work with structure has been evidenced in the excesses of restructuring and head count reduction that much management practice is focused on. The idea of control and the consequent accrual of financial benefit to the privileged minority from structure were inherent to scientific management (Hollway 1991). They also underpin the vast literatures looking at power, domination and industrial relations in organizations, which will not be covered in detail here, but are implicitly referenced in the positioning of this factor as a primary source of toxicity. This dominant attention to structure in organizations appears to be linked to a preference for using conceptual abstractions to contain the uncertainties inherent in collaborative work rather than working with the messiness of innovating.

This comfort with these structural control mechanisms is manifested in the ubiquitous nature of the organogram and the proliferation of codified processes and procedures that are designed to govern how people relate to each other and how work gets done. The diagrams that get produced in this process are drawn representations that get overlaid on the messiness of day-to-day working. Pflaegling (2014) critiques the current drawing conventions used in organizational design for the dysfunctional relationships they privilege and presents a very compelling account of the negative impacts of the informal and undrawn structure on organizations.

The current techniques of structural design in organizations leads us to create positions, comparative frames and boundaries and hence in-groups/out-groups and in parallel erases attention to much of the activity in the workplace that is critical to how things get done. Even when the attention moves to process descriptions the emphasis again is to clean out the baroque details of how we work together, rather than to work with them. Cross et al. (2002) in applying social network analysis to organizational functioning, illustrate how many essential connections are made invisible in the organizational representations that are produced which has two key consequences:

- Many of the connections critical to collaborative work are invisible and hence easily lost or disrupted in restructuring activities.
- This can hide the informal yet excluding in-group connections that are implicated in the perpetuation of unlawful discrimination in the workplace and more generally enable the slippage of accountability.

These structural representations can also actively and explicitly break the connection between the authority of a position and the accountability to others that any authority must carry. This creates toxicity in three distinct ways:

- It can lead to excesses of power through removing the necessary social control and self-regulation that accountability brings.
- It can create 'scapegoat' positions of being held accountable with no authority over the resources to be able to deliver. This is regularly described as role conflict or role ambiguity.
- It can create positions that have neither authority nor accountability, but that sit as servants to a task packaged in fragments that are then abdicated or micro managed. This is often described as disempowerment.

The poisonous nature of this abstract approach of 'drawing' the structure of organizations has become clear, consequent upon the evidence of the phenomenon of survivor syndrome (Baruch and Hind 1999). This is a well-researched and documented phenomenon that shows a repeating pattern of the following negative impacts:

- job insecurity;
- lack of management credibility;
- exclusion and poor communications;

- loss of support networks;
- increased levels of fatigue, stress and depression;
- risk aversion and slowed or stalled decision making;
- loss of shared purpose;
- active distrust;
- sense of betrayal;
- frustration, resentment and anger;
- anticipation of unfair treatment.

One significant consequence of this syndrome is the evidence of the activation of the associated 'imposter syndrome'; a term used to describe the defensive behavioural pattern associated with employees at all levels not believing that they have the right to their job. This manifests as external arrogance and hubris, coupled with internal stress and insecurity, profoundly damaging to the critical needs of crafting social identity necessary for effective collaborative work (Haslam et al. 2011).

Cognitive sources of toxicity

We process so much information that we need ways to handle this. The increased understanding of the heuristics (the rules of thumb) we all use when processing large quantities of information has evidenced the multitude forms of bias that exist in the ways we approach and process what is in front of us. This work has demonstrated the intimate connection between social context, cognition and human bias. The idea of 'thinking, fast and slow' (Kahneman 2011) has become an accepted frame of reference, and the importance of 'thinking slow' has been recognized as one means to manage bias. Paradoxically our growing understanding of heuristics has also demonstrated the importance of the 'thinking fast' as authentic intuition (Hodgkinson and Healey 2011) is increasingly being recognized as critical for effectiveness at work. Methods to engage and enable this as a practitioner are touched on in the overview of design thinking given in Chapter 4.

Simon (1956) introduced the ideas of bounded rationality and satisficing, the latter of which refers to a general human preference for the first decision option we find that meets all the basic requirements. Such an approach is a sensible response, given the limited mental capacity for thinking work that we all have (Maule and Hodgkinson 2002). As Tversky and Kahneman (1974: 1130) indicate 'these heuristics are highly economical and usually effective, but they lead to systematic and predictable errors'. The first three biases identified from their work were:

- Representativeness, where belief in the truth of something is based on how similar it is to something we already know.
- Availability, where a belief is based on how easy it is to call something to mind.
- Anchoring, where a starting position is considered to be more likely to be accurate, even though no thought has gone into this starting position.

There have been several attempts to list all the different types of bias that have been identified that are relevant for the workplace – an accessible version is given by Halvorson and Rock (2015). I will not repeat this here, but instead focus on the manner in which cognition can contribute as a source of toxicity. Although some may claim that these refer to processes internal to people and so do not belong in a section considering the macro level, I am concerned with the repeated patterns in social systems that have been created through these structures of mind. The significant ones for the workplace that will be covered are:

- discrimination, group-think and pluralistic ignorance – the in-group/out-group toxins;
- the interplay of confirmatory bias and framing bias into hubris and strategic persistence;
- failure to allow for authentic intuition and the increasing use of procedures that constrain discretion.

Bias associated with group boundaries and visible differences shows a repeating pattern of in-group/out-group (Tajfel 1978) and conformity pressures (Asch 1956) that lead to discrimination at work, is ubiquitous and increasingly the subject of legislation. This is a critical cognitive source of toxicity in the workplace based on the following attribution error:

- If someone you consider to be part of your in-group does something 'bad' you will blame this transgression on the context they find themselves in. However, when they do something positive it will be admired as an integral part of their character.
- If someone outside your in-group (i.e. a member of an out-group) does something 'bad' you will blame this transgression on the character of the individual involved. However, if they do something positive, this will be attributed to the conditions they are in and not to the character of the person.

This gets enacted through automatic social categorization and stereotyping processes at work coupled with the limited capacity we have to regulate our automatic and emotional reactions to social identity threats. Merely encouraging the conscious monitoring and adjustment of prejudices through reflective processes is insufficient to overcome them (Hodgkinson and Healey 2011) and while these automatic processes can be susceptible to self-regulation they are more prevalent when under heightened anxiety (which is the normal state in the contemporary workplace) as the capacity for reflexive self-monitoring and adjustment is reduced (Lowery et al. 2001; Maslach et al. 2001). This challenges the current investment in unconscious bias training, suggesting it may not have the desired impact (ECU 2013). Sexism, racism and a series of other identity-based biases are prevalent in organizations, with the consequent toxic impact on fairness, organizational productivity and resource distribution (see Chapter 12).

Groupthink (Janis 1982) is a consequence of the same group processes that cause unlawful (in some jurisdictions) and unfair discrimination and manifests the following group characteristics:

- excessive optimism with a belief in invulnerability;
- confirmatory bias and group rationalization;
- believe that they are good and inhabit the moral high ground;
- all out-groups become the enemy and the in-group holds highly negative views about those outside;
- internal compliance pressures on members coupled with self-censorship;
- pluralistic ignorance in the illusion of unanimity;
- self-appointed 'mind-guards' that block disconfirmatory information to help the group sustain its view of itself and its work.

The operation of bias to protect social identity and membership can generate a negative impact on safety, from unmediated compliance behaviour such as pluralistic ignorance, bystander effect and fear of retaliation all of which inhibit voicing of concerns and the capacity for role improvisation that increases organizational responsiveness and adaptability (Rankin et al. 2013). These compliance effects have been activated in the current UK NHS context, considered in Chapter 12.

There have been various suggestions that behavioural strategies (Lovallo and Sibony 2010) could address this, one of which is the impact of a diverse workforce mitigating groupthink. The mechanism suggested is that once visible difference rises above 30 per cent, this activates members of the norm group to be able to explore controversial issues or alternative solutions through the shift of attention away from identity group membership and towards the task (Phillips and Loyd 2006).

Framing bias concerns how a problem or issue is presented and the impact of presentation on the consequent decision or outcomes. The avoidance of threat appears to be the most significant factor in this effect (Hodgkinson and Healey 2011). Confirmatory bias is the tendency to seek out information that confirms a current perception, rather than testing the current perception by attending to disconfirmatory evidence. It has been suggested that the experience of identity threat and consequent disruption to self-concept caused by disconfirmatory information can generate resistance at all levels of the organization (Gioia et al. 2000; Haslam et al. 2003). A significant factor for organizational effectiveness is how decision makers handle their response to the receipt of conflicting and disconfirmatory information (Karlsson et al. 2009). Understanding both of these processes is critical when a practitioner wants to bring attention to new knowledge and ideas, because to simply provide knowledge that disconfirms something is likely to be experienced as an attack on identity.

Working together these biases lead to what has been described as strategic persistence. Strategic persistence is the continuing investment in a course of action that is not working. The emotional stickiness of these biases and the inertia they generate creates a significant concern about identity and can mean the fundamental identity of an organization becomes a trap that blocks adaptive capability (Teece 2007). This underpins the recommendations given in Chapter 3 that when considering approaches to change, we need to be aware of the need for clear and authorized fail fast processes. It also supports the assessment that our current approaches of performance management are toxic, which is covered in Chapter 10.

Executive hubris is an associated consequence of these cognitive sources of toxicity in the workplace. Executive hubris is a significant psychological bias (Li and Tang 2013), which affects the strategic decisions of a firm as well as the approaches to implementation. These manifest differently in different national and organizational cultures. High levels of flattery and opinion conformity can increase CEOs' overconfidence in their strategic judgement and leadership capability, which results in biased and sometimes catastrophic strategic decision making (Park and Westphal 2011). The concept of 'core self-evaluation' has been validated in the psychology literature and consolidates the common, overlapping portions of four previously unconnected dimensions: self-esteem; self-efficacy; locus of control; and emotional stability. High levels of this composite core self-evaluation align with assessments of hubris and organizational performance (Hiller and Hambrick 2005). Studies of the actions of highly hubristic CEOs suggest that they are more likely to pursue and spend heavily on acquisitions but that some hubristic CEOs use effective coping mechanisms to regulate the consequences of their biases. This can paradoxically make hubris positive in organizations as the use of active coping strategies leads to higher employee productivity and maintenance of more conservative capital structures (Mannor et al. 2012).

All the biases outlined so far would be classed as the toxic consequences of thinking fast, but thinking fast is essential to work, so the attempts to rid organizations of this aspect of human processing are also toxic in their consequences. As stated in Chapter 6, it is all about the dose. Intuition is commonplace among experienced professionals and there are reports of damaging consequences when expert decision makers overrule their intuitions and use 'slow thinking' mechanisms. Hodgkinson and Healey (2011) suggest that it is essential that professional practices reflect the psychological realities of how people actually make decisions and indicate that intuition manifests as decision makers reporting a strong feeling of knowing what they must do, without being able to explain exactly why, and they are often right. Hodgkinson (2013: 12) suggests that 'authentic intuition is borne of expertise that can take many years to acquire – and is not to be confused with snap judgments or prejudices'. The intuition developed in one domain based upon the acquisition of expertise, appears to a certain extent to be transferable to new domains. When working across domains of expertise, those people who have expertise in one area asked to make decisions in another area, make better decisions using intuitive processes than using deliberative (thinking slow) processes (Dijkstra et al. 2013). It has been suggested that one means of incorporating intuition is to reconfigure decision-making units with a requisite mixture of analytic and intuitive sensing style (Hodgkinson and Clarke 2007).

Behavioural sources of toxicity

These are wide ranging and a good coverage of impacts is given by Furnham and Taylor (2004). Bullying, exclusion, harassment and retaliation in the workplace have together been described as the growing yet silent epidemic (Einarsen et al. 2011) and there are extensive studies of these that cannot be covered in detail here. Bullying creates both victims and bystanders (Linstead 2013) and the nature of bystanding will be considered more deeply in Chapter 12. The research evidence indicates that victims of bullying report the same symptoms as for any other trauma (Hicks 2011) and bystanders have similar evidence of traumatic damage. Rejection generates a psychologically numb experience for those rejected which negatively impacts cognition and self-regulation. This numb quality appears to extend to others and reduce the capacity for empathy and compassion (Baumeister 2005). Unmanaged this leads to isolation and indifference that infuses a workplace.

Many of the structural and cognitive factors outlined previously are the antecedents of bullying (Salin and Hoel 2011). This has also been connected to destructive leaders (Hogan and Hogan 2001). The causes of abusive supervision (Hershcovis et al. 2007; Tepper et al. 2011; Hershcovis and Rafferty 2012) appear to be linked to perceptions of difference and coupled with low performance assessments are used as the basis to justify abuse of subordinates. Bullying has been evidenced to sustain inequalities at work and be a chosen tactic to get rid of people to avoid the payment of severance payments (Soylu and Sheehy-Skeffington 2015). The trauma experienced by bystanders is compounded by the act of staying silent, which again leads to the state of being psychologically numb, losing cognitive ability and the capacity to self-regulate. When the capacity for self-regulation is depleted it becomes much more likely that uncontained and unpredictable outbursts of aggression and anxiety will be expressed.

Again the concept of the toxic dose is critical. The reported general level of experiences of bullying varies depending upon how the question is asked, but base levels appear to be 4–10 per cent of the population ever experience treatment directly (Beswick et al. 2006). If we consider system toxicity, rather than interpersonal abuse, my experience has been that at these base line levels, bullying is distressing but does not appear to be destructive of the functioning of a community or organization. My perspective is that at these levels there is the scope or slack for active compassionate intervention of such situations by 'toxin handlers' (Frost 2003) containing this. Further, giving the rejected individual someone new to befriend or work with can reverse all of these impacts (Baumeister 2005). However, when the levels of reported bullying reach levels of 15 per cent and higher it appears that the whole system gets 'infected' and the organizational functioning becomes dominated by fear of rejection, rather than a concern with the work to be done, which inhibits the expression of necessary compassion (see next section). In this context it is insightful to consider the idea of carnival as a social regulation to provide a safe space for letting off steam and the extent to which this is permitted and designed into our highly economic rational model of the workplace (Ehrenreich 2006).

Research has also demonstrated that negative emotions can impact performance by directing an individual to focus on behaviours that can help manage the emotion (Lazarus 1991). This can negatively impact performance as it disrupts contribution through responses that are incompatible with work. In other words, emotion redirects focus from the task towards the circumstances surrounding the affective experience, thereby creating cognitive demands on the individual that can deplete their resources and interfere with performance activities.

Bullying and exclusion are not the only behavioural sources of toxicity. There are various employee activities associated with the fair balance of effort. This tends to be a consideration of productivity around matters of absenteeism, presenteeism and the impact on co-workers (Krol et al. 2013). The concept of 'social loafing' describes people deploying less effort due to being part of a group and the negative downward spiral from the sense of free-riding this induces across a work group, as equity adjustments around effort are made. This is described as the opposite of organizational citizenship behaviour (OCB), which is a term used to describe the discretionary effort an individual gives above the contractual requirement of the role (Hoon and Tan 2008). Leader–member exchange impacts OCB as do under-stimulation at work, co-worker lack of performance, organizational constraints, lack of expected rewards for pro-social behaviour and unjustified acts of bullying or disrespect (Specter and Fox 2010).

Both social loafing and organizational citizenship behaviour can have positive impacts but become sources of organizational toxicity at certain levels. Too much OCB resets the expectations on what is a reasonable amount of attention to give to work, often at the expense of other parts of life so has the potential to overload demand and so lead to damage. Contained levels of OCB can add the compassion and appreciation (see next section) that mitigate against difficult situations becoming toxic. Absence due to ill health or for other life reasons, or injury or disability, means an unequal distribution of effort will be perceived as fair as it points to a 'slack' in the workplace that all can access when in need. Toxicity emerges when too much free-riding leads to a general disengagement with work, a reduction in productivity and human well-being that comes from contributing meaningful work. Employee behaviour in this context can derail the total corporate identity communications process (Otubanio and Amuio 2012).

Symbolic or ritual sources of toxicity

By the time we are in the workplace we are all expert intuitive processors of meaning and can detect inconsistency, insincerity, BS and the attempt to deceive at lightning speed. The symbols and symbolic acts that populate the psychological environment at work are therefore critical potential sources of toxicity (and also the most significant points of intervention to mitigate this).

These symbolic factors are not just internal but can leak across boundaries, geographies and interest groups through a multitude of social media channels. Organizations are story rich environments (Gabriel 1995) and misalignment between the stories that symbols tell and the accounts that senior leaders in organizations give is a critical source of toxicity. The attempts to address this symbolic dimension at work with the 'audit rituals' of compliant 'tick box' processes and over-simplified measurement protocols are the most effective way of indicating the disconnect between 'talk and walk' (Wilson et al. 2010). When extrinsic and simple measures are used to compare and reward people or groups there are five broad unhelpful behavioural responses:

- we only concentrate upon what gets looked at leaving lots of work unattended;
- work becomes meaningless and extrinsic motivation takes over;
- effort gets directed to what is easy rather than what is necessary;
- people activate a self-serving bias in considerations of what they should do; and
- sophisticated ways of gaming the system are devised to 'beat it' (Osterloh 2014).

Although we apply the same rules on corporations as on 'persons' we judge corporations more stringently (Plitt et al. 2014). Additional practices in organizations that are of high relevance as symbolic and ritual sources of toxicity are: the practices around measuring performance and the private and public accounting for these and the practices around internal dispute resolution.

We know that giving stretch goals can have a negative impact on ethical behaviour (Zhang and Jia 2013). The use of ritualistic approaches to organizational regulation is a key source of toxicity. If regulators set general targets and use these to compare organizations, they symbolically activate competition and competition inherently generates losers. The ethos of winning and losing will strongly activate in-group/out-group processes and social comparisons that are an inherent aspect of human social behaviour. When the organization subject to regulation is health and social care, we need to contain the worst of these social comparison mechanisms rather than have an external authority symbolically activating them. To complete the toxic impact, when this symbolic activation of competition runs alongside generic, simplified ideas of 'a target' applied as the basis for deciding 'who wins and who loses', then we can predict that large amounts of effort will be directed to 'scoring the most goals' rather than attending to the complexities of signal detection needed to govern an enterprise.

Chapter 12 explores the psychosocial and symbolic factors involved in the damage caused to individuals and organizations through responses to whistleblowing. As background to this illustration, the over-engineering of ritual processes around internal dispute resolution means we have quasi-judicial procedures that are intended to denote that justice will be done, but because of the way they are designed they are inherently unfair.

The basic principle of a judicial system is that the judge is impartial. The grievance and disciplinary procedures used in the majority of western organizations have someone in the position of judge who, by the nature of their employment contract, cannot be impartial. The perception of lack of access to redress for

grievance damages and the felt unfairness in organizations have dramatic consequences both for organizational toxicity and for incidence of clinical depression
(Grynderup et al. 2013). When experiencing justice violations, relatively little is
known about how to enable victims' long-term recovery or the victim's role in the
recovery process (Barclay and Skarlicki 2009). There is a developing literature on
alternative restorative approaches to dispute resolution in inter-dependent communities that may provide a route through, but the emerging field evidence suggests
that we need to seriously re-design how we manage symbolic justice in organizations, to enable our approaches to justice to be healthful and be seen to be done.

Integrating the macro sources

There are various types of solution to these macro sources of toxicity offered and
when considering the model shown in Chapter 6, Figure 6.2, these tend to be the
usual focus of organizational change programmes, which are outlined in Table 7.1.

The critical issue when considering such solutions is the extent to which they
can in turn be a source of toxicity, either through bringing disproportionate attention to a single factor or through the lack of intelligent work with the psychosocial
micro processes outlined in Chapter 8.

These sources work together, so for example the issues with survivor syndrome
are linked to a single source; that of repeated restructuring, but will have impacts
across all four areas. A different structural matter, such as which organization division and hence budget allocation a function such as diversity and inclusion sits in,
can have far-reaching symbolic impacts (symbolically it is a legal problem if it sits
in HR yet it symbolizes business opportunity if it sits in Marketing). It could be
that for example an act of bullying is perceived as a behavioural factor, but it may
not be common enough in the context to be toxic. However, the root cause of the
behaviour could be a structural factor, such as role conflict, or a cognitive one such
as in-group/out-group processing hence meaning that each incidence may require

TABLE 7.1 Macro sources and current solutions

Macro factor	Types of solution
Structural factors	Organization design, process improvement, job design, succession planning, change management
Cognitive factors	Decision support including behavioural strategies and executive coaching, human factors, unconscious bias training, nudge initiatives
Behavioural factors	Positive management/leadership, management development, coaching, well-being and dignity at work, mindfulness, customer relationship management, diversity and inclusion initiatives
Symbolic factors	Culture change, leadership development brand and brand engagement, ethics training, communications, corporate social responsibility (CSR), employee consultation

attention to very different aspects of organizational function and also that it may be highlighting a deeper problem not directly linked to the behaviour.

Conclusion

This chapter has covered four broad sources of organizational toxicity that can operate individually or together. It is important to understand how each of these operates to build an understanding to support practice. Each of them already has a distinct set of solutions directed at the problems they cause but the manner in which each of these different approaches is implemented can cause problems. Organizational life does not unfold with opportunity, problems, causes and intervention all falling neatly into one box in this classification structure and intervention practice needs to consider all of these factors in an integrated manner including reference to the relevant micro processes outlined in the next chapter.

References

Asch, S. E. (1956) Studies of independence and conformity: A minority of one against a unanimous majority. *Psychological Monographs* 70(9): 1–70.

Barclay, L. J. and Skarlicki, D. P. (2009) Healing the wounds of organizational injustice: Examining the benefits of expressive writing. *Journal of Applied Psychology* 94(2): 511–523.

Baruch, Y. and Hind, P. (1999) Perpetual motion in organizations: Effective management and the impact of the new psychological contract on 'survivor syndrome'. *European Journal of Work and Organizational Psychology* 8(2): 295–306.

Baumeister, R. (2005) Rejected and alone. *The Psychologist* 18(12 December): 732–735.

Beswick, J., Gore, J. and Palferman, D. (2006) Bullying at work: A review of the literature. WPS/06/04. www.hse.gov.uk/research/hsl_pdf/2006/hsl0630.pdf.

Cross, R., Borgatti, S. and Parker, A. (2002) Making invisible work visible: Using social network analysis to support strategic collaboration. *California Management Review* 44(2): 25–46.

Dijkstra, K. A., Pligt, J. and Kleef, G. (2013) Deliberation versus intuition: Decomposing the role of expertise in judgment and decision making. *Journal of Behavioural Decision Making* 26(3): 285–294.

ECU (2013) Unconscious bias and higher education. Equalities Challenge Unit. http://www.ecu.ac.uk/publications/unconscious-bias-in-higher-education/.

Ehrenreich, B. (2006) *Dancing in the Streets*. New York: Holt Paperbacks.

Einarsen, S., Hoel, H., Zapf, D. et al. (eds) (2011) *Bullying and Harassment in the Workplace*. Florida: CRC Press, Taylor and Francis.

Frost, P. J. (2003) *Toxic Emotions at Work*. Boston, MA: Harvard Business School Press.

Furnham, A. and Taylor, J. (2004) *The Dark Side of Behavior at Work: Understanding and Avoiding Employees Leaving, Thieving and Deceiving*. Basingstoke: Palgrave Macmillan.

Gabriel, Y. (1995) The unmanaged organization: Stories, fantasies and subjectivity. *Organization Studies* 16(3): 477–501.

Gioia, D. A., Schultz, M. and Corley, K. G. (2000) Organizational identity, image and adaptive instability. *Academy of Management Review* 25(1): 63–81.

Grynderup, M. B., Mors, O., Hansen, A. M. et al. (2013) Work-unit measures of organisational justice and risk of depression: A 2-year cohort study. *Occupational and Environmental Medicine* 70(6): 380–385.

Halvorson, H. G. and Rock, D. (2015) Beyond bias: Neuroscience research shows how new organisational practices can shift ingrained thinking. m.strategy-business.com/article/00345.

Haslam, S. A., Eggins, R. A. and Reynolds, K. J. (2003) The ASPIRe model: Actualizing social and personality resources to enhance organizational outcomes. *Journal of Occupational and Organizational Psychology* 76(1): 83–113.

Haslam, S. A., Reicher, S. D. and Platow, M. J. (2011) *The New Psychology of Leadership: Identity, Influence and Power*. Hove: Psychology Press.

Hershcovis, M. S. and Rafferty, A. (2012) Predicting abusive supervision. In J. Houdmont, S. Leka and R. Sinclair (eds) *Contemporary Occupational Health Psychology: Global Perspectives on Research and Practice*, vol. 2. Chichester: Wiley-Blackwell.

Hershcovis, M. S., Turner, N., Barling, J. et al. (2007) Predicting workplace aggression: A meta-analysis. *Journal of Applied Psychology* 92(1): 228–238.

Hicks, D. (2011) *Dignity: The Essential Role It Plays in Resolving Conflict*. New Haven, CT: Yale University Press.

Hiller, N. J. and Hambrick, D. C. (2005) Conceptualizing executive hubris: The role of (hyper-) core self-evaluations in strategic decision-making. *Strategic Management Journal* 26(4): 297–319.

Hodgkinson, G. P. (2013) Shades of grey matter. *Financial Services Focus* March: 12–13.

Hodgkinson, G. P. and Clarke, I. (2007) Exploring the cognitive significance of organizational strategizing: A dual process framework and research agenda. *Human Relations* 60(1): 243–255.

Hodgkinson, G. P. and Healey, M. P. (2011) Psychological foundations of dynamic capabilities: Reflexion and reflection in strategic management. *Strategic Management Journal* 32(13): 1500–1516.

Hogan, R. and Hogan, J. (2001) Assessing leadership: A view from the dark side. *International Journal of Selection and Assessment* 9(1/2): 40–51.

Hollway, W. (1991) *Work Psychology and Organizational Behaviour: Managing the Individual at Work*. London and California: SAGE.

Hoon, H. and Tan, T. M. L. (2008) Organizational citizenship behavior and social loafing: The role of personality, motives, and contextual factors. *Journal of Psychology* 142(1): 89–108.

Janis, I. L. (1982) *Groupthink: Psychological Studies of Policy Decisions and Fiascoes* (2nd edn). New York: Houghton Mifflin.

Kahneman, D. (2011) *Thinking, Fast and Slow*. New York: Macmillan.

Karlsson, N., Loewenstein, G. and Seppi, D. (2009) The ostrich effect: Selective attention to information. *Journal of Risk and Uncertainty* 38: 95–115.

Krol, M., Brouwer, W. and Rutten, F. (2013) Productivity costs in economic evaluations: Past, present, future. *Pharmacoeconomics* 31(7): 537–549.

Lazarus, R. S. (1991) *Emotion and Adaptation*. New York: Oxford University Press.

Li, J. and Tang, Y. (2013) The social influence of executive hubris. *Management International Review* 53(1): 83–107.

Linstead, S. (2013) Organizational bystanding: Whistleblowing, watching the work go by or aiding and abetting. *M@n@gement* 16(5): 680–696.

Lovallo, D. and Sibony, O. (2010) The case for behavioral strategy. *McKinsey Quarterly* 2(March): 30–43.

Lowery, B. S., Hardin, C. D. and Sinclair, S. (2001) Social influence on automatic racial prejudice. *Journal of Personality and Social Psychology* 81(5): 842–855.

Mannor, M. J., Arrfelt, M. and Wowak, A. J. (2012) Arrogant but not ignorant? How CEOs manage their own hubris with conservative coping mechanisms. *Academy of Management Annual Meeting Proceedings* January.

Maslach, C., Schaufeli, W. B. and Leiter, M. P. (2001) Job burnout. *Annual Review of Psychology* 52(1): 397–422.

Maule, J. A. and Hodgkinson, G. P. (2002) Heuristics, biases and strategic decision-making. *The Psychologist* 15(2): 68–71.

Osterloh, M. (2014) Viewpoint: Why variable pay for performance in healthcare can backfire. Evidence from psychological economics. *Evidence Based HRM* 2(1): 120–123.

Otubanio, O. and Amuio, O. C. (2012) A holistic corporate identity communications process. *Marketing Review* 12(4): 403–417.

Park, S. H. and Westphal, J. D. (2011) Set up for a fall: The insidious effects of flattery and opinion conformity toward corporate leaders. *Administrative Science Quarterly* 56(2): 257–302.

Pflaegling, N. (2014) *Organize for Complexity: How to Get Life Back into Work to Build the High Performance Organization*. New York: Betacodex Publishing.

Phillips, K. W. and Loyd, D. L. (2006) When surface and deep-level diversity collide: The effects on dissenting group members. *Organizational Behavior and Human Decision Processes* 99(2): 143–160.

Plitt, M., Savjani, R. and Eagleman, D. (2014) Are corporates people too? The neural correlates of moral judgments about companies and individuals. *Social Neuroscience* 10(2): 113–125.

Rankin, A., Dahlback, N. and Lundberg, J. (2013) A case study of factor influencing role improvisation in crisis response teams. *Cognition Technology and Work* 15(1): 79–93.

Salin, D. and Hoel, H. (2011) Organisational causes of workplace bullying. In S. Einarsen, H. Hoel, D. Zapf et al. (eds) *Bullying and Harassment in the Workplace*. Florida: CRC Press, Taylor and Francis.

Simon, H. A. (1956) Rational choice and the structure of the environment. *Psychological Review* 63(2): 129–138.

Soylu, S. and Sheehy-Skeffington, J. (2015) Asymmetric intergroup bullying: The enactment and maintenance of societal inequality at work. *Human Relations* 68(7): 1009–1129.

Specter, P. E. and Fox, S. (2010) Counterproductive work behavior and organisational citizenship behavior: Are they opposite forms of active behavior? *Applied Psychology* 59(1): 21–39.

Tajfel, H. (1978) *Differentiation between Social Groups: Studies in the Social Psychology of Intergroup Relations*. London: Academic Press.

Teece, D. J. (2007) Explicating dynamic capabilities: The nature and microfoundations of (sustainable) enterprise performance. *Strategic Management Journal* 28(13): 1319–1350.

Tepper, B. J., Moss, S. E. and Duffy, M. K. (2011) Predictors of abusive supervision: Supervisor perceptions of deep-level dissimilarity, relationship conflict, and subordinate performance. *Academy of Management Journal* 54(2): 279–294.

Tversky, A. and Kahneman, D. (1974) Judgment under uncertainty: Heuristics and biases. *Science* 185: 1124–1131.

Wilson, D. C., Branicki, L., Sullivan-Taylor, B. et al. (2010) Extreme events, organizations and the politics of strategic decision-making. *Accounting, Auditing and Accountability Journal* 23(5): 699–721.

Zhang, Z. and Jia, M. (2013) How can companies decrease the disruptive effects of stretch goals? The moderating role of interpersonal- and informational- justice climates. *Human Relations* 66(7): 993–1020.

8

PSYCHOSOCIAL MICRO PROCESSES THAT MITIGATE OR MAXIMIZE TOXICITY IN THE WORKPLACE

Introduction

The dynamic nature of these psychosocial micro processes is represented in Chapter 6, Figure 6.7, in the wheel that encloses the sources of toxicity. When outlining the impact of such factors in the workplace, consideration is usually at the level of the individual, looking at the differences between individuals as the focus of explanation.

This text takes a different approach, focusing attention on relationships and their dynamics as the explanatory theme, so privileging the psychosocial processes at work above individual psychology. Emerging studies of trust, mistrust and distrust are providing a growing body of research insight into the manner in which the micro experience contributes to macro outcomes (Searle et al. 2014; Weibel et al. forthcoming). The human relationships that are manifested through these micro processes mitigate many of the issues caused by the macro sources of toxicity (see Chapter 7) until macro sources reach dose levels that cannot be contained any further. Many of the relevant micro processes have been listed in Table 8.1, together with an overview of the denatured functioning consequent upon toxic dose of the macro sources outlined in Chapter 7.

In this model of organizational toxicity, an integrated overview of four clusters of micro processes is provided, which are continuously in operation in any workplace setting:

- accountability
- compassion
- appreciation
- growth.

The synthesized titles of these clusters are deliberately chosen to be simple and to avoid the assumptions that come either with a popular workplace agenda or an existing area of research. There is not the scope (in this practice-focused discussion) to explore every psychosocial micro process listed in Table 8.1, as each is a research topic in its own right. My experience is that practice is better informed through synthesis of themes than by detailed research of any specific dynamic.

Accountability

Broadly, the micro processes relevant under the cluster heading *accountability* include considerations of the balance of authority and accountability, delegation, fair treatment, self-regulation, rumination and reflection. The broad evidence of denatured functioning manifests in abdication, micro management, being judgemental, bullying, role ambiguity, abstraction, discrimination, dwelling on mistakes, social loafing, disengagement and depression.

Accountability comes with authority, which tends to have a bad press in the organizational literature. The emphasis tends to be on the toxic manifestations of denatured authority as power rather than considerations of its importance as a psychosocial given in human relationships. I would suggest that it is important to engage with this concept from a more neutral position as the need for it to

TABLE 8.1 Four clusters of psychosocial micro processes

Psychosocial clusters	*Evidence of denatured functioning*
Accountability Authority and accountability, delegation, self-regulation, rumination and reflection, openness	*Denatured accountability* Abdication, micro management, bullying, being judgemental, role ambiguity, bystanding, dwelling on mistakes, discrimination, stereotypical thinking, social loafing, public whistleblowing
Compassion Compassion, affiliation and friendship, attention to well-being and work–life balance, support with coping strategies and job demand management	*Denatured compassion* Compassion fatigue, psychological numbness, isolation, exhaustion, stress, fear, absenteeism, presenteeism
Appreciation Inclusion and identity, double loop communications (cycle of 'listen, action, evidence of change') collaboration, recognition, story telling	*Denatured appreciation* Gossip, conflict, sabotage, exclusion, scapegoating, excessive competitiveness, cynicism
Growth Inquiry and learning, coaching and development, innovation practices, organizational citizenship behaviour (OCB), equal opportunities	*Denatured growth* Learned helplessness, feeling unvalued, disengagement, perfectionism, free-riding (not pulling your weight), inequalities

work well is evidenced in our expectations of fair treatment at work, suggesting that authority can either be benign, or often positive. Accountability/authority dynamics have been evidenced as critical in enabling healthy environments, indicating that benign function is supported by evidence of a shared responsibility for the nature of the psychological environment, together with clear, transparent and accountable 'authority holders'. Formal and informal leadership work is acknowledged and decision making is transparent (Haigh et al. 2012).

My understanding of authority and accountability has been influenced by the work of Jacques (1986, 1991). His notion of 'requisite authority' in organizations centres upon seeing authority as intimately connected with accountability. The attention then turns to identifying the social processes by which authority gets 'vested' into people and how inherent power is contained via a parallel process of vesting the equivalent requisite accountability. At times the investment of authority can be linked to the acceptance of a position or level of expertise leading to accountability for behaviour and representation of self. In organizations this process usually comes with an equivalent accountability/authority for the use of resources such as money, time and the contributions of others.

Teams led by 'empowering leaders', that is, those deploying accountability with their authority, experience higher and sustainable performance improvement over time through higher levels of team learning, coordination, empowerment and mental model development (Lorinkova et al. 2013). This is compared with directive styles (those using authority only) which generate quicker results, but these improvements are not sustained. Research into this process suggests a mismatch between a manager's assessment of the work involved and what is actually required. Subordinates experience the help and support available in the full use of accountability with authority as a powerful and proper use of position, whereas managers currently tend to see this active accountability work as discretionary behaviour that requires reciprocation (Toegel et al. 2013). This tends to suggest that systemically we have very confused ideas about what constitutes positive accountability/authority dynamics. To address this problem it has been suggested that selection of leaders for their capacity to role model accountability when deploying authority is critical to mitigate against business disasters (O'Toole and Bennis 2009).

Authority/accountability dynamics can also be activated via expertise. There is a subtlety around the psychosocial process involved in making assessments of expertise-based authority which points to the critical importance of status and its cues. The reciprocal affirmation of recognized expertise is positively related to team performance, hence pointing to the impact of attention to the accountability dynamics for the effective functioning of work teams (Grutterink et al. 2013). This psychosocial difference in the way in which accountability/authority works for technical experts and managers in the line underpins many of the tensions about the placement of technical experts in accountability hierarchies (Bunderson 2003). The difference between 'collegial' or expertise-based and executive hierarchy-based accountability/authority dynamics is shown in Table 8.2.

TABLE 8.2 Different accountability/authority frames (drawn from Jacques 1986)

	Nature of accountability	How authority is 'vested'	The decision processes available in this context
Executive hierarchy	Accountable upwards for the work of those you have delegated responsibility to and for all other impacts of your use of resources and position	Vested through the connections of different levels, divided up and delegated, with clear review mechanisms. This allows an individual to be the arbiter of a final decision	As this is enabled through a conventional executive decision-making approach it sits with an individual. The style used can range from authoritarian to participative but is inherently vested via the corporate structure
Collegium	Relatively autonomous accountability within the broad frame of membership rules that allows peers to comment on each other's work and to veto actions but no one member is accountable for another member's work	Vested in the 'college' or group – which constitute all the members and so decision making is either autonomous or fully participative	The various mechanisms that can be used to enable a group of members to come to decision are: consensus; veto; democracy; moderated consensus; delegated topic-based executive style authority

I have found the idea that requisite authority requires explicit levels of account-ability extremely helpful in working with client organizations, as it leads us to ask questions about how, when and if authority is separated from accountabil-ity. When these two aspects are properly connected acts of effective delegation and review are possible, but delegation is not possible if these two processes are uncoupled in the minutiae of organizational micro processes. Uncoupling these in the day-to-day psychosocial interactions is a critical indicator of toxicity in a complex workplace and is evidenced in the detachment apparent in board func-tioning (Searle et al. 2014). Unfortunately, the decoupling of authority from accountability is becoming ubiquitous in organizations, leading to dangerous and uncontained workplaces where people have no role clarity, either about what they are authorized to do or what they will be held accountable for. This uncou-pling also leads to the heightened risk of unpredictable blame (what it feels like when held to account for something without the authority to control or influence the outcome).

Disconnections between accountability and authority are implicated in all the evidence about the precursors of bullying and violence in the workplace. There is substantial evidence of the negative impact of aggression and unfair treatment (see Chapter 7). The individual decision to disengage from work, to minimize decision taking and to withdraw creative (i.e. uncertain) effort from organizational problems, is a rational response in these circumstances as it minimizes the likelihood of punishment. It has been suggested that 'moral' collapse in organizations is associated with breakdowns in the collective social structures anchored through accountability/authority in regulatory pathways (Shadnam and Lawrence 2011).

The desire for clarity about accountability and authority was evidenced in research with CEOs asked about the input they wanted from boards (Sonnenfeld et al. 2013). This indicated that energetic, constructive debate, with no tendency to rubber-stamp approval of their plans was desired. Underpinning this was a request for board members to overcome any conflict aversion and work intelligently to make the inherently fraught decisions about who is accountable and so has authority. This is a clear articulation of the need for active accountability and the importance this brings in creating psychological safety, even for those with the highest levels of authority in the system. When I have participated in positive authority relationships they have provided the containment for decision making and action, the basis of trust and hence the freedom to think and act. I have experienced this in relationship with teachers, supervisors, team members, students, managers, coaches, peers, senior leadership teams and those reporting to me.

There are two other arenas that this accountability/authority dynamic is enacted in workplaces. The first is in the mechanisms around unfair treatment. Benign accountability/authority relationships are evidenced in the productive management of unfair treatment through conditions being set that enable apologies, making amends, extending forgiveness and fostering re-connection (Goodstein and Aquino 2010). In workplace settings the provision of just social accounts, such as apologies, justifications and admission of wrong-doing is necessary but not sufficient to repair injustice. Concrete actions including the removal of offenders from the workplace to ensure that injustice will be prevented in the future are effective ways of repairing injustice (Beugre 2011). Working in community settings directly integrating ideas of individual and community responsibilities in the response to violence and violent situations has been impactful in the repair of damaged trust and lowering the sense of injustice. Such approaches use the authority of story telling, of being an author, so creating explicit co-authored narratives to explain transgression and contain further damage (Kim 2010).

However, we rarely see such a collective approach to 'authority' – who gets to tell the story – when cases of unfair treatment are raised in organizations. Neither do we see the full demonstration of accountability used in the way such complaints are handled. More commonly we see breaches of natural justice perpetrated through organizational processes used to manage grievances and disciplinary procedures (see Chapter 12) that deploy authority without the balancing accountability, hence enacting toxic power.

The second arena is in the internalized accountability/authority dynamics that are described as self-regulation, supported by self-reflection in the workplace context. Self-regulatory models of goal pursuit provide a useful explanatory approach to how we contain accountability/authority (Moberly and Watkins 2010). The impact of self-regulation and the way the resource for this diminishes with use has also been implicated in increases in bullying levels (as workplaces get more demanding). The depletion effect happens when individuals who exert self-control in a task (i.e. depleted individuals) then exhibit less self-control on a subsequent task. This depletion appears to be linked to the cues in the environment and so is inherently socially activated (Agrawal and Wan 2009). Self-regulation can denature with brooding and can cause depressive symptoms particularly when linked to passive coping strategies. This is in contrast to reflection, which can with positive supervisory or coaching type relationships, help externalize problems and create scope for effective coping (Marroquin et al. 2010).

When considering behavioural transgressions, we are really clear about how the behaviour of others negatively impacts us, as this evidence is readily available to us in our own responses. However, we are much less aware of how our behaviour negatively impacts others, hence creating an 'availability' bias in the data available for us to process. Self-reflection and self-regulation requires working against this bias, using 'thinking slow' principles to overcome instinctive responses, which is resource depleting. The provision of time and support to encourage the rebuilding of this self-regulation resource has been advocated as a key positive response for organizational toxicity and probably explains much of the investment we have seen in coaching over the past 10 years as we strip embedded support out of organizations through 'head count reduction'.

Compassion

Broadly, the micro processes relevant under the cluster heading compassion include considerations of compassion, affiliation and friendship, attention to well-being, work–life balance, coping strategies and job demand management. The broad evidence of denatured functioning includes compassion fatigue, psychological numbness, isolation, exhaustion, stress, absenteeism, presenteeism and fear.

As outlined in Chapter 6 social support (and more specifically its absence) in the workplace, has been classed as a psychosocial hazard. Affiliations, friendships at work and support for coping strategies are critical to mitigating the experience of pain and suffering at work. The sense of being valued at work is created (or destroyed) day-to-day in the interactions around suffering and attention to coping has been identified as a significant factor in psychological well-being at work (Landen and Wang 2010). Workplaces are steeped in emotion and 'lows' at work can be painful, as individuals' feelings, desires and needs collide with organizational realities. Inadequate control at work causes burnout and hurtful behavioural transgressions are on the rise in our workplaces (Lee 2000). The lack of ongoing psychosocial attention to these workplace realities, builds into denatured organizational functioning that contaminates a whole workplace, manifesting in phenomena such as compassion fatigue, indifference to suffering, isolation, exhaustion, stress at work and disaffection.

Compassion is an interpersonal process associated with the response to and management of suffering. The safe expression of negative emotions to those who are trusted improves relationships and motivates connection (Driver 2007; Dutton et al. 2014). Compassionate acts can be found everywhere in an organization; from office workers who listen and respond empathetically to their friends (Frost 2003; Kanov et al. 2004), managers who contain the anxieties and concerns of team members (Donaldson-Feilder et al. 2008) to boards that create and govern the systems and structures designed to buffer against the suffering of their employees.

Where compassion is present in the workplace, there is less anxiety and greater attachment to the workplace (Grant et al. 2008). Compassion is also 'infectious' and those who have seen and/or received compassionate acts tend to take less punitive action against others who make errors in work or transgress in any way (Condon and Desteno 2011) and it is more likely to foster a 'forgiveness' climate in organizations (Fehr and Gelfand 2012). Frost (2003) has also highlighted that experiencing compassion (or not) impacts how connected people feel in the working environment and it has been associated with a range of positive attitudes, behaviours and feelings (Dutton et al. 2002).

Frost (2003) writes of the importance of having 'toxin handlers' in the workplace to mitigate the worst excesses of suffering. By activating the relational possibility of compassion these 'toxin handlers' mitigate against the worst excesses of the overly economic-rationalistic (masculine) characteristics of contemporary organizations. There are key routines in organizations that appear to enable compassion evidenced in an 'enabling environments' approach (Haigh et al. 2012). These routines include a clear sense of organizational purpose, the permission to speak of suffering, the nature of social support, the role modelling of vulnerability in high status individuals and responsiveness to expressions of pain (Gerada and Wilde 2015). The freedom to act in accordance with one's chosen values also enables compassion (Atkins and Parker 2012).

There are emotional and self-regulation costs to participating in a compassionate exchange (for both carer and sufferer), which draw on the limited resources we each have for self-regulation. It is therefore unsurprising that compassionate exchanges are more forthcoming in a workplace if there are only a few 'victims' (be that from experiences of bullying or working with ill patients and their worried families) than if the organization is full of people suffering (Dickert and Slovic 2009). In high suffering contexts, there is the real risk of increased 'secondary trauma'; the strain that comes from watching the suffering of others (Halifax 2011). One of the biggest protectors against secondary trauma and associated 'compassion fatigue', particularly where there are large numbers of 'victims', is the time made available to activate social support, coping mechanisms and reflective practices which allocate resources to the processing of pain and suffering (Lois 2001).

In field settings, I have encountered suggestions that compassion can be increased through 'compassion training' workshops, but this suggestion fails to understand the psychosocial nature of this protective micro process. I think suggesting that people in a toxic environment need training in 'compassion' is an act of abuse. Being 'accused' of a lack of compassion compounds the pain caused for those who are already 'victims' of the toxicity of the system they are unfortunate enough to work within. Compassion is not a skill that sits in an individual, but is a product of the quality of relationships enabled in the work context. The suggestion of individual training implies that needing to take time to undertake essential recovery, reflection and self-regulation to stay well in high suffering contexts is a failure of the individual rather than a reality of the context.

Appreciation

Broadly, the psychosocial connections clustered under the heading appreciation include considerations of identity, collaboration, story telling, inclusion and the way double loop communications unfold in the workplace. The broad evidence of denatured functioning includes groupthink, sabotage, blame, exclusion, excessive competition, gossip, inter-group conflict, scapegoating and cynicism.

It is important for our capacity to function and contribute, to be recognized and appreciated by others and the various dynamics around appreciation have a profound impact on the experiences of work and our capacity to absorb and handle sources of toxicity. Appreciation is evidenced in the nature of interpersonal exchanges and the literature on interactional justice is relevant in this context. In addition it is evidenced in the functioning of 'double loop communications', which refers to the process where there is the opportunity for voice, this being listened to and there being clear feedback that shows how this input has contributed. If a communication process does not have this action impact, it is much more likely that it will lead to cynical interpretations by those involved. Particularly relevant here is the evidence of micro processes rooted in a deep-seated motivation to maintain positive self-esteem, and an underlying reluctance about giving negative feedback (Larson 1989). Chapter 10 covers the problems with performance management. The loss of a valued social identity also leads to decline of mental and physical health (Haslam 2014). In the context of ethical organizational practices, this suggests that careful attention to positive social identity at work (inclusion) and the associated increase in appreciation that follows is a critical need for creating acceptable levels of psychological safety.

There is evidence that workplace environments characterized by high appreciation have open inquiry and positive feedback in their work groups and show higher productivity than those characterized by more sceptical and challenging feedback interactions (Losada and Heaphy 2004). Psychological theories of attachment applied to the workplace suggest that those who are appreciated by their employing organizations are more likely to exhibit organizational citizenship behaviour, that is, you do things that your employment contract does not require of you (Desivilya et al. 2006 and Chapter 7). The rationale for inclusion at work, participation, co-creation and engagement are increasingly linked to the contention that people give more when they are appreciated.

Atewologun and Nitu (2015) indicate that inclusive leadership requires alignment between organizational strategy and the relational aspects of the workplace, so clearly establishing the macro–micro link. The work of constantly reinforcing social identity is a critical requirement from team and organizational leaders, explicitly ensuring their decisions affirm distinct social identities shared by employees (Haslam and Platow 2001).

Unfortunately, the growing literature on workplace diversity and particularly ethnicity at work points to the negative health impact on minority groups from exclusion and the lower levels of expressed appreciation consequent on this. Singh et al. (2013) found that employees from minority ethnic backgrounds were more vulnerable to psychologically unsafe environments and so more at risk from the negative health consequences. In considering the treatment of black and white footballers celebrating their success while celebratory black and white players were perceived as being equally arrogant, black players were penalized with lower compensation whereas white players were not (Hall and Livingston 2012). Also minority employees in psychologically unsafe environments were, self-protectively, less likely to extend themselves in their roles, resulting in lower perceived performance and disadvantaged career achievement, which in turn reinforce the perceptions of unfairness. This is broad evidence of these patterns of exclusion in the workplace and their impact on appreciation, well-being and organizational performance (Kamenou and Fearfull 2006; Tepper et al. 2011; Guillaume et al. 2013; Luksyte et al. 2013).

Effective diversity and inclusion practices within an organization have been shown to have positive impact on the productive use of 'voice and identity'. This has been demonstrated at strategic decision-making levels through the positive outcomes from gender balanced boards on organizational performance (CTPSR 2015). Well-managed, balanced and visible differences in a group appear to enable the non-visible difference (thought diversity) to be brought productively into play at work (Phillips and Loyd 2006). Positive contact reduces prejudice and anxiety between groups can help to develop inter-group appreciation (Stathi and Crisp 2010), which has been activated by asking people merely to imagine positive inter-group experiences (Miles and Crisp 2014). Positive contact also supports increased discussion-based cooperation despite diversity (Meleady et al. 2013). Creating salience for identity linked with higher-level and inclusive (superordinate) belonging across groups also reduces bias (Stone and Crisp 2007).

When new entrants to a workplace meet and work with people that they appreciate, they are more likely to stay and contribute. Studies of socialization into a workplace indicates the distinct roles played by peers and leaders to build trust (Schaubroeck et al. 2013) and lack of appreciation leads to much higher turnover rates for poorly socialized employees (Somers 2010). There is also interesting evidence that high status organizations generate a feeling of positive social identity and consequently a sense of appreciation in people, which can lead paradoxically to inappropriately high levels of retention, together with high levels of free-riding behaviour (Swider et al. 2011). Evidence from the voluntary sector indicates that retention is not linked to abstract ideas of the 'mission' of the organization, but is much more closely linked to the interpersonal appreciation forthcoming from the specific places within which individuals work (Brown and Yoshioka 2003; Hustinx and Handy 2009).

Growth

Broadly, the micro processes relevant under the cluster heading growth include considerations of inquiry and learning, coaching and development, equal opportunities and the dynamics that enable play and innovation. Denatured functioning can be evidenced in learned helplessness, 'jobs worth', disengagement, inequality and the failure to innovate.

The inherent vulnerability of learning underpinned the development of ideas of psychological safety in the workplace and the impact of the environment on organizational productivity (Edmondson 1999). The psychosocial dynamics around growth are internalized models of the parent–child relationship, of schooling and the various social settings in which human development is enabled and constrained. Building on this requires role modelling, didactic practices and action learning as the scaffolding for the development approaches in the workplace. Previous experiences of development will impact and a critical issue in this context is the trust needed to accept developmental input which is not always straightforward or comfortable, so self-reliance can be experienced as a safer alternative (Gianakos 2013).

A major challenge for workplace learning theories (particularly in the context of substantial technological driven changes in the way we access information) is to illuminate how particular kinds of learning experiences and environments promote the development of expertise. This development appears to rely on the roles of expert modelling, peer feedback, self-reflection and participation in a supportive learning community: growth is inherently a social process (Ge and Hardre 2010).

Teams in workplaces whose members have 'growth mindsets' work better with each other, are more innovative, push themselves harder, set higher standards and generally outperform teams whose members have more predominantly fixed mindsets (Dweck 1999, 2006). Organizations can unintentionally disrupt these benefits and also encourage such people to leave.

There has recently been a major increase in coaching in organizations. This includes the purchase of external coaching input and the development of coaching skills in managers within organizations. Part of the rationale around this development is linked to the suggestion that experience-based learning is more productive and generates a better return on investment than sending people out of organizations. However, when we consider the toxic impacts of continuous restructuring as outlined in Chapter 7 and the importance of social support, outlined in Chapter 6, I consider that this increase in the coaching relationship is often a field-based response to the structural damage done, rather than having particular relevance to growth dynamics in workplaces.

Asking people to think creatively with rules around voice, elaboration and creation that inhibit the right to critique, challenge or reject has a direct impact on brain function and output and the creation of places to play which illuminates the requirement for psychological safety. Creativity is inhibited by a climate of stress and tension (Sternberg 1999) as such a climate increases stereotypical thinking and inhibits learning. How we feel is integral to cognition and intrinsic to learning, reasoning and action (LeDoux 2000) and so to expertise and organizational effectiveness.

Thriving is closely linked to learning; the growth that comes from gaining knowledge and skills. The psychosocial environment is critical to this. Factors that help, all link to the mechanisms of growth: providing discretion; sharing information about the organization and its strategy; minimizing incivility; and offering feedback (Spreitzer and Porath 2012). The study found that a learning organization culture, as evidenced in employee engagement, made a direct and indirect impact on employees' innovative work behaviours (Park et al. 2014). Openness in organizations appears to be a critical precursor to enabling both effective development of organizational memory (the collective growth of accessible knowledge). It also appears to be a pre-requisite to enabling individual learning, suggesting that there are aspects of organizational routines that inhibit the capacity for effective growth-based relationships (Cegarra-Navarro and Sanchez-Polo 2011).

Learning situations if carefully managed do make people more receptive to negative feedback as long as this is constructive and focused on the need to learn rather than the failure of an objective (Cianci et al. 2010 and Chapter 10). Growth dynamics are supported through very careful use of feedback, where anything negative needs to be focused on what people do rather than who they are and also needs to be explicitly linked to practical steps that can improve the situation (Sommer and KulKarni 2012). The dynamics around growth and learning are complex and both goal difficulty and goal specificity appear to mediate the relationship between how leaders get on with people and the level of engagement that is invested in learning (Bezuijen et al. 2010).

The current dominance of competency frameworks that give simple pathway accounts of what growth and learning look like are counter-productive and will disrupt the environment that enables this openness and probably warrants research for their toxic impacts on development of individuals and growth of expertise in organizations.

Conclusion

This chapter has outlined some of the dynamics of psychosocial relationships that are critical to workplace functioning and mitigation of toxicity. It also indicates some of the consequences when our approaches to relating become denatured.

Intervention is properly enabled through brokering a balance of participation and orchestration, as the model presented in Chapter 3, Figure 3.5 outlines. This not only works to enable demand-effective (and cost-effective) change, but also builds in a framework that is predicated upon the essential connectivity between macro and micro levels in organizations.

The psychosocial risks associated with structural re-design means denatured micro processes are at their most active and this chapter gives an overview of the clusters of psychosocial dynamics that must be addressed. The predominant concerns will become those about position (the work of social comparison) rather than purpose (the work of social identity) and so the very act of restructuring brings an increase in damaging types of relating with toxic consequences. Enabling a flow between micro experiences to inform macro initiatives has the capacity to resonate and shift what it is that 'feels possible' in any context.

References

Agrawal, N. and Wan, E. W. (2009) Regulating risk or risking regulation? Construal levels and depletion effects in the processing of health messages. *Journal of Consumer Research* 36(3): 448–462.

Atewologun, D. and Nitu, M. (2015) What is inclusive leadership? A systematic literature review of the empirical evidence. *DOP Conference Proceedings*. British Psychological Society, Glasgow, January.

Atkins, P. W. B. and Parker, S. K. (2012) Understanding individual compassion in organizations: The role of appraisals and psychological flexibility. *Academy of Management Review* 37(4): 524–546.

Beugre, C. D. (2011) Repairing injustice in organisations: Beyond social accounts. *Journal of General Management* 37(1): 47–63.

Bezuijen, X. M., van Dam, K., van den Berg, P. T. et al. (2010) How leaders stimulate employee learning: A leader–member exchange approach. *Journal of Occupational and Organizational Psychology* 83(3): 673–693.

Brown, W. and Yoshioka, C. (2003) Mission attachment and satisfaction as factors in employee retention. *Nonprofit Management and Leadership* 14(1): 5–18.

Bunderson, J. S. (2003) Recognizing and utilizing expertise in work groups: A status characteristics perspective. *Administrative Science Quarterly* 48(4): 557–591.

Cegarra-Navarro, J.-G. and Sanchez-Polo, M. T. (2011) Influence of the open-mindedness culture on organizational memory: An empirical investigation of Spanish SMEs. *International Journal of Human Resource Management* 22(1): 1–18.

Cianci, A. M., Klein, H. and Seijts, G. (2010) The effect of negative feedback on tension and subsequent performance: The main and interactive effects of goal content and conscientiousness. *Journal of Applied Psychology* 95(4): 618–630.

Condon, P. and Desteno, D. (2011) Compassion for one reduces punishment for another. *Journal of Experimental Social Psychology* 47(3): 698–701.

CTPSR (2015) What happens when women have more power and influence? www.coventry.ac.uk/CTPSR.

Desivilya, H. S., Sabag, Y. and Ashton, E. (2006) Prosocial tendencies in organizations: The role of attachment styles and organizational justice in shaping organizational citizenship behavior. *International Journal of Organizational Analysis* 14(1): 22–42.

Dickert, S. and Slovic, P. (2009) Attentional mechanisms in the generation of sympathy. *Judgment and Decision Making* 4(4): 297–306.

Donaldson-Feilder, E., Yarker, J. and Lewis, R. (2008) Line management competence: The key to reducing stress at work. *Strategic HR Review* 7(2): 11–16.

Driver, M. (2007) Meaning and suffering in organizations. *Journal of Organizational Change Management* 20(5): 611–632.

Dutton, J. E., Frost, P. J., Worline, M. C. et al. (2002) Leading in times of trauma. *Harvard Business Review* 80(1): 54–61.

Dutton, J., Workman, K. M. and Hardin, A. E. (2014) Compassion at work. *Annual Review of Organizational Psychology and Organizational Behavior* 1: 277–304.

Dweck, C. S. (1999) *Self-Theories: Their Role in Motivation, Personality, and Development.* Philadelphia, PA: Taylor and Francis/Psychology Press.

Dweck, C. S. (2006) *Mindset.* New York: Random House.

Edmondson, A. (1999) Psychological safety and learning behavior in work teams. *Administrative Science Quarterly* 44(2): 350–383.

Fehr, R. and Gelfand, M. J. (2012) The forgiving organization: A multilevel model of forgiveness at work. *Academy of Management Review* 37(4): 664–688.

Frost, P. J. (2003) *Toxic Emotions at Work: How Compassionate Managers Handle Pain and Conflict.* Boston, MA: Harvard Business School Press.

Ge, X. and Hardre, P. (2010) Self-processes and learning environment as influences in the development of expertise in instructional design. *Learning Environments Research* 13(1): 23–41.

Gerada, C. and Wilde, J. (2015) Care, compassion and concern in the NHS. *Journal of Psychological Therapies in Primary Care* 4(S): 47–68.

Gianakos, I. (2013) Counterdependence at work: Relationships with social support, control beliefs, and self-monitoring. *Journal of Career Development* 40(1): 23–39.

Goodstein, J. and Aquino, K. (2010) And restorative justice for all: Redemption, forgiveness, and reintegration in organizations. *Journal of Organizational Behavior* 31(4): 624–628.

Grant, A. M., Dutton, J. E. and Rosso, B. D. (2008) Giving commitment: Employee support programs and the prosocial sensemaking process. *Academy of Management Journal* 51(5): 898–918.

Grutterink, H., Van der Vegt, G. S., Molleman, E. et al. (2013) Reciprocal expertise affirmation and shared expertise perceptions in work teams: Their implications for coordinated action and team performance. *Applied Psychology: An International Review* 62(3): 359–381.

Guillaume, Y. R. F., Dawson, J. F., Woods, S. A. et al. (2013) Getting diversity at work to work. *Journal of Occupational and Organisational Psychology* 86(2): 123–141.

Haigh, R., Harrison, T., Johnson, R. et al. (2012) Psychologically informed environments and the 'enabling environments' initiative. *Housing, Care and Support* 15(1): 34–42.

Halifax, J. (2011) The precious necessity of compassion. *Journal of Pain Symptom Management* 41(1): 146–153.

Hall, E. V. and Livingston, R. W. (2012) The hubris penalty: Biased responses to 'celebration' displays of black football players. *Journal of Experimental Social Psychology* 48(4): 899–904.

Haslam, S. A. (2014) Making good theory practical: Five lessons for an Applied Social Identity approach to challenges of organizational, health and clinical psychology. *British Journal of Social Psychology* 53(1): 1–20.

Haslam, S. A. and Platow, M. J. (2001) Your wish is our command: The role of shared social identity in translating a leader's vision into followers' action. In M. A. Hogg and D. J. Terry (eds) *Social Identity Processes in Organizational Contexts.* Philadelphia, PA: Psychology Press.

Hustinx, L. and Handy, F. (2009) Where do I belong? Volunteer attachment in a complex organization. *Administration in Social Work* 33(2): 202–220.

Jacques, E. (1986) *A General Theory of Bureaucracy.* Portsmouth: Heinemann.

Jacques, E. (1991) *Requisite Organization*. Virginia: Cason Hall.

Kamenou, N. and Fearfull, A. (2006) Ethnic minority women: A lost voice in HRM. *Human Resource Management Journal* 16(2): 154–172.

Kanov, J. M., Maitlis, S., Worline, M. C. et al. (2004) Compassion in organizational life. *American Behavioral Science* 47(6): 808–827.

Kim, M. E. (2010) Moving beyond critique: Creative interventions and reconstructions of community accountability. *Social Justice* 37(4): 14–35.

Landen, S. M. and Wang, C. D. C. (2010) Adult attachment, work cohesion, coping, and psychological well-being of fire-fighters. *Counselling Psychology Quarterly* 23(2): 143–162.

Larson, J. R. (1989) The dynamic interplay between employees' feedback-seeking strategies and supervisors' delivery of performance feedback. *Academy of Management Review* 14(3): 408–422.

LeDoux, J. E. (2000) Emotion circuits in the brain. *Annual Review of Neuroscience* 23: 155–184.

Lee, D. (2000) An analysis of workplace bullying in the UK. *Personnel Review* 29(5): 593–610.

Lois, J. (2001) Managing emotions, intimacy and relationships in a volunteer search and rescue group. *Journal of Contemporary Ethnography* 30(2): 131–179.

Lorinkova, N. M., Pearsall, M. J. and Sims Jr, H. P. (2013) Examining the differential longitudinal performance of directive versus empowering leadership in teams. *Academy of Management Journal* 56(2): 573–596.

Losada, M. and Heaphy, E. (2004) The role of positivity and connectivity in the performance of business teams: A non-linear dynamics model. *American Behavioural Scientist* 47(6): 740–765.

Luksyte, A., Waite, E., Avery, D. R. et al. (2013) Held to a different standard: Racial differences in the impact of lateness on advancement opportunity. *Journal of Occupational and Organizational Psychology* 86(2): 142–165.

Marroquin, B., Fontes, M., Scilletta, A. et al. (2010) Ruminative subtypes and coping responses: Active and passive pathways to depressive symptoms. *Cognition and Emotion* 24(8): 1446–1455.

Meleady, R., Hopthrow, T. and Crisp, R. J. (2013) The group discussion effect: Integrative processes and suggestions for implementation. *Personality and Social Psychology Review* 17(1): 56–71.

Miles, E. and Crisp, R. J. (2014) A meta-analytic test of the imagined contact hypothesis. *Group Processes and Intergroup Relations* 17(1): 3–26.

Moberly, N. and Watkins, E. R. (2010) Negative affect and ruminative self-focus during everyday goal pursuit. *Cognition and Emotion* 24(4): 729–739.

O'Toole, J. and Bennis, W. (2009) What's needed next: A culture of candor. *Harvard Business Review* 87(6): 54–61.

Park, Y. K., Song, J. H., Yoon, S. W. et al. (2014) Learning organization and innovative behavior: The mediating effect of work engagement. *European Journal of Training and Development* 38(1–2): 75–94.

Phillips, K. W. and Loyd, D. L. (2006) When surface and deep-level diversity collide: The effects on dissenting group members. *Organizational Behavior and Human Decision Processes* 99(2): 143–160.

Schaubroeck, J. M., Peng, A. C. and Hannah, S. T. (2013) Developing trust with peers and leaders: Impacts on organizational identification and performance during entry. *Academy of Management Journal* 56(4): 1148–1168.

Searle, R. H., Legood, A. and Teoh, K. (2014) *Trust Boards and Governance: Composition and Behavioural Styles in Implementing Culture Change in the NHS*. Contributions from Occupational Psychology; BPS Shop.

Shadnam, M. and Lawrence, T. B. (2011) Understanding widespread misconduct in organizations: An institutional theory of moral collapse. *Business Ethics Quarterly* 21(3): 379–407.

Singh, B., Winkel, D. E. and Selvarajan, T. (2013) Managing diversity at work: Does psychological safety hold the key to racial differences in employee performance? *Journal of Occupational and Organizational Psychology* 86(2): 242–263.

Somers, M. J. (2010) Patterns of attachment to organizations: Commitment profiles and work outcomes. *Journal of Occupational and Organizational Psychology* 83(2): 443–453.

Sommer, K. L. and KulKarni, M. (2012) Does constructive performance feedback improve citizenship intentions and job satisfaction? The roles of perceived opportunities for advancement, respect, and mood. *Human Resource Development Quarterly* 23(2): 177–201.

Sonnenfeld, J., Kusin, M. and Waltonz, E. (2013) What CEOs really think of their boards. *Harvard Business Review* 91(4): 98–106.

Spreitzer, G. and Porath, C. (2012) Creating sustainable performance. *Harvard Business Review* 90(1/2): 92–99.

Stathi, S. and Crisp, R. J. (2010) Intergroup contact and the projection of positivity. *International Journal of Intercultural Relations* 34(6): 580–591.

Sternberg, R. J. (ed.) (1999) *Handbook of Creativity*. Cambridge: Cambridge University Press.

Stone, C. H. and Crisp, R. J. (2007) Superordinate and subgroup identification as predictors of intergroup evaluation in common ingroup contexts. *Group Process and Intergroup Relations* 10(4): 493–513.

Swider, B., Zimmerman, R., Boswell, W. R. et al. (2011) Understanding your standing: Multiple indicators of status and their influence on employee attachment. *Corporate Reputation Review* 14(3): 159–174.

Tepper, B. J., Moss, S. E. and Duffy, M. K. (2011) Predictors of abusive supervision: Supervisor perceptions of deep-level dissimilarity, relationship conflict, and subordinate performance. *Academy of Management Journal* 54(2): 279–294.

Toegel, G., Kilduff, M. and Anand, N. (2013) Emotion helping by managers: An emergent understanding of discrepant role expectations and outcomes. *Academy of Management Journal* 56(2): 334–357.

Weibel, A., Den Hartog, D. N., Gillespie, N. et al. (forthcoming) The role of control in organisational trust and trustworthiness. *Human Resources Management*.

PART III

Learning from practice to intervene in toxic organizations

These chapters cover the work of intelligent activism and what can be learned from intervention practice.

Chapter 9 provides reflections on the three diagnostic themes (included in the integrated model of organizational toxicity) that I use to understand the current state of any psychological environment: belonging; contributing; and meaning. These common sense headings have been synthesized using a wide range of disciplines and experience. The 'shadow-side' toxic justice, attachment and accountability disorders are also covered.

Chapter 10 illustrates contributing and toxic justice disorders in outlining why performance management does not work. Performance management technologies are widespread and used to manage most individual contributions in complex organizations, but are damaging. This chapter covers the six key ways in which these technologies damage collaborative contribution and human well-being.

Chapter 11 illustrates the complexity of belonging and the basis of toxic attachment disorders. It brings brokering in belonging to the foreground through two case illustrations of effective social network moderation. This highlights the varying realities of group structures, how a limited view of human connection can lead to organizational dysfunction and what can be done about it.

Chapter 12 probes the processes around meaning and toxic accounting disorders in organizations via two distinct topics. One explores equal pay patterns in a single context to explore how patterns get hidden in our current measurement approaches in organizations. The other considers the psychosocial processes around bystanding, whistleblowing and the impact of current quasi-judicial HR management protocols. It offers six design challenges to mitigate toxic accountability disorders.

9

DIAGNOSTIC THEMES FOR EXAMINING THE PSYCHOLOGICAL ENVIRONMENT

Introduction

I work with three diagnostic themes – *contributing*, *belonging* and *meaning* – to explore function and toxicity for any workplace client engagement. The use of these themes is also informed by my growing understanding of three patterns of organizational toxicity that are manifesting:

- The contributing theme manifests as toxic justice disorders.
- The belonging theme manifests as a series of toxic attachment disorders (detachment, exclusion or over-attachment).
- The meaning theme manifests as toxic accountability disorders.

These diagnostic themes are synthesized from a combination of client experience and breadth of reading and knowledge across psychology, social science, management studies and critical management, anthropology, ethics, philosophy and law. The reflections presented later will demonstrate the way in which breadth rather than depth helps inform practice. I neither see nor deploy a hierarchy around these themes but instead hold them 'loosely' and work deliberately with their dynamic and interacting nature, using them to assess the specific psychological environment within a workplace and to help discern starting points, organizational capabilities and sensitive and current 'no-go' zones. To help, we are obligated to start from where our client is not where we wish they were, nor where the state of external knowledge may be or even where a client may think they are, as we cannot initiate any sensible intervention from an imagined starting point.

Diagnosis as a practice capability

Diagnosis (as a form of organized insight) is a practice capability listed in Chapter 1, Table 1.2 and requires a specific approach to inquiry – one that is quite different from a formal 'research' endeavour. The awareness of the interplay of macro factors and micro processes feeds into this diagnostic work, but the specific topics given in Chapters 7 and 8 are not used to frame or define the inquiry process I undertake in a client context. I would not expect to have a detailed examination of each of the macro environment factors (structure, behaviour, cognition and symbols) or the functioning of each psychosocial micro process cluster (accountability, compassion, appreciation and growth) before commencing intervention as I do not consider that investment in complex analytic processes is generally the best use of resources or attention once a client request has been activated. Diagnostic methods inherently unfold in the process of working with a presenting problem or question, supporting consideration of what needs to be done in the specific and emerging situation.

These three themes – contributing, belonging and meaning – are therefore not intended to be 'research' concepts. They do not come with tight definitions that constitute them as 'entities with properties' but instead they are dialogic terms (see Chapter 4) designed to enable context specific examination in a way that has some conceptual integration across different client assignments. To do this they are:

- designed to encourage *inquiry for intervention* in the 'field' rather than to enable research in the 'lab';
- *common sense notions* open for all to understand without complex definitions and have been *synthesized* from field experience rather than using academically pre defined concepts;
- focused on the 'emergent description' of psychosocial *relationships* rather than being interested or focused upon individual experiences;
- designed to *be 'elaborative' in use*, which means they are to be used to generate exploration and dialogue and access context specific ways of talking and acting;
- chosen as *cross-culturally accessible* descriptors that can enable dialogue around an expressed 'client problem' in any context or country.

In using these themes diagnostically, the intent is not to 'control' or define how things are seen or 'measured'. Instead the focus is to be able to intervene helpfully in the functioning of a complex psychological environment. Using loosely defined common sense terms enables us to 'include in' the variability that exists in the client context. This is in contrast to a research 'problem definition' approach that would exclude out this variability as a set of confounding factors needing to be controlled.

When using these themes, there are instances when I do not use the descriptors given here, but instead attend to the language used in the client organization and adapt my terminology; sometimes working with the internal language to blend in and sometimes very deliberately introducing a different way of framing an issue to introduce dialogic space for a different perspective (see framing bias, Chapter 7). As the purpose is to free up established ways of talking and thinking to enable intervention, the practical engagement with these subtle cues from the psychological environments in each workplace is critical.

Too often ideas of 'diagnosis' in management studies and workplace psychology tacitly accept a 'managerialist' view of the need for 'organizational change management' and locate the need for change and the point of the problem in individual 'resistance to change'. The notion of resistance to change troubles me, as it appears to position 'resistance' as a problem. By contrast resistance (e.g. in the form of an immune system) is a critical requirement for the health for any living entity and individuals and organizations warrant having these active forms of resistance in operation – it is not the job of any outsider to try and take them down. This implicit assumption about 'resistance as wrong' directs imagination, emotion and cognition about organizational change management to people as the 'source of the problem' rather than seeing them both as the victims of the conditions they are expected to work in and as the key enablers of improvement through subtle adjustments to the way they engage in psychosocial processes in the workplace.

We are still at the stage where we need to use these environmental themes to repair psychological environments to make them 'safe' workplaces. My hope is that there will be a time when we understand deeply and practically how these dynamics work and are able to focus upon the design of beautiful and elegant psychological environments where psychological safety is taken for granted.

Reflections on the diagnostic theme of contributing

This section offers a brief reflection on the theme of contributing and outlines its toxic manifestation as 'justice disorders' in complex workplaces. There are various other common sense words that I could have used here. Concepts such as engagement, empowerment and motivation are all alternative ways that this theme has been addressed. The reason that I have used the term 'contributing' is that this points to the purpose rather than an individual state of mind or behaviour. Contributing is about collaboration. Two people working together are always more proficient than the most proficient individual working alone (Koriat 2012) and three or more people in a group are more effective than two people (Laughlin et al. 2006). Further, being self-centred damages individual performance in action (McKay et al. 2015).

When I apply the diagnostic theme of contributing I will variably draw on topics such as creativity and innovation, performance management (see Chapter 10), social comparison theory, grievances, discipline and conflict resolution, process and outcome fairness. I will also consider the emerging literature on restorative justice, equality, diversity and inclusion (D&I), pay structures, competency frameworks, organizational values systems and ideas of hierarchy and structure.

All aspects of 'contributing' are active in any client context and need to be open to consideration. While a 'lab-based' approach would properly focus down on one or two of these areas of consideration and develop a substantial knowledge base around the chosen focus, this is not viable for intervention design. Instead a light touch wide view approach to gaining insights and evidence about these dynamics is critical.

Contributing is a significant human drive linked to the significant relationship we all have with our creativity, and there is fascinating research indicating how this is primed socially (Kounios et al. 2006; Jung-Beeman et al. 2008). This drive supports the connections with other human beings in mutually beneficial social structures and organizations and provides the means to enable people to work together. Our relationship with 'doing' is central to ideas of flow (see Csikszentmihalyi 2002 and the more recent material from Seligman 2006) raising the impact on well-being from productive and active engagement in work and creativity.

Innovation involves dynamic organizational processes associated with collaboration leadership roles that solve critical innovation problems related to recombination across boundaries. While dominating and consensus leadership processes are associated with less innovation, a rotating leadership process is associated with more innovation (Davis and Eisenhardt 2011).

Over my 30 years of professional practice, I have increasingly asked clients direct questions about how 'contributing' is enabled in their context, as these questions generate clear and relatively undefended conversations about organizational purpose and the difficulties associated with the alignment of complex activities. This can be used to frame inquiry about the structure or contents in the design of a specific department, task or job, to understand and engage with the purposes, explanations and often hidden frustrations that permeate the workplace.

Raising this theme brings with it the awareness that there is always something wider, bigger or external to the person. Implicit in the term 'contributing' is collaboration as an essential part of what we do in complex organizations. It implies a social purpose in the work, hence building in the social and the relational, even in the most individualistic of cultures:

- We have a significant relationship with our creativity, our outputs and the social recognition we obtain that is consequent upon these.
- To produce a contribution of any merit requires substantial input from others, whether this is from colleagues, 'subordinates', leaders, 'bosses', teachers or service users.
- Often the collaborative requirement is rendered invisible, unrecognized and hence undervalued in our workplaces.
- The group processes involved in collaborative work will inherently include attention to and engaging in what we refer to as 'political' behaviour.

Contributing 'includes in' workplace ideas about engagement, considerations of job demand, stress or well-being and issues of absence, presenteeism and capability management. We can also explore human needs for development and growth, for careers, achievement, making a difference and obtaining respect and social standing. It draws our attention to the process of becoming qualified, of professionalism and the nature of trades unions and guilds, which in turn raises questions about how inter-organizational relationships impact approaches to contributing across boundaries.

There are considerations of conflict inherent in the theme of contributing. The question about whether people pull their weight or whether there is 'social loafing' (see Chapter 7) in operation is one example. This also frames questions about exchange and payment and how this complexity is fairly and properly addressed (which is explored in Chapter 12). It includes questions about equal opportunities, considerations of how integrated contributions across work and home lives can be facilitated, questions about 'dis-ability' and the positive duties to make reasonable adjustments to enable contribution. These questions are animated by the complexities of employment law and the express and implied contract terms around the employment relationship as a paid contract linked to service. With this comes a consideration of wrong-doing, power, oppression, conflict, mediation and litigation and how such tensions are handled in any workplace.

A couple of illustrations give a flavour of the day-to-day use of these themes. For example, absence levels are a regular concern for organizations. An article on absence management that I have used repeatedly with clients comes from Nicholson and Johns (1985) who pointed to the 'trade off' made between individual benefits from absence and the cost to colleagues, pointing to this issue of contributing in human decision making at work.

There is a considerable literature in social sciences about motivation, but this predominantly is viewed as a property of an individual person. In this context, I see the process of motivating as a psychosocial dynamic rather than an individualistic decision. Conventional and yet inaccurate models of motivation such as Maslow (1943) are unhelpful because they suggest that physical needs are more important than psychological, which given our preparedness to die for social identity (Hicks 2011) is clearly questionable. This matters because working with motivation as inherently collaborative ensures that we downplay the role of heroic individuals in achieving outcomes. Individualistic and 'heroic' notions of people who 'save the day' are actually implicated in lowered safety in high stakes environments, as this heroic narrative draws attention away from understanding how the interactions between different functions and contributions join up to deliver things that are greater and safer than any individual can do alone (Lewis et al. 2011).

A note on justice disorders

I have characterized the toxic manifestations around contributing as *justice disorders*. The substance of these toxic manifestations includes equity adjustments, activation of reputation damaging complaints and processes, the over-use of quasi-judicial approaches to conflict in workplaces and alarming increases in mental ill health caused by work (see Chapter 6). These disorders emerge when contributing is not adequately or fairly enabled and appreciated. There is extensive literature suggesting that our current approaches to performance management lead to significant and damaging unfairness as discussed in detail in Chapter 10.

Reflections on the diagnostic theme of belonging

Belonging is one description of the experience of being social animals that depend deeply on each other for the lives we lead and there is a wide range of relevant literature, built upon the recognition of the drive to attach; and we attach to people, to places, to ideas and to identities. Attachment styles have been found to predict emotion regulation (Towler and Stuhlmacher 2013) and turnover intentions (Somers 2010). They also predict customers' preferences for closeness and loyalty intentions better than ideas of customer segmentation (Mende et al. 2013). Through my practice career from working in construction, outsourcing, brand and marketing, creating strategic partnerships and enabling multi-disciplinary (cross-silo) working, my attention was steadily drawn to the wider considerations around belonging. All of these experiences brought the 'edges' of 'group' into focus.

These edges were regularly points of creativity and innovation, but much more work was needed to enable them to work without conflict and protectionism. There were also the points where issues of team, dyadic authority relationships and individual brand/identity issues mutated, showing the taken for granted internal 'kinship' assumptions and the limits of their impact. However, much of this research has been constrained by rather 'managerialist' assumptions about the dominance of team, close peer relationships and role-based accounts of individual leaders and managers. The networked environments we are creating and working in cannot be understood using only these ideas.

My thinking about belonging as a key diagnostic theme in workplaces was much more helpfully influenced by structural anthropology (Lévi-Strauss 1969; Jones 2010), which asserts the existence of a universal 'grammar' of kinship structures. Psychological safety in social structure has long been recognized as a critical requirement in human environments and it has been managed through the interplay of micro processes and macro factors. Rather than this being a 'primitive' need based on superstition, which is often the rhetoric in western dominated anthropological treatises, I would suggest that this is a fundamental human right. This universal kinship 'grammar' is alive and well and operating in every complex workplace. The theme of belonging is used to bring this human need back clearly into focus as a legitimate concern in our working lives.

My interest in the idea of belonging developed from reflecting on issues of 'kinship' and attachment in the workplace. This is complex as we attach to people, to purposes and to ideas and, despite our disembodied western fantasies of having totally rational working lives, our workplaces are not neutral but generate powerful emotional connections around people, places and identity (personal and brand). We do not put down our need to belong or our drive to connect at the entrance to the work place, space or PC screen. I have increasingly observed that organizations are seeking to engage these extended connections as a 'resource' without demonstrating any awareness of the dynamics that underpin kinship or what is involved in containing the human experience of psychological risk inherent in extended belonging dynamics.

Kinship role relationships always imply two positions with a relationship between them – aunt/nephew, father/daughter, sister/brother – that are based on rules around legitimacy. Kinship boundaries bring a universal sense of danger (Douglas 1966). Inherent in this understanding of danger are the realities of human attachment and loss and how these are contained through belonging structures and rituals. The identification of this universal sense of danger informs the recent observations about the impact of psychological safety (or its absence) in the workplace. This perspective allows us to consider aspects of work that are less often addressed in rationalist models of organization. There are three kinship boundaries of relevance: transitions in identity; dynamic relationships with place; and inter-group boundaries.

Identity transitions, such as that from husband to father, from prisoner to free man, from job to job, are ubiquitous. Hicks (2011) outlines that the basis of major human conflict is the experience of dignity violations caused by perceived attacks on identity. Haslam et al. (2011) have highlighted the importance of actively working with social identity as critical to effective workplaces. Emotionally sophisticated cultures use complex kinship ritual processes to manage such transitions, but as yet our western identified workplaces do not appear to have the requisite sophistication to be effective in this symbolic work with identity, despite the fact that these workplaces regularly activate such identity challenges. Applying these ideas to the workplace is deeply relevant for job loss as there is evidence that the manner of job loss is more important than the fact of job loss in the extent to which there will be negative outcomes for individuals (Maertz et al. 2010).

In considering issues of place, the movement of work from visceral to virtual connections is a substantive issue in diagnosis using the theme of belonging. The emerging issue around managing the boundary tension between work identity and home identity is important. Different places of belonging are predominantly a source of enrichment for employees who are enabled to have 'integrated identities' (Rothbard 2001). However for those employees that are not enabled to have 'integrated identities' managing this 'place fracture' has been identified as emotionally depleting. The consequence of this depletion is lower resource acquisition and lowered peace of mind (Dahm et al. 2015). The extra work that needs to be done to manage identity tension between the work and community personas of those from minority ethnic groups is a clear example of this (see Chapter 11, case two). The other key example is the distinction between workplace and nurturing non-work personas, linked to childcare, elder care and other care responsibilities, that still sit predominantly with women (Rothbard 2001).

Forming inter-group alliances is critical to protect against 'incest', which in the workplace could realistically be characterized as 'groupthink' (Janis 1982). 'Incest' causes kinship structures to quickly become dysfunctional and prone to dying out. In the context of the workplace, groupthink is where a group of decision makers is so inwardly referent (incestuous) that they collude in distorted ways of seeing the world, so making problematic decisions leading often to disastrous outcomes. The recent social psychological research indicates, as would be predicted by this view of kinship structures, that ensuring variability in the senior workplace decision groups is the most effective form of mitigation (CTPSR 2015). Intercultural capability is recognized as an increasingly critical aspect of work as these identity boundaries are brought more into relief. This is shifting our focus to the importance of adaptive or flexible capabilities instead of current ideas of fixing statements of competence (Leung et al. 2014).

Granovetter's (1973) now classic conceptualization of the 'strength of weak ties' in network structures raises some interesting issues for our theme of belonging. His study found that while all groups were well networked, the differentiating factor of the belonging structures to enable gain was through the connections to those in power positions. Burt's (2000) follow-up work explored the structural holes between networks. This reinforced the importance of what are considered brokerage or boundary roles in making these belonging structures work, following the delicate process through which 'boundary people' are gradually able to mediate between groups. Mckelvey et al. (2013) demonstrate that 'groupthink' results from strong ties whereas novelty and entrepreneurship come from enabling weak ties (Granovetter 1973). It has been demonstrated that the investment in building new and shared practices (social norms) for groups prevents discriminatory behaviour (Chatman 2010) and builds effective group identification (Willer et al. 2012). Currie and White (2012) demonstrated that even in one of most institutionalized contexts, such as healthcare, where professional hierarchy is all-pervasive, social structures may be mediated and the group affiliation in healthcare around knowledge is more malleable beyond occupational affiliation.

Network theory articulates three distinct structures of human connection for collaborative endeavour that operate in very different ways:

- bonding connections
- bridging connections
- brokerage connections.

The insights from network theory enable us to design and implement different ways of approaching belonging at work that do not impose a 'one size fits all' model on working relationships. By making informal networks visible, social network analysis helps practitioners systematically assess and support strategically important collaboration (Cross et al. 2002).

Bonding connections are the orthodoxy in workplaces. This means it is the implicit assumption that underpins most of the work in organizational psychology and management studies. The focus is the functioning of long-term connections (that mirror 'family' style relationships) established between people who know each other and act with reciprocal intent that generates individual value for all the parties involved. This structure also activates all the issues with groupthink and in-group/out-group boundaries and is the basis for ideas of silos in workplaces.

The recent contribution outlining the human limits on maintaining such bonding connections (Dunbar 2003) has been articulated as the Dunbar number, which suggests we can maintain 7 close connections and 154 reciprocal bonds (i.e. people that we actively know). This understanding has animated the design and structuring of some large-scale social media platforms to enable collaboration despite/beyond these human 'visceral' constraints. The success of social media at enabling collaboration beyond the Dunbar number suggests we need to rethink human connection for collaborative endeavour, acknowledging that bonding is only one model, with clear benefits and also clear limitations. These limitations are currently managed by hierarchy but we believe they will increasingly be managed through brokerage work (see below). Accepting that there are different models of connection that can support collaborative endeavour also gives us alternative and potentially beneficial lines of enquiry acknowledging the recognized problems with bonding such as groupthink, silos, discrimination and low trust that are becoming increasingly problematic.

Bridging connections describe loosely coupled multiple short-term role-based exchanges that create membership and identity but are not characterized by interpersonal reciprocation. Instead the value of these connections is generated from membership of a specific group (either formal or informal) that brings specific benefits, barriers, badges and protocols. These are the types of relationship that we see across membership organizations, union structures and professional bodies. Granovetter (1973) identified that the fixed structures built from such connections are now widespread. He also identified the groups that are excluded from them (see Chapter 11, case two). Just existing in the known membership organizations has a profound impact on the individuals engaged in these connections and on the flow of information through the consequence networks, described as the 'strength of weak ties'.

Bridging networks are paradoxically a more stable form of network structure than bonded ones as they are not dependent on specific individuals. 'Managing' such structures requires a very different way of thinking about human endeavour and role design. In addition, they have a tendency to regress to a baseline level of contribution to ensure fair benefit. This structure tends to encourage more positive citizenship (or identity) values (Geys and Murdoch 2010), rather than individual gains (Urwin et al. 2008). For members of networks operating in a bridging mode the negative consequences can be over-identification, an internal downward levelling process based on strong peer pressure and a relative lack of individually directed social support.

Recent research indicates that activating these identity type membership connections on a social media platform leads to greater use of the platform than if the site moderation approach attempts to activate interpersonal style bonds (Ren et al. 2012). This indicates that bridging is not a second choice mechanism for human connection but is prevalent and important. It has also been recognized that individuals who can activate these bridging networks are effective 'change agents' in large organizations (Battilana and Casciaro 2013).

Brokerage connections describe the processes by which different types of networks are joined together and leveraged. Connection between different structures will become an increasingly important consideration in our networked world (Galunic et al. 2012). Studies of networks have been illustrating the invisible work of connecting across teams in organizations for a while (Cross et al. 2002), and the importance of what is described as 'bridging capital' on the performance of local communities (Menahem et al. 2011). Working with multiple memberships has also been identified as a critical aspect of the contribution of 'tempered radicals' (Meyerson and Scully 1995) trying to speak to multiple constituencies. Tempered radicals might seek compromise, which can be seen as too radical for some and too conservative for others. Brokerage work is increasingly visible and valued as critical to boundary-spanning challenges and is inhibited in psychologically unsafe contexts (Cross et al. 2002). This connecting function between different types of belonging structure will become an increasingly important consideration in our networked world and ideas of 'brand' and 'reputation' are increasingly being activated as brokers for corporate reputation across the 'leaky walls' that social media enabled networks create.

The rapid increase of social media use in organizations coupled with the requirement for 'cross-organizational partnership work' and 'crowd sourcing' are making visible the range of belonging structures that can support collaborative work. It is also bringing to the foreground the work required to create and sustain these necessary and differing structures and requires a re-frame of the relative 'value' of different types of connecting and belonging and challenges preconceived ideas of 'team' and 'leadership'.

A note on attachment disorders

Toxic manifestations of belonging or *attachment disorders* emerge as detachment, exclusion, conflict and over-attachment. The eroding of positive social identity through organizational trauma (such as repeated restructuring or public scandals) has led to what has been described as 'engagement deficit' as people *detach* their identity from their work and hence self-protect through establishing distance and isolation. Groupthink is evidence of a form of toxic *over-attachment* where desire for group consensus overrides the proper assessment of risks. Group belonging also creates discriminatory behaviour and *exclusions* with all the associated inter-group conflict, legal and organization risk this creates. This conflict can manifest in the gaming of information in response to targets set, withholding of information for group-protective reasons and fraud and violence, both physical and psychological. These toxic manifestations can lead to catastrophic organizational failure.

Reflections on the diagnostic theme of meaning

This section offers a brief reflection on the theme of meaning and outlines the toxic manifestation of 'accountability disorders' in complex organizations. Explicitly working with narrative underpins ideas of brand, brand engagement, marketing, accounting and accountancy and is also inherent to the idea of creating a strategy or building pathways for employee development. When I use the diagnostic theme of meaning I draw on literatures from the anthropology of myth and story telling, cultural studies, media studies including studies of narrative and genre, psychologies of identity and reputation, studies of art and artefact in management studies, critical accounting, cross-cultural psychology and the psychology of values. I am also now mindful of media stories about corporate governance and corporate social responsibility as these give the emerging data about how this narrative process is shaping the 'reality' in which complex workplaces operate.

The importance of interpretive work in organizations is not a new idea. Weick (1995) has written extensively of a sense-making process in organizations. In this sense-making process, it is suggested that people extract cues from their environment and interpret them and the resulting impressions take on an aura of truth in the workplace and elsewhere. The diagnostic theme of meaning extends this beyond trying to make sense of workplace events to the recognition that every individual is participating daily in the creation of their own stories, not merely engaged in sense making focused on what is required of them in the workplace.

Various scholars have addressed the importance and impact of story in organizations (e.g. Gabriel 1995; Boyce 1996), suggesting that they have increasing importance now as a means to manage sensory overload and function as a vehicle for learning in organizations. Ideas of story and character are impacting thinking about change in public service (Needham et al. 2013) to address the specific need for purpose-centred approaches to work. I have found Gabriel's (1995) examination of the manner in which stories animate the unmanaged parts of organizations and act as the glue that keeps compliance and resistance in balance to be of practice use. We read meaning into what happens at work, and specifically in the gap between espoused and actual behaviour. A significant part of complex work resides in the identities and narratives that are created, both deliberately within the fabric of organizational practice and in the gaps and unmanaged spaces that human beings at work inhabit. The most common stories that Gabriel's work identifies fall into the following three categories:

- cock up stories – with the self as hero;
- humorous stories – with the self as heroic survivor;
- gripes and tragic stories – the self as victim.

When these stories cross over from the unmanaged spaces in organizations into the managed spaces this can be the cause of much pain and difficulty. This is the point at which the authority of the individual to tell their life story meets the authority of the organization, and the way this is currently addressed is problematic (see section on symbolic sources of toxicity in Chapter 7). This dynamic is touched upon in the exploration of whistleblowing in Chapter 12. Given this tension when the personal story is 'over-written', it is of note that the quality of the story told and the narrative structure constructed during a court hearing have been found to be very impactful in judicial decision-making processes (Pennington and Hastie 1986; Kahan 2015).

Studies of political skill (Silvester et al. 2014) point to the capacity to work deliberately with meaning making in organizations as a distinct and teachable capability. The ability to respect the importance of relationship building, opinion and pluralistic views is critical to effectiveness. The nature of these relationships at work impacts meaning making. Leaders who have the power to incite and influence knowledge creation activities play a central role in how organizations function (Kumar et al. 2013). Employees who work for ethical leaders tend to judge acts of workplace deviance as morally inequitable and acts of organizational citizenship as morally equitable. The recent rhetoric around authenticity touches upon this personal narrative idea and brings with it subtle considerations of fixed and adaptable character and how these denote authenticity (Ibarra 2015).

The impact of working with meaning and behavioural control has contributed to the range of 'nudge' (Haynes et al. 2010) techniques being used to animate social policy intent. One of the recent approaches to intervention practice of interest in this context is the theory of planned behaviour (Ajzen 1991). This postulates that the biggest predictor of action is intent, a notion that centres on the work of people creating narratives about their future. This proposes a set of relationships between norms, attitudes and behavioural control factors that feed into the intention formation process. It is helpful to consider this intention formation process as an act of narrative creation that projects both forwards and backwards in time and activates the personal 'authority' inherent in meaning. It actively works with the understanding that agency sits in the individual rather than in the message sender.

This work indicates the value of organizational stories as significant sources of insight. These gems of internal evidence manifest in gossip, through the accounts around the creation of informal networks, in the jokes told and the resistance they offer. Organizational stories can point to the biggest points of tension that need to be worked with when intervening. Organizations that use the structures of carnival, designed to 'send up' the status of those in senior positions (Ehrenreich 2006) are explicitly using the power of story to keep the resistance–compliance dynamic regulated.

This diagnostic theme is developed to bring attention to our underlying drive to create coherent accounts of why and how we do the things we do and how we respond to what is done to us. Central to the 'mono-myth' or 'hero's journey' (Vogler 2007) is the importance of identity and how it is constituted socially. The social psychology of leadership (Haslam et al 2011) suggests that it is the work of crafting identity that is the critical differentiator for successful work. It is also being explored as the underpinning of the notion of the heroic leader in complex organizations that appears to be implicated in high stakes environments that have problems with safety (Lewis et al. 2011). With knowledge of death comes a clear understanding of the impact and trajectory of time and there is well-documented evidence of us working with a 'grammar' of narrative that enables us to record, create and re-create our selves through time (Lacey 2000). A narrative activates ideas of cause and effect, morality and social structure and the need for resolution, which, it is suggested contribute to enhanced oxytocin levels and the probability of acts of compassion (see Chapter 6).

Creating accounts out of organizational life is active work and involves choice. It is never possible to share all that happens, so accounts are always partial. The process of creating an account always implies an audience who we encourage to participate in the narratives we create and to accept the trajectories (or story arcs) that we build. This is also implicit in the industry of accounting where socially determined structures of 'finances' are used to generate confidence. Critical accounting examines the power of the finance narrative as the core agent in organizations stories (e.g. Czarniawska 2010) with the consequent rationalist approaches to organization, many of which have contributed to the level of toxicity we are now having to live with

We all have the 'authority' to create personal stories about the place where we work. This suggests that the idea that an organization can claim the 'hearts and minds' of its employees is a completely misleading endeavour (and one that I consider to be morally dubious). Personal authority over the meaning in our lives is fully active alongside all the other socially constituted accountability/authority dynamics at play. We make our own meanings out of the experiences in our lives and these are also heavily framed by the social and cultural contexts we operate within. The studies of myth, narrative and genre give frameworks to understand the structures and dynamics of this human activity.

A key theme played out when we make meaning in the workplace links to the power of responses to just and unjust treatment and the acts of truth telling to authority. The developing interest in co-creation approaches in the workplace adds a complexity to this work. It raises the need to work with the tension around enabling multiple stories to build into an identity-based set of connections with a workplace, rather than organizations working institutionally towards the imposition of a single dominating organizational 'myth'. In the 'reputation economy' (Chamorro-Premuzic 2015) the issue of individual authority over meaning is an increasingly dominant factor in organizational strategy.

A note on accountability disorders

The consistency between what is said and what is done is a primary factor in the 'meaningfulness' of the job (May et al. 2004) and in the narratives that get created. This reading of intent is particularly directed at those in authority. This can be evidenced in public statements from an organization, running counter to what it actually does or the internal tensions between having a policy of no bullying and a senior leader who behaves inappropriately and is not called to account. These have profound and negative impacts on the internal and external trust levels for the organization. These issues with 'meaning' in organizations manifest as a variety of 'accountability disorders'. Such disorders can also manifest in the institutional processes and denatured psychosocial micro processes that silence individuals at work and which have led to catastrophic failure. Accountability disorders also manifest in the operational impact from reputation damaging reports written about organizations that become widely distributed (see Chapter 12, case two). The gaming and manipulation of measuring and target systems is a critical issue (Osterloh 2014).

Conclusion

This chapter introduces and reflects upon three diagnostic themes and their associated toxic disorders. These themes provide fluid and broad categories that enable us to work with the emerging vicissitudes of organizational life, rather than fixing on a single issue. They can help us identify entry points and tension points for intervention. This chapter has provided reflections on what we know about these diagnostic themes and how they unfold in field situations. The approach to these diagnostic themes also illustrates the value of the breadth of exploration of different literatures and the patterns that we can recognize from accessing this range of scholarly input. The remaining chapters in this part outline, in different ways, manifestations of toxicity under these themes and some key actions that clients have taken to mitigate through innovative interventions.

References

Ajzen, I. (1991) The theory of planned behavior. *Organizational Behavior and Human Decision Processes* 50: 179–211.

Battilana, J. and Casciaro, T. (2013) The network secrets of great change agents. *Harvard Business Review* 91(7): 62–68.

Boyce, M. (1996) Organizational story and storytelling: A critical review. *Journal of Organisational Learning* 9(5): 5–26.

Burt, R. S. (2000) The network structure of social capital. *Research in Organizational Behavior* 22: 345–423.

Chamorro-Premuzic, T. (2015) Talent identification in the reputation economy. *DOP Conference Proceedings*. British Psychological Society, Glasgow, January.

Chatman, J. A. (2010) Norms in mixed sex and mixed race work groups. *Academy of Management Annals* 4(1): 447–484.

Cross, R., Borgatti, S. and Parker, A. (2002) Making invisible work visible: Using social network analysis to support strategic collaboration. *California Management Review* 44(2): 25–46.

Csikszentmihalyi, M. (2002) *Flow: The Classic Work on How To Achieve Happiness*. London: Rider.

CTPSR (2015) What happens when women have more power and influence. www.coventry.ac.uk/CTPSR.

Currie, G. and White, L. (2012) Inter-professional barriers and knowledge brokering in an organisational context. *Organisation Studies* 33(10): 1333–1361.

Czarniawska, B. (2010) Translation impossible: Accounting for a city project. *Accounting, Auditing and Accountability Journal* 23(3): 420–437.

Dahm, P. C., Glomb, T. M., Manchester, C. F. et al. (2015) Work–family conflict changes how you do your job. *Journal of Applied Psychology* 100(3): 767–792.

Davis, J. P. and Eisenhardt, K. M. (2011) Rotating leadership and collaborative innovation: Recombination processes in symbiotic relationships. *Administrative Science Quarterly* 56(2): 159–201.

Douglas, M. (1966) *Purity and Danger*. London and New York: ARK Paperbacks.

Dunbar, R. (2003) *Grooming, Gossip and the Evolution of Language* (2nd edn). London: Faber.

Ehrenreich, B. (2006) *Dancing in the Street*. New York: Holt Paperbacks.

Gabriel, Y. (1995) The unmanaged organization: Stories, fantasies and subjectivity. *Organization Studies* 16(3): 477–501.

Galunic, C., Ertug, G. and Gargiulo, M. (2012) The positive externalities of social capital: Benefiting from senior brokers. *Academy of Management Journal* 55(5): 1213–1231.

Geys, B. and Murdoch, Z. (2010) Measuring the 'bridging' versus 'bonding' nature of social networks: A proposal for integrating existing measures. *Sociology* 44(3): 523–540.

Granovetter, M. S. (1973) The strength of weak ties. *American Journal of Sociology* 78(6): 1360–1380.

Haslam, S. A., Reicher, S. D. and Platow, M. J. (2011) *The New Psychology of Leadership: Identity, Influence and Power*. Hove: Psychology Press.

Haynes, L., Service, O., Goldacre, B. et al. (2010) Test, learn, adapt: Developing public policy with randomised controlled trials. http://www.behaviouralinsights.co.uk.

Hicks, D. (2011) *Dignity: The Essential Role It Plays in Resolving Conflict*. New Haven, CT and London: Yale University Press.

Ibarra, H. (2015) Adaptive authenticity: The authenticity paradox. *Harvard Business Review* January/February [online].

Janis, I. L. (1982) *Groupthink: Psychological Studies of Policy Decisions and Fiascoes* (2nd edn). New York: Houghton Mifflin.

Jones, D. (2010) Human kinship, from conceptual structure to grammar. *Behavioral and Brain Sciences* 33(5): 367–381.

Jung-Beeman, M., Collier, A. and Kounios, J. (2008) How insight happens: Learning from the brain. *Neuro-Leadership Journal* 1: 20–25.

Kahan, D. M. (2015) Laws of cognition and the cognition of law. *Journal of Cognition* 135: 56–60.

Koriat, A. (2012) When are two heads better than one and why? *Science* 336(6079): 360–362.

Kounios, J., Frymiare, J. L., Bowden, E. M. et al. (2006) The prepared mind: Neural activity prior to problem presentation predicts solution by sudden insight. *Psychological Science* 17(10): 882–890.

Kumar, K. K., Jain, K. K. and Tiwary, R. R. (2013) Leadership activities and their impact on creating knowledge in organizations. *International Journal of Leadership Studies* 8(1): 19–31.

Lacey, N. (2000) *Narrative and Genre: Key Concepts in Media Studies*. Hampshire: MacMillan Press.

Laughlin, P. R., Hatch, E. C., Silver, J. S. et al. (2006) Groups perform better than the best individuals on letters to numbers problems: Effect of group size. *Journal of Personality and Social Psychology* 90(4): 644–651.

Leung, K., Ang, S. and Tan, M. L. (2014) Intercultural competence. *Annual Review of Organizational Psychology and Organizational Behavior* 1: 489–519.

Lévi-Strauss, C. (1969) *The Elementary Structures of Kinship*. Trans. J. Bell and J. von Sturmer. Boston, MA: Beacon Press.

Lewis, G., Vaithianathan, R., Hockey, P. M. et al. (2011) Counterheroism, common knowledge, and ergonomics: Concepts from aviation that could improve patient safety. *Millbank Quarterly* 89(1): 4–38.

McKay, B., Wulf, G., Lewthwaite, R. et al. (2015) The self; your own worst enemy: A test of the self-invoking trigger hypothesis. *Journal of Experimental Psychology* 68(9): 1910–1919.

Mckelvey, B., Li, M., Xu, H. et al. (2013) Re-thinking Kauffman's NK fitness landscape: From artifact & groupthink to weak-tie effects. *Human Systems Management* 32(1): 17–42.

Maertz Jr, C. P., Wiley, J. W., LeRouge, C. et al. (2010) Downsizing effects on survivors: Layoffs, offshoring, and outsourcing. *Industrial Relations* 49(2): 275–285.

Maslow, A. H. (1943) A theory of human motivation. *Psychological Review* 50(4): 370–396.

May, D. R., Gilson, R. L. and Harter, L. M. (2004) The psychological conditions of mean-ingfulness, safety and availability and the engagement of the human spirit at work. *Journal of Occupational and Organizational Psychology* 77(1): 11–37.

Menahem, G., Doron, G. and Haim, I. (2011) Bonding and bridging associational social capital and the financial performance of local authorities in Israel. *Public Management Review* 13(5): 659–681.

Mende, M., Bolton, R. and Bitner, M. (2013) Decoding customer–firm relationships: How attachment styles help explain customers' preferences for closeness, repurchase inten-tions, and changes in relationship breadth. *Journal of Marketing Research* 50(1): 125–142.

Meyerson, D. and Scully, M. (1995) Tempered radicalism and the politics of ambivalence and change. *Organization Science* 6(6): 585–600.

Needham, C., Mengan, C. and Dickinson, H. (2013) The 21st century public service work-place: Eight lessons from the literature. www.birmingham.ac.uk/psa.

Nicholson, N. and Johns, G. (1985) The absence culture and the psychological contract: Who's in control of absence. *Academy of Management Review* 10(3): 297–407.

Osterloh, M. (2014) Viewpoint: Why variable pay for performance in healthcare can back-fire: Evidence from psychological economics. *Evidence Based HRM* 2(1): 120–123.

Pennington, N. and Hastie, R. (1986) Evidence evaluation in complex decision-making. *Journal of Personality and Social Psychology* 51(2): 242–258.

Ren, Y., Harper, F. M., Drenner, S. et al. (2012) Building member attachment in online communities: Applying theories of group identity and interpersonal bonds. *MIS Quarterly* 36(3): 841–864.

Rothbard, N. (2001) Enriching or depleting? The dynamics of engagement in work and family roles. *Administrative Science Quarterly* 46(4): 655–684.

Seligman, M. (2006) *Authentic Happiness, Using the New Positive Psychology to Realize Your Potential for Lasting Fulfilment*. London: Nicholas Brealey.

Silvester, J., Wyatt, M. and Randall, R. (2014) Politician personality, Machiavellianism, and political skill as predictors of performance ratings in political roles. *Journal of Occupational and Organizational Psychology* 87(2): 258–279.

Somers, M. J. (2010) Patterns of attachment to organizations: Commitment profiles and work outcomes. *Journal of Occupational and Organizational Psychology* 83(2): 443–453.

Towler, A. J. and Stuhlmacher, A. F. (2013) Attachment styles, relationship satisfaction, and well-being in working women. *Journal of Social Psychology* 153(3): 279–298.

Urwin, P., Di Pietro, G., Sturgis, P. et al. (2008) Measuring the returns to networking and the accumulation of social capital: Any evidence of bonding, bridging, or linking? *American Journal of Economics and Sociology* 67(5): 941–968.

Vogler, C. (2007) *The Writer's Journey: Mythic Structure for Writers*. US: MIchael Wiese Productions.

Weick, K. E. (1995) *Sensemaking in Organizations*. Los Angeles, CA: SAGE.

Willer, R., Flynn, F. and Zak, S. (2012) Structure, identity, and solidarity: A comparative field study of generalized and direct exchange. *Administrative Science Quarterly* 57(1): 119–155.

10

HOW CURRENT PERFORMANCE MANAGEMENT SYSTEMS MAKE WORKPLACES TOXIC

Introduction

Exploring the issues around contribution is a key element of organizational diagnosis (described in overview in Chapter 9). Linked to this theme as a practitioner, you may get asked the following types of questions:

- How can we improve the performance of our business?
- How can we better manage the performance of our people?
- How do we engage our staff to increase the discretionary effort we can access?
- What can we do to empower our people to deliver effectively?

One of the most ubiquitous responses to this type of inquiry has been the wide implementation of *normal distribution performance management* (performance management) with the associated investment in complex information technology (IT) solutions to manage the data required for and generated by this mechanism. I now consider this ubiquitous western-designed approach to managing contribution in the workplace to be a significant source of toxicity in our organizations. Increasingly, I am seeing organizations commission expensive engagement and empowerment programmes, which are fundamentally attempting to deal with the problems that performance management causes. A more cost effective approach would be to remove the cause of the problem. This mechanism generally has five relevant steps shown in Table 10.1.

The content of this chapter illustrates a practice-driven evidence review and critique. What is presented here is not an academic review of literature, as it does not start with a focused stage of problem definition. Instead it has been built up iteratively in response to emerging field-based concerns and observations.

TABLE 10.1 The key steps in performance management

Overview	Brief description
1. The 'desired output' step	The annual cycle of goal setting: manager to subordinate, predicated on the assumption that the organization knows what is coming and can prescribe what is needed
2. The 'in-group' step	The collection of what is described as 360-degree feedback from people inside and outside of a workplace variously chosen by individual and manager
3. The 'assessment' step	Each manager assesses each individual they manage against a pre-determined set of criteria and gives everyone a 'grade'
4. The 'comparison' step	All grades across an organization are adjusted so the whole can be mapped onto a normal distribution curve to determine the relative 'position' of each person on this curve compared with the rest of the employees in the organization
5. The 'consequences' step	This is widely variable, appropriately legally constrained and often produces nothing but pain and irritation in the system. When action is taken, it largely ignores the bulk of people working diligently and effectively in the interests of the shared purpose of the organization, so building resentment and disengagement

The evidence presented in the following critique has been collated over several years. I sought it out to help me address repeated client problem presentations focused on business performance. These increasingly included concerns about disengagement, bullying, other counter-productive behaviour and disempowerment at work. This review has led me to the general insight that we need a systemic re-design of how we align the contribution of individuals in the workplace, as our current attempts to manage collaboration are poisoning the environments we require people to work in. The critique outlines why ethical practitioners should stop advocating such practices, as we now have sufficient evidence that they cause harm. This review has been organized into six insights outlined in Table 10.2.

Performance management is individualistic and yet placed in a collaborative context

Performance management has no psychological or behavioural science built into its design. Instead it came from economic theory using mathematical modelling of theorized employee movement. In was originally developed in the 1970s and then unfortunately re-invigorated in the 1990s. The authors successfully convinced organizations that they could increase the productivity and ability of their employee pool by 'marking' individuals, comparing these marks, removing those with low marks from the organization and replacing them with external 'better' people. This simplistic formulation has been very attractive to organizations, I assume because

TABLE 10.2 Why performance management does not work

Why normal distribution performance management as we know it does not work

1. *Performance management is individualistic*: it is competitive by design and placed in a context which requires collaboration
2. *Performance management is psychologically naïve*: it takes no account of the social psychological and cultural realities of feedback dynamics
3. *Performance management is inherently biased*: it uses assessment practices that enable inherent (or unconscious) biases to flourish
4. *Performance management is decontextualized and culturally specific*: it ignores the importance of context and flexibility around what can be accomplished and is a subtle form of colonization across global employment organizations
5. *Performance management causes ill health*: low levels of organizational justice are predictive of clinical depression and psychosocial hazards cause stress-related illness
6. *Performance management is analytically weak*: it demonstrates confusion over the use of statistical distribution and the impact of levels of analysis (Simpson's paradox – see main text) on how it conceptualizes performance

it appears to 'make sense'. However, this formulation made no use of the widely available psychological evidence which points to the damaging consequences of encouraging such social comparisons within collaborative work.

Indeed, the very idea of 'performance' at work (compared with contributing which is my preferred frame for exploring these matters with clients) creates an inherently individualistic 'display-based' perspective. Talking about performance contradicts the basic premise behind creating an organization, which is to enable people to come together, to contribute to a wider purpose that any individual can deliver alone and to contain and support collaboration. To concentrate upon such an individualistic notion as 'performance' when thinking about workplaces draws attention away from the social processes of shared purpose, authority, accountability, inter-dependence, communication and building an understanding of a complex task.

Instead it puts each individual 'on a stage' as if they are doing something on their own that is neither context dependent or intimately connected with the work of others. It also uses an implicit assumption that business performance relies on the simple sum of employee activity rather than the generative capacity that comes from collaboration at the system level. *Speaking metaphorically: this is like the difference between listening to a single voice and a choir – a choir creates sounds out of the resonance between voices – it is more than the sum of each individual part.*

The longitudinal research evidence of implementation of this individualistic design indicates that it makes each employee focus specifically on survival, threat and insecurity rather than on shared productivity. The unintended threat-based impacts found in a longitudinal study of implementation (McBriarty 1988) were as follows:

- organizational disaffection and disengagement by employees;
- lowered trust in managers' intentions;

- lowered employee assessments of manager competence and fitness to lead;
- the emergence of 'visibility syndrome'; 'face-time' not output the priority;
- crucial organizational work requiring steady persistence over several years did not get done, as short-term impact work was always prioritized;
- highly effective employees refused challenging assignments and promotion, as they did not want to risk their ratings;
- people stopped helping each other.

Despite these well-documented problems, the approach continued and was strongly revitalized by the work of Grote (2005). A mathematical 'simulation' was used to demonstrate the proposed benefits of performance management centred on identifying those individuals who were the 'lowest performers'. The formulation focused on the proposed benefits from 'staff turnover' as they claimed that organizational improvement would come from the '10 per cent of workers to be fired in each cycle' (Scullen et al. 2005: 3).

Experimental tests of this assertion found that productivity is significantly higher in 'forced distribution' conditions (by about 6 per cent to 12 per cent), but only when implemented under tightly controlled circumstances. When the experimental conditions were changed to allow 'workers' to have a simple option to sabotage each other, they did so (Berger et al. 2013) and consequently all the productivity benefits were lost as discretionary effort was directed to the act of sabotage. In laboratory conditions we can control for sabotage, but we cannot do this in any live organizational context.

Grote (2005) suggested that this approach would force managers to differentiate individual 'talent', stating that 'it is reasonable to expect that an organization would be able to improve the performance potential of its workforce by firing the workers judged to be performing most poorly and replacing them with its most promising applicant'. This has three assumptions built in:

- that every manager can effectively differentiate individual contribution in what is collaborative output;
- that people can be easily replaced;
- that people would want to work in such a competitive situation.

These assumptions are not sustainable when applied in the field. The focus on the importance of 'differentiating talent' fails to address a key factor in individual output. In complex work, any individual is dependent upon a complex set of relationships crossing organizational boundaries, physical barriers and hierarchical levels in order to be able to contribute effectively (Cross and Cummings 2004). There is research evidence that raters are not able to differentiate an individual's performance from the unit level performance (Yammarino et al. 1987) as complex work is built on inter-dependency. Parker et al. (2013) further demonstrate that social and structural support improves role performance and impacts how individual contribution is perceived. Social inter-dependency has an impact on not just what can get done but also on how the actual output and person is perceived.

Experimental work has examined prospective employee perceptions of performance management, where they were presented with different ways in which their contribution could be managed in the workplace. All respondents were particularly attracted to the systems with less stringent treatment of low performers. Those with high cognitive ability were most comfortable with a comparative aspect but the way low performers would be treated was nearly twice as influential in the attractiveness rating than any other dimension measured (Blume et al. 2009). This research evidence suggests that approaches predicated upon firing people are not likely to be attractive, undermining the assumption that an annual 'firing' round would then enable the recruitment of 'better' people; it is much more likely that this would become known and actively discourage people from applying. The relevant social processes at work also include altruism and care and not the competitive individualistic ethos this design assumes.

Grote (2005) did caveat his claim for organizational productivity improvement with the statement that using performance management methods for any longer than two years is likely to be counter-productive. The external findings suggest that even two years is too long, but worryingly, my field experience is that *this caveat around time limits is not noted* when organizations implement these claimed best practice mechanisms. Instead the implementation decision is made based on a broad acceptance that performance management is 'best practice' in the Human Resource Management (HRM) field and so is set it up to run 'in perpetuity'. Usually there is a major investment in technology to be able to run this process, so there is a vested interest in keeping it running to justify the costly process of implementation.

In recognizing these problems, there has been some research exploring how the dis-benefits and harms can be managed. For example, Phillips and Kruger (2006) link the use of performance management with consequent dysfunctional internal competition and explore a range of techniques for managing this. Such an approach requires too much effort for insufficient benefit. My assessment (given all the material collated so far) is that we would be better suggesting that *implementing performance management well is neither possible, nor the solution*. We need an organizational de-clutter. We need to start again with the small bits that we know are productive and explore how we can fit them together differently.

Performance management is psychologically naïve

It appears that we (people in organizations) are more psychologically savvy than those that have designed such systems. We know that giving feedback is a socially complex activity and also potentially damaging. We know that the manner in which we give and receive feedback will have long-standing and serious relationship consequences for us and also impact everyone's capacity for organizational contribution.

If someone rates you as average or failing in your goals this constitutes negative feedback. The model only allows for 10 per cent of the organizational population to be praised through this process, leaving 90 per cent of the workforce considering that they have been negatively rated. If someone rates you negatively for your contribution in the workplace context, they know they are compromising your dignity. The pain of a dignity violation has been compared to experiencing someone deliberately breaking your leg (Eisenberger and Leiberman 2004).

The action of our mirror neurons (Iacobani 2008) means that we tend to 'feel' the impact we are having on other people. This means that we also experience the pain we cause in implementing these unintelligently designed systems. I have repeatedly observed in client organizations a situation where an otherwise kind and competent manager avoids those they have given low ratings, so they do not have to experience the pain they have caused. This avoidance further compounds the dignity violation against the individual, while clearly being an entirely rational piece of self-protection on the part of the manager. Considering the growing issue with stress, it is helpful to note that future burnout is explained by sensitivity to social rejection and the social evaluation of mistreatment in stress responses in the workplace (Ronen and Baldwin 2010).

I have explored this feedback dilemma with senior people in effective organizations by asking how they actually get the relevant problematic issues raised with other members of staff. In response they show a sophisticated understanding of all the psychosocial mechanisms at play – the identity issues, the role of mentoring and supervision, the role of friendship and kinship groups and the relative priorities of task requirements – when deciding how to orchestrate the delivery of 'negative' messages without also delivering a dignity violation. Three key things have emerged from these client discussions:

- they ensure that the information comes from a safe source;
- this feedback is actively separated from any individual appraisal process;
- this feedback is given in a 'learning frame' about the political context, rather than as a goal-based comment.

This intuitive wisdom at play in effective organizations is also supported by the experimental outputs from psychological and behavioural science. Studies of the impact of negative feedback on output demonstrate that the ability to achieve a goal deteriorates following negative feedback (Cianci et al. 2010). The only exception to this pattern is when the goal is an individually defined one focused on learning something new. With a 'self-chosen learning goal' negative feedback activates a *lowering of positive affect*. This means we feel a gentle dip in our self-esteem, which we feel able to address through getting more practice. This experience can aid trial and error and hence learning if undertaken in a psychologically safe environment.

In contrast, if we are given negative feedback about our achievements (which the performance management is predicated upon) such feedback does not lead to a lowering of positive affect but instead *actively generates negative affect*. This means that we experience an unfair and dangerous attack meaning our threat response is activated (see Chapter 6). This generates immediate self-esteem and identity protecting behaviour, evidenced in a predictable tendency to fierce disagreement and a reduction in the capacity for behavioural self-regulation (Ilies et al. 2007).

Another direct consequence of being given negative feedback is that any individual given such feedback will stick more strongly to behaviour that is generating poor organizational performance (Brockner et al. 1986).

There are situations where comparative feedback can be productive, but it must be positively framed (Murthy and Schafer 2011), for example, 'Jane is brilliant at analysis and John superb at stakeholder management – support each other and learn from each other', suggesting that positively framed social comparison can be helpful. However studies of the social impact of public comparative feedback as required in performance management (where only 10 per cent can be positively graded) have found that this causes covert victimization of 'high performers' and overt victimization of 'low performers' in the workplace (Jensen et al. 2014). Such complex psychological processes and possibilities of backlash caused by social comparison have substantial negative implications for subsequent organizational effectiveness and hence business performance.

There have been some suggestions that we can fix this performance management 'feedback problem' by training people in having 'difficult conversations' and so enabling them to give negative feedback well. However, the general evidence is that such attempts fail. Regardless of the extent to which assessors are trained to give negative performance feedback or experienced in running these mechanisms, the tendency is to give poor and confusing feedback that individuals cannot act upon (Govaerts et al. 2013) and which feeds into the public process of comparison. This causes distress both for the recipient and the individual giving the feedback.

By contrast, positive feedback increases effective contribution and business performance. Privately delivered positive feedback leads to the highest evaluations of procedural and interactional justice in organizations (Westerman and Westerman 2013). Employees whose supervisors used positive constructive feedback felt more respected by their supervisors and perceived greater opportunities for advancement within the organization. These variables, in turn, predicted better mood at work, greater job satisfaction and prosocial intentions (Sommer and Kulkarni 2012). These studies also indicate that low-performing workers improved their output following positive feedback significantly more than average and high-performing workers.

Mollick (2012) found that variations in the behaviour of middle managers have a particularly large impact on firm performance (much larger than senior leaders or that of individuals who are assigned specialist roles) suggesting that it is the day-to-day relational work involved in effective management that is most strongly related to overall organizational effectiveness. These middle managers required to use such performance management systems are compromised in their ability to do their managerial job well (Lawler 2003). The use of comparative performance management approaches tends to be associated with lower effectiveness in managing performance, as managers are concerned about how they will be viewed as a consequence of the assessments they make. This worry is a very rational concern and the negative impact on the perceived competence of managers caused by applying this approach has been confirmed (McBriarty 1988).

Forcing raters to compare individuals rather than working with each individual on their own merits leads to raters making bad judgements in many cases which has serious impacts on fair pay outcomes (Lawler 2003). Larkin et al. (2012) indicate that the psychological costs from social comparison reduce any potential positive gains from using pay for performance. The use of performance management coupled with pay secrecy causes negative inferences of an organization's fairness and, among high performers, leads to increased intentions to leave (Belogolovsky and Bamberger 2014).

Positivity, mutual inquiry and the tolerance of difference (visible difference, and range of opinions and thinking styles) in working relationships are well established as a powerful contributor to good team output (see Chapter 8). There is evidence that specialist contribution to team performance is compromised by intra-group competition and that project teams work together better when they have a healthy disregard for imposed performance management mechanisms. The ability to ignore these imposed mechanisms varies and quality output is closely linked to the ability to ignore intra-group competition reward distribution rules (Navaresse et al. 2014).

Well-managed task-focused positively expressed conflict in teams enhances team contribution to the wider business goals. It also generates consistency between the objective and subjective evaluation of overall team performance. However managers vary greatly in their capacity to tolerate such conflict, which has knock-on impacts on how they evaluate their subordinates. Team members who enable and encourage this productive conflict are likely to be marked down by conflict averse managers (Breugst et al. 2012). The insistence on using performance management in team contexts clearly interrupts collaboration either by inhibiting individuals from fully engaging or by wasting valuable self-regulation resources that are directed to mitigating unfair practices.

The use of 360-degree feedback includes all levels in an organization and the impact of social compliances pressures on upward feedback is a cause for serious concern. Ingratiation tends to be the general tone of upward feedback, with people rarely being prepared to give negative feedback to those with power over them. We know that telling the truth to power is a socially dangerous act, so we would predict this tone of feedback in these circumstances. When ingratiation, flattery and opinion conformity is directed at the CEO, evidence indicates that this acts to support strategic persistence (see Chapter 7) by encouraging senior leaders to become overconfident in their strategic judgement. This decreases the likelihood that senior leaders will notice and act to mitigate evidence of poor organizational performance (Park and Westphal 2011).

The neurobiology of the stock market (Coates 2012 – Chapter 6) indicates that central bank actions designed to create an enhanced sense of certainty were a significant factor in the financial collapse of 2008. It worked to lower the perceived threat to traders, thereby increasing their dopamine levels, which in turn increased their preparedness to take unacceptable risks. Coates' recommendation for managing the stock market to prevent another catastrophic collapse is to ensure that traders are kept at a level of requisite uncertainty to constrain their neurobiology and hence risky behaviour; this is an insight we would do well to consider for our CEOs when considering how we deploy feedback in organizations.

Performance management is inherently unlawfully biased

This performance management mechanism is fraught with all the biases, preconceptions and cognitive flaws outlined in Chapter 7. The assumption made in the design of these mechanisms is that the same criteria will be used for assessing anyone, regardless of our gender, ethnicity, age, disability, sexuality and so on. This simplistic assumption does not stand up to scrutiny. In-group preference is a significant problem in performance management. Leniency towards in-groups is viewed as fair (Bol 2011) but we appear to be blind to the impacts on 'outgroups' of systems claiming to be meritocratic. At the most simple level, personal acquaintanceship, physical proximity and an alma mater link with subordinates lead to relatively lenient ratings and compressed ratings from supervisors (Chen 2014). However, it is a more deep-seated issue than individual nepotism. Research indicates that when an organization explicitly describes itself as meritocratic and objectively fair in its assessment of employees, individuals in managerial positions will favour a male employee over an equally competent female employee by awarding him a larger monetary reward (Castilla and Benard 2010).

In addition to gender, there is a consistent pattern of minority groups being given lower performance ratings on average (Sackett and DuBois 1991). There are serious concerns with the associated consequences of this uncontrolled bias operating in performance management processes because deep level dissimilarity, when supervisors perceive subordinates as having low performance, is predictive of abusive supervision (Hershcovis et al. 2007; Tepper et al. 2011) and all the associated discrimination and mental ill health consequences of unfair treatment.

Wilson (2010) found that there was evidence of different implicit theories of performance in operation for different ethnic groups in a financial services employment context. This study looked at high, medium and low performance assessments across Asian, Black and White members of staff. In addition to the scores allocated, narrative explanations of performance assessments were analysed based on themes of action, personal characteristics and outcomes. There were two key findings from these studies:

- The narrative accounts given of performance were less positive for minority ethnic groups, even when they were given high ratings.
- Different models of good and bad performance were used to evaluate each of the different ethnic groups; these different ethnic groups were not compared using either the same standards or the same constructs.

For the Asian group high performance was based on perceptions of accuracy and diligence, for the Black group high performance was linked to perceptions of being a team player and demonstrating leadership, while for the White group high performance was associated with broad ideas of 'high standards'. For those at the other end of the performance rating scale the accounts indicated that there was a clear negative pattern for Black staff around business awareness and punctuality as the reasons for low evaluations but for the other two groups the accounts were more diffuse.

The allocation of different interpretations of the same behaviour when evaluating the worth of members of different ethnic groups is widely illustrated in other research (see Chapter 8 on appreciation). Managerial interpretations of the meaning and treatment of lateness varies significantly based on ethnicity. Tardiness has no impact on performance appraisals of White employees or Hispanic employees but does have a significant negative impact on the performance appraisal and advancement opportunities of Black employees (Luksyte et al. 2013). Evaluators engage in goal-based stereotyping by perceiving that Black leaders (and not White leaders) fail because of negative leader-based attributes and succeed because of positive non-leader attributes. This systemic bias undermines the capacity for Black employees to be appointed to hold leadership roles in a straightforward manner (Carton and Rosette 2011).

Also when considering 360-degree feedback we also need to recognize that 'customers' or 'service users' can be subjective and biased too. Many companies are tying employee incentives to customer ratings of satisfaction, service quality or employee performance. One potential drawback to these practices is that customers' evaluations of employees appear to be biased, based on race rather than treatment received (Lynn and Sturman 2011) hence organizations could be using inherently discriminatory feedback to make pay and performance judgements which raises issues of vicarious liability and unlawful practice in various jurisdictions that use this approach.

This substantial body of research clearly indicates that we do not use the same performance models for all people but instead demonstrates that members of each ethnic group will be judged on different criteria; what makes a 'high-performing' Black employee is not what makes a 'high-performing' White employee. The other area is the belief that what a 'high-performing' man is entitled to financially, is different (and greater) from that of a 'high-performing' woman. The intersection of these two stereotypes is touched upon in the equal pay illustration given in Chapter 12.

Although we are clearly aware that the outcome measures of organizational equality – progression, pay levels and seniority – demonstrate high levels of unfairness linked to race and gender, organizations continue to implement and use these performance management systems, which work to reinforce these inequalities. There is a quasi-authority given via the implementation of the performance management process at an individual level, which both enables and disguises the systemic organizational processes that disadvantage some groups and privilege others. With this research evidence that performance management works to support unlawful discrimination there is a clear need to publicize this evidence and ensure that such mechanisms are not used as a means for subjective and unfair decisions to be allowed to hide behind the pseudo-objectivity of an abstract and widely applied process.

Performance management is decontextualized, culturally specific and potentially colonizing

My field experience of contexts where performance management is used have led me to identify two broad concerns with the way in which context completely undermines the justification for the implementation of this abstract design. The first is a micro level concern and the second a macro cultural issue:

- Goal setting (Step 1 in Table 10.1) rarely takes place effectively, for a whole variety of very good reasons, but later adherence to the other process steps means everything that is output is perception-based rather than evidence-based.
- Performance management is culturally specific based on one cultural dimension that is just about tolerable in high individualism cultures, but is deeply violating of social cohesion in different cultural contexts.

Goal setting

This rarely happens as required by the design for two very good contextual reasons articulated by many people in different organizations that I have collected as evidence by experience:

- The increased need for flexibility and course correction in work makes it very difficult to specify individual objectives as tightly and as clearly as the design assumes is possible and also requires.
- There are large numbers of managers who manage technical experts and they expect them to act as decision makers and course correctors as their work unfolds. The managers have very little understanding of how this work breaks down.
- To do this goal setting work properly is extremely time consuming and in already high pressure environments there is not the confidence that investing the requisite time will make much material difference to the overall outcome of the work or ultimate organizational performance.

As this avoidance of Step 1 is rarely sanctioned in practice, failing to set goals is reinforced by organizational habit. However, the acceptance of the Step 1 failure does not get converted into the clarity that therefore none of the other steps should be applied. Instead people are subjected to the later performance management assessment and comparison steps without having participated in a goal setting process and so legitimately experience the assessment as unfair, divisive and bullying.

There have been some suggestions that we need to impose this goal setting step in organizations as a solution to this, but this ignores the need for collaborative flexibility over time. The organizational resilience literature is increasingly suggesting that effectiveness is linked to the organisational capacity to course correct based on learning from the environment. Resilience is also predicated upon the ability to stop unnecessary work (Tranfield et al 2002). The imposed goal setting approach inherent in performance management undermines the capabilities needed for organizational resilience.

The research evidence clearly supports the need for a far more flexible approach to goal setting than performance management suggests (and that has already in effect been rejected in practice). In workplace studies, adaptive performance is positively associated with task performance indicating that overly constrained objectives can inhibit the best contribution (Shoss et al. 2012). There is also substantial evidence that flexibility in role, role crafting and role improvisation are capabilities critical to organizational productivity. Daily job crafting improves performance through the positive impact of work enjoyment on output (Tims et al. 2014). There is also evidence that a top–down, control model for managing the minutiae of work is unhelpful and relational factors (i.e. relationships with co-workers) and empowerment (i.e. how employees can take charge of matters themselves) are fundamental to job design for effective performance (Grant and Parker 2009).

We now have substantial evidence that goal/target setting causes gaming and unethical behaviour. At the individual level setting demanding goals increases the level of unethical behaviour and relationship conflict in an organization, which in turn exposes the organization performance and organizational reputation to risk (Zhang and Jia 2013). This is compounded in complex systems like healthcare and a consideration of some of the studies of organizational performance in healthcare settings is illustrative. A longitudinal study of a collaborative and emergent approach to infection control across populations (Halpin et al. 2013) demonstrated the importance of trust between politicians and managers and the wider encouragement of inter-organizational co-operation, which enabled improvements in infection control outcomes. The opposite is evidenced by Osterloh (2014) who points to the gaming practices consequent upon simplistic targets/goals as a means to control performance.

We have evidence of serious problems when accountability is entirely located in an individual and then this is used to mitigate complex service user risk in high stakes environments (i.e. healthcare). The research evidence suggests that if an organization focuses on individual accountability as its mechanism to prevent error, this actually generates a negative impact on patient safety. The psychosocial reasons for this are the unmediated compliance behaviours such as pluralistic ignorance, bystander effect, fear of retaliation and equity adjustments. An equity adjustment is when feeling unfairly treated is re-balanced by actions such as taking free time during working hours, taking paper or pens home from the office or bad mouthing your employer to friends. All of these responses operate to inhibit the voicing of concerns and so stop acts that could enhance organizational performance (Dodds and Kodate 2011).

On this basis there have been calls for performance management practitioners to shift their design paradigm from 'a dyadic perspective to a systems perspective' (Abernathy 2014: 235) using team and organizational goals rather than reducing the unit of measurement down to the individual and the specific sub-goals they are set.

Culturally

The performance management design comes from the North American context and so pre-supposes an organizational culture, employment market and legal environment that actually does not exist in very many other parts of the world, so is clearly culturally specific. Despite this cultural specificity, it has been used elsewhere without any consideration of the impact on a different cultural context from using a 'colonizing' approach to its implementation. There is evidence that when organizations expand across different cultures, the way in which this performance issue is approached is subtly flexed to address the worst problems associated with this mono-cultural design deficiency. In addition to pointing to the additional complexity of cross-cultural organizational functioning (that we ignore at our peril) it also gives clear evidence that performance management does not offer the 'objective assessment' outputs that are claimed, as cultural intelligence fortunately impacts practice (Varma et al. 2008).

Applying this to our critique of performance management, such practices create a 'climate for autonomy' and research into the impact of this climate indicates it is generally neutral in impact in US workplaces, but is widely reported as a substantial cause of workplace stress in other cultures. However, when high demands are added to the context such a climate causes stress and dramatically reduces productivity across all cultures, US culture included (Hirst et al. 2008). For a detailed exploration of the issues in cross-cultural performance management see Varma et al. (2008).

There are alternative approaches to supporting individual contribution to collective endeavour. By way of a cultural contrast, the Yoruba Oriki practice has been recently redeveloped for use in organizations (Okonkwo 2010) and was included in the Appreciative Inquiry example given in Chapter 4.

The cultural specificity is not only evidenced in the damage done to subtle forms of social interaction, but in the fact that the basic premise of performance management is not supported by many of the legal frameworks in countries other than the US. My experience in a wide variety of client contexts is that this performance management mechanism is rarely used to fire people, and certainly not the 10 per cent figure that is the requisite in the mathematical model to gain predicted benefits. Contract termination is far too complicated in the majority of employment jurisdictions for this simple dynamic to work. Therefore these mechanisms cannot deliver the benefits the model intends in different cultural settings, even if it were productive to do so. In different jurisdictions these approaches are inherently inappropriate and have the added impact of upsetting everybody.

Performance management causes ill health

This approach activates psychosocial hazards. As outlined in Chapter 6, psychological safety at work is essential for sustained productivity and health. It enhances workplace productivity through the positive impact it has on creativity, learning, role improvisation and innovation. The risk of negative feedback works to reduce a sense of control and increase an experience of demand. The competitive quality of the design and the experience of negative feedback associated with the financial risk of job loss causes what is described as a 'blame culture'. Through this performance management is implicated in a lowering of peer support and in damaging relationships. With this apparently simple performance management system, organizations have fully activated the psychosocial workplace hazards that have been identified in the stress literature.

When employees feel they are treated fairly, positive outcomes result and negative outcomes can be avoided (Westerman and Westerman 2013) and perceptions of justice at work are also recognized as an inherent part of psychological safety and the review above indicates the variety of ways in which performance management generates perceptions of unfairness. Grynderup et al. (2013) demonstrated through in-depth longitudinal study across multiple work contexts that employment in an organization with low workplace justice predicted the onset of clinical depression in employees. An outline of the literature on psychological safety, psychosocial hazards and the global costs of mental ill health is given in Chapter 6.

The critical factor in improving justice perceptions is encouraging employee participation, which is in contrast to the individualistic and competitive ethos of performance management. A longitudinal study of the impact that participative interventions have on justice perceptions from a two-year large-scale study showed that these dramatically improved employees' justice perceptions at both individual and work group levels (Linna et al. 2011). A further study indicated that participative interventions undertaken by organizational leaders have a positive and sustainable impact on organizational outcomes (Neilsen 2013). The research on performance management and participation supports this view, with perceptions of appraisal fairness closely linked to the frequency of informal discussions (Dewettinck and van Dijk 2013). Indeed, these authors identified that the perception of performance management system fairness and effectiveness is disabled through the application of the formal aspects of the performance review process.

Performance management is analytically weak

Performance management is predicated upon three key assumptions, none of which holds up to scrutiny:

- that the assessments made of individuals are objective, valid and reliable 'measures' of performance;
- that the statistical distribution of performance follows a normal distribution curve;

- that there is a causal connection between 'performance' as assessed by this mechanism at different levels – the individual, the group and the whole organization.

Objective, valid and reliable measurements

The previous sections substantially challenge any claims to objectivity, validity or reliability and will not be repeated here.

Normal distribution

I find it curious that it is considered statistically appropriate to use a normal distribution curve for the phenomenon that we describe as individual 'performance'. Good practice in managing people in the workplace involves actively selecting people for specific roles in an effective and productive way, followed by training and developing them to maximize their contribution. These HR processes which together are called 'high performance HR' in practice are focused upon ensuring that any organization is not managing and deploying a 'random' set of individuals in a normal distributed population, but instead working with a specifically selected group. This means that we would predict a skewed distribution in performance assessment. To then assume that the organization is a normally distributed sample for the purposes of performance management is erroneous; it has not been randomly selected and indeed there is substantial expense and effort deployed to ensure it is not random. The difference between these two distribution curves is illustrated in Figure 10.1.

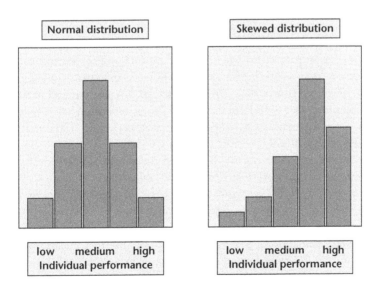

FIGURE 10.1   Normal and skewed distribution curves for performance

Independent assessments of individual performance in the workplace for a research study indicated that 'performance' does not follow a normal distribution curve but instead shows a skewed distribution towards the high performance end (O'Boyle and Aguinis 2012). This same research also indicated that this statistical reality is well recognized by both those being rated and those doing the rating. They report that the use of a normal distribution is both inaccurate and unfair.

Inferring a connection between individual performance rating and company performance

At a simplistic level of analysis, if we consider the distribution curve for individual performance using the performance management mechanism, we assume the same distribution of individual performance regardless of how the whole organization is actually performing comparatively with other organizations. An organization that was about to cease trading due to severe losses would show the same distribution of individual performance ratings when using this approach, as one that is really successful, so clearly indicating that the individual assessments in this process have no connection to overall business performance. Despite this self-evident truth, most large western employers use this mechanism and apply these distribution curves to their whole population of staff and act on the confidence that this helps improve business performance.

This however is not the only problematic assumption about how organizational, team and individual level performance assessments are related (or not). The *actual strength and direction of an association* at the individual level may be weakened or reversed within the sub-groups comprising that organization or at the total organizational level. This means that organizations could be rewarding people for actions that look good at the individual level (or punishing people for what looks bad at an individual level), but are actively bad for overall organizational performance (or are actively good at an organizational level).

This discrepant pattern has been explored in studies of workplace experience, for example in the relationship between performance and organizational commitment (Conway and Briner 2012). In exploring the dynamics around performance and commitment, they found that there was a strong association between unit level performance and commitment, indicating the existence of differential relationships at different organizational levels. In accounting for this, they point to the work of employees targeting 'discretionary' behaviours to achieve organizational goals by, for instance, avoiding work that is redundant and noticing the gaps to be filled. Such behaviour may not necessarily contribute to individual performance (it may even worsen) but it is likely to contribute to the unit's performance. Acting to compromise the delivery of one's own task in the interests of group performance in generating organizational performance gains does not fit with the competitive and individualistic assumptions of performance management and so would also suggest that there is likely to be a negative correlation between measures of team performance and the assessments of individual performance.

The existence of discrepant relationships at different levels in a data-set is a striking observation known as Simpson's paradox, and has negative impacts on inferences drawn based upon a human tendency to causal bias. This has been observed in many data-sets recognized as very significant, for example medical tests:

> treatment that appears effective at the population-level may, in fact, have adverse consequences within each of the population's subgroups. For instance, a higher dosage of medicine may be associated with higher recovery rates at the population-level; however, *within* subgroups (e.g., for both males and females), a higher dosage may actually result in *lower* recovery rates.
> *(Kievit et al. 2013: 1, emphasis in original)*

To illustrate I have constructed the illustration shown in Figure 10.2. This diagram represents how a series of measures of 'coping strategies' and task performance could appear in a data-set impacted by Simpson's paradox. For each individual, four different measures from different times are aggregated into the following three types of data-set:

- one whole population data-set comprising all the measurement points taken;
- two data-sets based on gender comprising all the measurement points taken for each gender;
- multiple data-sets at the individual level.

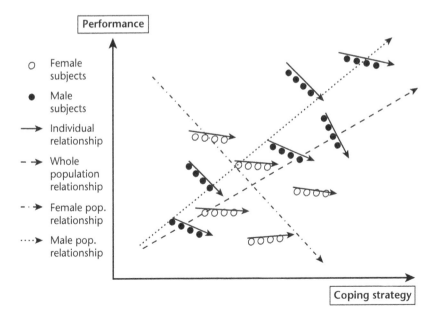

FIGURE 10.2 Data patterns described as Simpson's paradox

Although the whole population data-set shows a positive correlation between coping strategy and performance (see solid dash line) when these measures are divided into two gender-based sub-sets, this positive correlation holds for the male sub-group (see dotted line) and not the female sub-group (see the dot-dash line). Further, regardless of gender the majority of individuals show a negative correlation between coping strategy and performance, with a few exceptions among the female individuals who show a positive relationship between coping strategy and performance.

Kievit et al. (2013: 2–3) state that this 'phenomenon is not actually a paradox, but a counterintuitive feature of aggregated data, which may arise when causal inferences are drawn across different explanatory levels: from populations to subgroups, or subgroups to individuals, or from cross-sectional data to intra-individual changes over time' and 'to be able to draw causal conclusions, we must know what the underlying causal mechanisms of the observed patterns are, and to what extent the data we observe are informative about these mechanisms'.

The evidence available about what can impact organizational performance points to various factors, rarely linked to individual behaviour, but mostly at the ways people work together as evidenced in the critical impact of managerial behaviour towards others. There has been a relationship established between unit level and organizational performance (Harter et al. 2002), the use of balanced gender and other balanced boards for governance of large corporations improves financial outcomes, governance processes and positive management behaviour (see Chapters 8 and 9).

It is worth considering that this elaborate attention to an internally focused individualized approach to 'explaining' and rewarding 'performance' through performance management is merely an expensive form of making sure we have our biases legitimized in workplaces. I would contend that it is functioning to distract time, effort and intelligence away from attention to the overall productivity of the internal collaborative working relationships and how they are responding to the external operating environment.

Conclusion

This chapter presents the significance that external evidence can have for the development of psychosocial priorities in practice. It represents a full illustration of the insight phase of knowledge translation. Based on this knowledge translation, we can now be confident that we have sufficient psychological, social science, management and neuroscience evidence to show that current approaches to performance management in the workplace are flawed and dangerous. There is clear evidence, both from external research (and on the ground investigations in client organizations) that performance management actually causes disengagement, disaffection and depression. Given the extent to which these practices activate organizational toxicity, it is not surprising that as the use of performance management has extended across our employment organizations, there has also been a parallel increase in the reported levels of bullying, harassment, victimization and the feeling that workplaces have lost their humanity.

The solution to the current concern with the 'engagement' problem is not to spend more on ill-conceived interventions but instead to remove a significant cause – the over-engineered and process heavy performance management machinery from our organizations (and this extends to grievance and disciplinary procedures too – but that is a different story). We do not need more and different 'engagement' and 'empowerment' programmes to mitigate these unintended consequences of performance management, but instead we need to remove the torturous organizational clutter that has built up from the belief in the value of performance management practices, and let people work together without this unhelpful and damaging process.

Employers are beginning to engage with these manifest problems. Recently Buckingham and Goodall (2015) shared an in-depth internal review of performance management in a large professional services firm, which indicated that the performance management process consumes 2 million hours of billable time each year with no evidence of any return on this investment. Consequently they re-designed the whole approach to aligning individual work.

Imagine how much money and pain we would save, how much more impactful our efforts would be and how much workplace-induced depression we could prevent by removing performance management and replacing it with regular human dialogue that would enable us to engage in real time with the impact of changing requirements and expectations and allow us work together with a reasonable, contextually relevant understanding of the constraints on possible outcome.

References

Abernathy, W. B. (2014) Beyond the Skinner Box: The design and management of organization-wide performance systems. *Journal of Organizational Behavior Management* 34(4): 235–254.

Belogolovsky, E. and Bamberger, P. A. (2014) Signaling in secret: Pay for performance and the incentive and sorting effects of pay secrecy. *Academy of Management Journal* 57(6): 1706–1733.

Berger, J., Harbring, C. and Sliwka, D. (2013) Performance appraisals and the impact of forced distribution: An experimental investigation. *Management Science* 59(1): 54–68.

Blume, B., Baldwin, T. and Rubin, R. (2009) Reactions to different types of forced distribution performance evaluation systems. *Journal of Business and Psychology* 24(1): 77–91.

Bol, J. C. (2011) The determinants and performance effects of managers' performance evaluation biases. *Accounting Review* 86(5): 1549–1575.

Breugst, N., Patzelt, H., Shepherd, D. A. et al. (2012) Relationship conflict improves team performance assessment accuracy: Evidence from a multilevel study. *Academy of Management Learning & Education* 11(2): 187–206.

Brockner, J., Houser, R., Birnbaum, G. et al. (1986) Escalation of commitment to an ineffective course of action: The effect of feedback having negative implications for self-identity. *Administrative Science Quarterly* 31(1): 109–126.

Buckingham, M. and Goodall, A. (2015) Reinventing performance management. *Harvard Business Review* April: 40–50.

Carton, A. M. and Rosette, A. S. (2011) Explaining bias against black leaders: Integrating theory on information processing and goal-based stereotyping. *Academy of Management Journal* 54(6): 1141–1158.

Castilla, E. and Benard, S. (2010) The paradox of meritocracy in organizations. *Administrative Science Quarterly* 55(4): 543–576.

Chen, Y. L. (2014) Determinants of biased subjective performance evaluations: Evidence from a Taiwanese public sector organization. *Accounting and Business Research* 44(6): 656–675.

Cianci, A. M., Klein, H. and Seijts, G. (2010) The effect of negative feedback on tension and subsequent performance: The main and interactive effects of goal content and conscientiousness. *Journal of Applied Psychology* 95(4): 618–630.

Coates, J. (2012) *The Hour between Dog and Wolf: Risk Taking, Gut Feelings and the Biology of Boom and Bust.* London: Harper Collins.

Conway, N. and Briner, R. (2012) Investigating the effect of collective organizational commitment on unit-level performance and absence. *Journal of Occupational and Organizational Psychology* 85(3): 472–486.

Cross, R. and Cummings, J. N. (2004) Tie and network correlates of individual performance in knowledge-intensive work. *Academy of Management Journal* 47(6): 928–937.

Dewettinck, K. and van Dijk, H. (2013) Linking Belgian employee performance management system characteristics with performance management system effectiveness: Exploring the mediating role of fairness. *International Journal of Human Resource Management* 24(4): 806–825.

Dodds, A. and Kodate, N. (2011) Accountability, organisational learning and risks to patient safety in England: Conflict or compromise? *Health Risk and Society* 13(4): 327–346.

Eisenberger, N. I. and Leiberman, M. D. (2004) Why it hurts to be left out: The neuro-cognitive overlap between physical pain and social pain. *Trends in Cognitive Sciences* 8(7): 294–300.

Govaerts, M., Van de Weil, M. and van der Vleuten, C. (2013) Quality of feedback following performance assessments: Does assessor expertise matter? *European Journal of Training and development* 37(1): 105–125.

Grant, A. M. and Parker, S. K. (2009) Redesigning work design theories: The rise of relational and proactive perspectives. *The Academy of Management Annals* 3(1): 317–375.

Grote, D. (2005) Forced ranking: Making performance management work. http://hbswk. hbs.edu/archive/5091.html.

Grynderup, M. B., Mors, O., Hansen, A. M. et al. (2013) Work-unit measures of organisational justice and risk of depression: A 2-year cohort study. *Occupational and Environmental Medicine* 70(6): 380–385.

Halpin, H. A., McMenamin, S. B., Simon, L. P. et al. (2013) Impact of participation in the California Healthcare-Associated Infection Prevention Initiative on adoption and implementation of evidence-based practices for patients. *American Journal of Infection Control* 41(4): 307–311.

Harter, J. K., Schmidt, F. L. and Hayes, T. L. (2002) Business-unit-level relationship between employee satisfaction, employee engagement, and business outcomes: A meta-analysis. *Journal of Applied Psychology* 87(2): 268–279.

Hershcovis, M. S., Turner, N., Barling, J. et al. (2007) Predicting workplace aggression: A meta-analysis. *Journal of Applied Psychology* 92(1): 228–238.

Hirst, G., Budhwar, P., Cooper, B. K. et al. (2008) Cross-cultural variations in climate for autonomy, stress and organizational productivity relationships: A comparison of

Chinese and UK manufacturing organizations. *Journal of International Business Studies* 39(8): 1343–1358.

Iacobani, M. (2008) *Mirroring People: The New Science of How We Connect with Others*. New York: Farrar, Straus & Giroux.

Ilies, R., De Pater, I. and Judge, T. (2007) Differential affective reactions to negative and positive feedback, and the role of self-esteem. *Journal of Managerial Psychology* 22(6): 590–609.

Jensen, J. M., Patel, P. and Raver, J. (2014) Is it better to be average? High and low performance as predictors of employee victimization. *Journal of Applied Psychology* 99(2): 296–309.

Kievit, R. A., Frankenhuis, W. E., Waldorp, L. J. et al. (2013) Simpson's paradox in psychological science: A practical guide. *Frontiers in Psychology* 4(513): 1–14.

Larkin, I., Pierce, L. and Gino, F. (2012) The psychological costs of pay-for-performance: Implications for the strategic compensation of employees. *Strategic Management Journal* 33(10): 1194–1214.

Lawler III, E. (2003) Reward practices and performance management system effectiveness. *Organization Dynamics* 32(4): 396.

Linna, A., Väänänen, A., Elovainio, M., et al. (2011) Effect of participative intervention on organisational justice perceptions: A quasi-experimental study on Finnish public sector employees. *International Journal of Human Resource Management* 22(3): 706–721.

Luksyte, A., Waite, E., Avery, D. R. et al. (2013) Held to a different standard: Racial differences in the impact of lateness on advancement opportunity. *Journal of Occupational and Organizational Psychology* 86(2): 142–165.

Lynn, M. and Sturman, M. (2011) Is the customer always right? The potential for racial bias in customer evaluations of employee performance. *Journal of Applied Social Psychology* 41(9): 2312–2324.

McBriarty, M. A. (1988) Performance appraisal: Some unintended consequences. *Public Personnel Management* 17(4): 421–434.

Mollick, E. (2012) People and process, suits and innovators: The role of individuals in firm performance. *Strategic Management Journal* 33(9): 1001–1015.

Murthy, U. S. and Schafer, B. A. (2011) The effects of relative performance information and framed information systems feedback on performance in a production task. *Journal of Information Systems* 25(1): 159–184.

Navaresse, D., Yauch, C. A., Goff, K. et al. (2014) Assessing the effects of organizational culture, rewards, and individual creativity on technical workgroup performance. *Creative Research Journal* 26(4): 439–455.

Neilsen, K. (2013) How can we make organizational interventions work? Employees and line managers as actively crafting interventions. *Human Relations* 66(8): 1029–1050.

O'Boyle Jr, E. and Aguinis, H. (2012) The best and the rest: Revisiting the norm of normality of individual performance. *Personnel Psychology* 65(1): 79–119.

Okonkwo, J. (2010) Coaching for leadership using myths and stories: An African perspective. In J. Passmore (ed.) *Leadership in Coaching: Working with Leaders To Develop Elite Performance*. London: Kogan Page.

Osterloh, M. (2014) Viewpoint: Why variable pay for performance in healthcare can backfire: Evidence from psychological economics. *Evidence Based HRM* 2(1): 120–123.

Park, S. H. and Westphal, J. D. (2011) Set up for a fall: The insidious effects of flattery and opinion conformity toward corporate leaders. *Administrative Science Quarterly* 56(2): 257–302.

Parker, S. K., Johnson, A., Collins, C. et al. (2013) Making the most of structural support: Moderating influence of employees' clarity and negative affect. *Academy of Management Journal* 56(3): 867–892.

Phillips, A. R. and Kruger, C. J. (2006) Minimizing dysfunctional internal competition: A strategy enabler model. *South African Journal of Information Management* 8(1): 4.

Ronen, S. and Baldwin, M. W. (2010) Hypersensitivity to social rejection and perceived stress as mediators between attachment anxiety and future burnout: A prospective analysis. *Applied Psychology: An International Review* 59(3): 380–403.

Sackett, P. R. and DuBois, C. L. Z. (1991) Rater–ratee race effects on performance evaluation challenging meta-analytic conclusions. *Journal of Applied Psychology* 76(6): 873–877.

Scullen, S., Bergey, P. and Aiman-Smith, L. (2005) Forced distribution rating systems and the improvement of workforce potential: A baseline simulation. *Personnel Psychology* 58(1): 1–31.

Shoss, M. K., Witt, L. A. and Dusya, V. (2012) When does adaptive performance lead to higher task performance? *Journal of Organizational Behaviour* 33(7): 910–924.

Sommer, K. L. and Kulkarni, M. (2012) Does constructive performance feedback improve citizenship intentions and job satisfaction? The roles of perceived opportunities for advancement, respect, and mood. *Human Resource Development Quarterly* 23(2): 177–201.

Tepper, B. J., Moss, S. E. and Duffy, M. K. (2011) Predictors of abusive supervision: Supervisor perceptions of deep-level dissimilarity, relationship conflict, and subordinate performance. *Academy of Management Journal* 54(2): 279–294.

Tims, M., Bakker, A. B. and Derks, D. (2014) Daily job crafting and the self-efficacy–performance relationship. *Journal of Managerial Psychology* 29(5): 490–507.

Tranfield, D., Denyer, D. and Marcos, J. (2002) Management and the development of high reliability organisations. *Management Focus* 19: 16–18.

Varma, A., Budhwar, P. S. and De Nisi, A. (eds) (2008) *Performance Management Systems: A Global Perspective*. London and New York: Routledge.

Westerman, C. and Westerman, D. (2013) What's fair? Public and private delivery of project feedback. *Journal of Business Communication* 50(2): 190–207.

Wilson, K. (2010) An analysis of bias in supervisor narrative comments in performance appraisal. *Human Relations* 63(12): 1903–1933.

Yammarino, F. J., Dubinsky, A. J. and Hartley, S. W. (1987) An approach for assessing individual versus group effects in performance evaluations. *Journal of Occupational Psychology* 60(2): 157–167.

Zhang, Z. and Jia, M. (2013) How can companies decrease the disruptive effects of stretch goals? The moderating role of interpersonal- and informational-justice climates. *Human Relations* 66(7): 993–1020.

11

RE-DESIGNING BELONGING DYNAMICS FOR AN INTERCONNECTED WORLD OF WORK

Introduction

Two case illustrations are used to share client work I have been involved in that has engaged directly with the emerging complexity of extended belonging structures impacting contemporary workplaces. This is not so much an exploration of toxicity, but of responses to emerging attachment disorders. Both stories relate to the 'wicked problem' of extended belonging relationships at work and to the design, implementation and support phases of knowledge translation involved in addressing this. The types of client problems statements that underpin this work are illustrated in the following:

- 'How do we get our customer to repeat buy?'
- 'How do we get service user voice into our ideas about development?'
- 'How do we make our organization inclusive?'
- 'How do we work productively with tribalism?'
- 'How do we build our brand effectively?'
- 'What do we do about all our silos?'
- 'How do we increase workplace satisfaction and commitment?'
- 'How do we get our customers to recommend us?'

These questions point to 'belonging dynamics' at the edges of groups and organizations. People outside the organization (customers) are generally positioned differently than those within. The idea of 'customers' and 'customer relationship management' tends to create distance and disconnect rather than invoke people. Internally to organizations, the considerations of human belonging in mainstream psychosocial literature about the workplace predominantly focuses upon 'team building', 'engagement surveys' and 'leadership' as the focus of positive interventions to increase productivity, none of which include the human connection with customers.

This internal status quo does not cover all of the critical belonging factors at work and indeed many of the interventions built from these conventions are toxic in their impacts. The 'blindness' caused by these conventional frames about belonging at work, limits our approach to design. In order to meet the real and emerging design challenges around belonging in the workplace, and to avoid creating unintended toxicity, we must critique this convention, based as it is on implicit assumptions about the need for 'bonding' at work to be able to do good work (see definition of bonding in Chapter 9). In addition to this being a limited view (as the design stories that follow illustrate) I am also concerned that the way we implicitly approach human belonging at work causes many of the problems it claims to solve. When interventions are designed to enhance 'bonding', in-groups are privileged over other types of attachment structure, which reinforces systemic exclusion and lack of innovation. In practice I have seen the unintended consequences of using team bonding approaches without care make silos stronger, exclude minority groups, enable and reinforce groupthink and cause systemic toxic attachment disorders at work.

Designing from the edge in the cabin crew world (case one)

Airlines have managed remote, flexible and mobile workforces for nearly a century. This industry was one of the 'early adopters' of what is now a much more prevalent way of working; working through the deployment of emergent virtual groups, pulled together for particular tasks and then disbanded. While we now enable this widely through social technology, the aviation industry developed these practices over time to support an earlier technological change.

In aviation the work undertaken on board a flight includes a range of distinctive working relationships. All airlines offer pretty much the same practical offering, so distinctiveness is embedded in the nature of how these human connections between strangers in a very constrained context (a thin metal tube in the air) are realized. Instead of considering that work stops at the bounds of the employment contract, it is important to re-frame this to recognize that an important contemporary *working relationship* (i.e. not merely a service relationship) is that between each individual customer and each individual front line service provider. This is a trust-based relationship involving the meeting of strangers, where each member of the cabin crew acts in a key 'management' role with the customer group and the idea ('brand') they have chosen to put their trust in.

A significant current concern for all airlines is the market research evidence in this sector that *inconsistency in service experience* (i.e. not poor quality but unpredictable experience) is one of the most significant factors impacting customer intent to rebook or recommend. Psychosocially, why is consistency important in this context? To really engage with this question we need to recognize the significance of psychological aspects of safety and security in the very particular airline 'service transaction'. Although flying is now a commonplace, it is a purchase that requires making a choice to trust and then submit to being 'trapped' in a metal cage with a large number of people you do not know, from which there is no escape. There are very few other service transactions of this nature.

To engage with this, it is necessary to explore belonging in working relationships, which includes the customer experience of belonging and the role clarity that customers/service users need. Organizations that have focused consciously on increasing customer role clarity through socialization and participation techniques have identified additional commercial advantages through the increased customer motivation to take a defined role (e.g. buy own food on board or to actively engage in the recommendation of service providers). Such approaches are enabling businesses to generate higher margins through integrating the customer as an explicit 'working resource'. Lack of predictability generates role confusion for the customer, decreases felt safety and security and so undermines the psychosocial safety that underpins participation and hence work.

A fully functioning bridging structure

The virtual, flexible, mobile cabin crew workforce is one of the oldest active examples of a bridging structure (see Chapter 9) established through an employment contract. The crew communications grapevine is a perfect illustration of what Granovetter (1973) described as the 'strength of weak ties'; the speed with which information flows. For him it was a theoretical suggestion which is being demonstrated through the 'viral memes' that social media is enabling. For decades before this test of theory was made possible through these social media research programmes, viral communication via weak ties was alive in the crew community. Each airline has a different descriptor of this phenomenon, but all have to work with it. In a crew community of 8K operating with a full international hub airline service, any new story will be communicated 'virally' through these regularly changing team structures. The mathematically modeled review (I got all geeky about this living 'proof of concept') of information flow demonstrates that it takes a maximum of six days for an 8K crew community to have directly heard the new story from another member of crew.

A quick account of the crew workflow will help to outline the design issue. Before each flight there is a rapid pre-flight briefing at the airport which is the first time each crew member will meet their new colleagues, and it is through this rapid briefing that the working organization for the duration of the flight is established, creating a workforce made up of people who are all strangers to each other. Achieving this successfully (which airlines manage day after day without incident) relies on specific qualities of discipline and relationship skill manifested in the behaviour of the cabin crew. This self-regulation covers presentation and regulation of self in role, time management and the management of time changes, work–life balance management, the management of daily new working relationships, the management of customers who are committed to the journey, the management of personal isolation and regular displacement and the management of back office (often regulatory) updates to provision and practice.

This is not only a psychosocial design issue, it is also business critical as the functioning of this bridging structure has clear benefits. It is cost effective and without these people operating in this structure, the cost of flying would be prohibitive. Those employment jurisdictions (that could afford to) enabled some airlines to trial an alternative team bonding structure for crew, which produced interesting (and unpublished data). The headline findings were:

- This bonded team model costs 40–60 per cent more for the business to implement.
- In approximately 80 per cent of flights the team-bonded relationships in crew teams produces better customer reference-ability outcomes.
- However in the other 20 per cent of flights the manner in which bonded team dynamics derailed led to serious problems with the operation, the flight experience and generated highly negative customer outcomes.
- This polarized experience generates the same overall customer reference-ability outcomes as for a bridging structure.

An emotionally dysfunctional team on the ground is one thing, but in a small metal tube in the air this is quite another.

The work done to support the business of flying takes place in a more conventional bonded hierarchical structure in the organizational head offices; for example there are bonded teams managing rosters, routes, aviation authorities, safety and security infrastructure and aviation medicine requirements. This difference in belonging type has led to unexpected problems. 'Bonded' teams work on implicit assumptions of reciprocity dynamics via 'strong ties' which are built into 'intimate kinship structures'. Bridging structures do not work like this. The long-term established crew bridging structures have consolidated instead into 'extended kinship structures' based on mutual recognition with high individual autonomy.

As the rhetoric about the importance of 'team' has grown, airlines running this virtual bridging model have been encouraged to create 'normal' team approaches for crew, akin to those that they find in their head offices (and that most of us are more used to at work) and this has disrupted functioning.

This bridging framework means that meeting the reciprocity and affiliative support needs, recognized as critical for personal resilience at work, will not be forthcoming in the same way for the crew community as for the head office teams. Instead resilience for this community is based upon membership determining a predictable form of role-based exchange. If this predictable exchange gets disrupted, then there is a degree of uncertainty that leads to felt insecurity, particularly if working in high stakes/security alert environments. The experience of inconsistency in treatment, which disrupts the drivers of mutual recognition, either from other cabin crew, from subtle changes to things like uniform or procedure or unclear communications into this bridged network, will generate higher levels of felt insecurity than such symbolic factors would in a predominantly bonded environment. How organizational symbols such as uniform, use of procedures, communication style and the presentation of self are used will have serious impacts (either negative or positive) on the resilience, confidence and well-being of members of this community.

As customers on any flight are also invited to participate in this bridging structure, they are subject to similar impacts from inconsistency. The value for an airline from the service delivery point working relationship comes from the *brand brokerage* that the crew on board offers. As this is not a bonded environment, but instead one characterized by the meeting of strangers, there is not the luxury of time to get to know the others you are working with or being served by. What makes the workplace demands extreme for crew is that they are undertaking this significant brokerage role for customers when working alongside other crew as part of a bridging structure; a world of strangers. On a flight this means we are working in contexts that are physically uncomfortable, relatively tedious and high stakes. In such a context, behavioural predictability through 'role clarity' for both crew and customers is critical to the experience of psychological control. Predictability is important for the psychological safety of all on board. Customers need to know their own role in this exchange and to build their sense of role clarity and to do this they need predictability in the role behaviour of the service providers. Mutual investment in role consistency, rather than individuality, is the fabric from which the sense of psychological safety is built between strangers.

In addition to the mutual recognition issue, interference with crew member autonomy undermines their perceptions of employer fairness as this is inconsistent with the 'bridging deal'. The imposition of a conventional 'management approach' onto a bridging structure is not felt as fair as it inherently challenges autonomy. This is not to suggest that management is not needed, but instead to recognize that bridging structures are already highly 'managed' spaces, with 'self-management', 'self-regulation' and 'self-determination' the norm. (This has really interesting impacts for absence management, work–life balance and progression questions but these are not the substance of this short account.) By contrast those working in head office using a more bonded ethos get very upset when members of these bridged communities appear to break bonding structure reciprocity rules; the collision of the two structures generates breaches of trust and confidence in both parties.

Defining a design challenge around brokerage in organizations

The design challenge is therefore not about management or leadership or teamwork but instead a need to explore how to create a connection between two different worlds and world views without compromising how the two different worlds function. Instead of imposing bonding on the cabin crew community, the challenge is how to work with the power of ideas, identity, bridging and brokerage in belonging at work. For the purpose of this story this is my articulation of the revised and elaborated design challenge:

> How can we effectively broker connections between the head office bonding structure (and their working assumptions) with the cabin crew bridging

structure (and their working assumptions)? How can we to add support and resilience to the bridging structure? How do we give a sense of reciprocity to those in the bonded structure? How do we allow information to flow between these two different structures? Further how can we activate this to increase the customer sense of consistency in service experience?

Figure 11.1 outlines the prototype design we developed to address our revised understanding of the 'team' problem when we looked beyond the idea of teamwork being dependent upon bonding structures. The attempt to impose a team approach from one context to another has been the most informative example

---

THE PROTOTYPE DESIGN: ACTIVATING BROKERAGE

The design re-framed the understanding of 'management' for a bridging structure. Instead of trying to fit an implicit model of a bonded structure as the basis for 'managing' the crew to increase consistency of customer experience, a 'brokerage' role was developed and protoyped. The subtle shift was that a broker's role was to explicitly manage the connection (the boundary) between the cabin crew community and the head office teams. In contrast the existing idea behind a crew manager's role was to have a manager responsible for the performance of each crew member (a person they rarely met or worked with).

A group of 20 senior cabin crew was recruited for the trial on a voluntary basis. The importance of autonomy in a bridging structure meant the volunteer nature was critical and having control of lifestyle and roster was part of the bridging deal. A short training period was provided where the group was given key information, including an introduction to the company's employment policies (the constraints in this context) as well as articulating what a broker role was.

Two broker colleagues were rostered to work together each day to provide support for each other and to be able to respond to whatever personal or service queries any member of the crew raised – very much in the way in which the client would expect the crew to respond to a customer. The important factor here is that they were still subject to roster, still in uniform and still in the bridging community. The main focus of the protoype was focused on brokers provided coaching to rostered crew as issues emerged. What was compelling about this trial was that brokers recruited were from senior crew who were used to working autonomously on board and dealing with critical incidents at 35,000 feet for which there may be no easy solution.

This experience was evident and impressed the head office teams when they worked on the ground. They were adept at using their initiative and finding innovative solutions to problems and were particularly competent at forming new working relationships quickly across all levels of the head office structure and using these to be able to respond quickly to crew queries and needs.

Another aspect of the role which proved to be a success was the support it gave to the launch of a new internal social media tool. The broker group was an early adopter of this and prolific users of the medium, using it to communicate with, and support their colleagues who were working across the globe so staying embedded in the bridging structure via this mechanism. The overriding feedback was that this prototype was a commercial success and good for employee wellbeing across both pre-existing structures.

FIGURE 11.1 Prototype design of brokerage role

of the importance of understanding context and consequent constraint in intervention design. It shows the 'design as conversation' between the knowledgeable designer and the realities of context. Bad design happens when a pre-determined a-contextual solution/knowledge is implemented without this 'conversation' (Farrands 2013). (See Chapter 4 for a brief coverage of design thinking.) To do design well requires a translation process that engages with the client world. Insights can be found from anywhere, but the design challenge can only be created from within the specific context. The use of evidence in this context to 'get under the skin' of a client question by really understanding what the evidence from the field is indicating, allows two things:

- a properly formulated design challenge statement to commence the work;
- far better identification of relevant external evidence that can help with insight to support the design work.

Using evidence in these various ways means that we can move beyond thinking of evidence as enabling decision support, to recognizing a much wider range of evidence as impactful in the creative collaboration between client and intelligent activist.

This cabin crew story was focused very much on the design aspect of translation enabled through being active in the various relevant organizations. The next account also covers a belonging-based design challenge, but working as a practitioner remote from the client site in a coaching capacity, needing greater emphasis on client dialogue and co-creation to ensure that the client was comfortable to use the design through the vicissitudes of implementation and course correction.

Coaching the 'tempered radical' in a career challenging ethnicity innovation (case two)

I was fortunate to be able to offer psychosocial design and coaching services to a Black professional employee committed to social change in his workplace. It is not often you have the opportunity to work with a client who is genuinely in the role of 'tempered radical [. . .] engaged in the dual project of working within the organization and working to change the organization' (Meyerson and Scully 1995: 586). He worked for a global services business and had gained the authority to implement an ethnicity-led innovation (the process of getting the authority to do this is another story). This ran in parallel with his professional role in the organization. The programme was designed as an ethnicity-based, yet inclusive externally facing innovation initiative, to be led from within the business, rather than from a more conventional idea of diversity and inclusion (D&I) as operating separately from the business. Most such innovation undertaken by organizations is positioned as corporate social responsibility (CSR) and so focused on impacting externally for reputation benefit; a type of marketing activity.

The client organization was US dominated and the approach had been developed and successfully rolled out across the US offices. The opportunity arose because the model they had been using effectively in the US had failed in the UK context. The problem for the client organization was how to develop a model of Black Networks (BNs) in the Europe, Middle East and Africa (EMEA) context (starting with the UK), that would both work in situ and be aligned with the US-led approach. The programme was impactful against the design challenge articulated in this work. Figure 11.2 outlines the impact summary of the ethnicity programme as background for the account of the innovation challenges such work brings with it.

Undertaking design/co-creation

The design work for the programme was undertaken in 2009 when the majority of the UK 'diversity' rhetoric available was around gender (which is critical but brings a different set of issues). Ideas of 'unconscious bias' and 'intersectionality' were just beginning to make their way into the diversity discourse, but consideration

---

THE SUMMARY IMPACT STATEMENT FROM THE THREE-YEAR UK-BASED ETHNICITY PROGRAMME

- The UKBN membership increased nine fold over the three years.
- Three impactful UK Black History Month (BHM) celebrations were delivered across a range of community locations.
- A black performance charity was sponsored and they provided disruptive and positive images for display across the UK business for each annual UK BHM.
- A large number of Black staff from across the UK were brought together for a development and 'Brand Ambassador' programme.
- Their previous predominant experience was being 'the only one', but this programme provided the opportunity for an integral identity experience where self, home, work and ethnicity identities all aligned.
- An inclusive career development and mentoring programme was developed and distributed via this UKBN network to all EMEA employees.
- Connections across a wide range of large organizations were brokered through this work, positioning this organization favourably with several of their large clients.
- The community contribution enabled through the BN became actively recognized in the performance management content in the UK.
- A resourced workspace was built in the Black community for general community use.
- A number of talented and socially disadvantaged young minority ethnic performers were sponsored to receive full training.
- A range of career advice programmes was supplied to 16–18 minority ethnic students across various locations, leading to successful degree applications from more than 35 per cent of them.
- Interest in the approach from all Black, Asian and Minority Ethnic (BAME) MPs in the UK.

FIGURE 11.2 Impact from 'positive identity through partnership' three-year ethnicity led programme

of ethnicity in the workplace was relatively invisible. This was evidenced by the lack of information about senior Black executives in the UK, a lack of UK-based published material about ethnicity initiatives in organizations and no regulatory requirement for reports of minority ethnic representation in organizational hierarchies. The available material has changed considerably since this work started (Haslam et al. 2011; Atewologun and Nitu 2015). In addition, there was a lack of 'built in' models for innovation (organizational change) either linked explicitly to working with ethnicity or for change programmes more generally. There were also very specific expectations in the business and very explicit D&I strategic goals.

Working in the area of ethnicity in the UK is politically and personally challenging. Accepting the leadership of this programme was exposing for my client and potentially career limiting. This meant that the first anchor point for me working as a coach was to name and address the insights around psychological safety from the literature. This was a consideration both for my direct client contact and also for all of those who were drawn into this work. Workplaces are not inclusive and leading this change, regardless of organization position, creates vulnerability.

One of the fallacies in the D&I rhetoric (based on my practical experience) is the view that a senior sponsor will guarantee change. Senior sponsors are just as susceptible to the pressures of psychological safety as anyone else and thinking about sponsorship requires the 'intelligent activist' to consider this need for all people. Reviewing psychological safety for all participants was an ongoing part of the coaching relationship and this deliberate awareness also helped frame the ways in which course correction was managed over the three-year programme. A key part of the overall design challenge was to identify how psychological safety for all those engaged would be managed and maintained.

Combined, these factors generated a tricky design challenge. The 'do no harm' ethic (Chapter 5) that is inherent to organizational psychology intervention was active and guided by the considerations of psychological safety. The global organization already had a Black employee structure operating in the USA and active Black Networks (BNs) across the USA. There was growing business pressure for this to become a global network structure linked to key business drivers. The pressing corporate issue was a challenge from an influential senior African American client. The predominant business need was the development of new clients across the EMEA (Europe, Middle East and Africa) division of the business.

A key existing business strategy was investment in diverse supply chain innovations across emerging economies. The nature of the UK business meant that the ethnic minority grouping was more diverse and intersected than its counterpart in the USA and so a different approach was needed to create apparently the same structures. When my client was authorized to lead this work in the UK, there had been two recent failed attempts to set up a UKBN. In the UK, the D&I focus was viewed as necessary to manage legal risk, so was more of a 'bolt on' approach to D&I than in the US. This meant that there would be some disconnect in D&I understanding that would need managing as part of the design solution.

The new design was co-created with my client, who from his knowledge of the context indicated there were three simple questions relevant to potential BN members that needed to guide the choices of action: These questions were: How will I profit from being involved? When will I profit from being involved? Who says I profit from my contribution? The potential answers to these challenges emerged from my client's conversation with potential allies and underpinned the focus of the planned work.

The insights used for design

The client insight into the context pressures (see Figure 11.3) was combined with my years of experience as a practitioner with some key of insights from network theory (Granovetter 1973; Burt 2000) and insights from social identity theories.

When moving into creativity and innovation I have found that 'systematic' approaches to the consideration of evidence hinder design, and so techniques are needed to move into a different way of working. In addition, there was not much literature relevant for this work and so I used what I describe as my 'quirky review' process to feed my creative thinking about a psychologically sound design for this specific problem. The dictionary definition of quirky 'having or characterized by

---

WORKPLACE EVIDENCE

- Operating in the UK workplace claiming a Black identity was described as 'unsafe'.
- African American, Native American and Hispanic employees had different identity groups in the USA, but the ethnicity/identity landscape in the UK was much more intersected.
- There was an authorized structure around the African American identity group, sponsored at senior levels in the USA that provided the infrastructure for this programme.
- The USA Black History Month (BHM) was in the corporate calendar in February each year but there was nothing equivalent for the UK BHM in October each year.
- The UK Black employees were widely distributed across different UK offices, so tended to be isolated rather than being co-located in each office, as they were in the USA.
- Understanding of the structures of progression and career development were not well shared internally in the UK.
- The US corporate objectives around minority ethnic progression had not been translated into UK performance management practice for senior executives.
- Claiming a workplace identity in a UK Black community context did not feel permitted by the organization.
- Work on new projects started virtually in the UK and the impact of turning up after establishing virtual relationships and 'being Black' was complex and uncomfortable.
- There was a redundancy programme running.

FIGURE 11.3 Workplace evidence for design

peculiar or unexpected traits or aspects' is chosen deliberately to point to the use of evidence to support a creative process rather than a fact-based knowledge process. A quirky review process involves free thinking to generate a few key headline criteria to source interesting material that will generate a distinctive idea. Usually I will find something helpful in the papers, literature and ideas I have already collected on the way and this is sufficient. (Occasionally I will turn to EBSCO – a business research database – but this can be pretty cumbersome.) My approach is then to read material afresh with design intent – that is, to ask 'what does this tell me needs to be designed to help with this challenge?'

In this case I first thought 'Black progression and networks' and remembered that Granovetter (1973) had used Black Networks and finding a new job as his data. So I drew insights from the same source as the previous story, but for a different purpose and different reason. Ignoring all the material on network theory in the article, I scanned the case material and picked up on the statement that Black Networks tended to be internally referent rather than externally referent, and consequently disconnected from other networks that can offer powerful help in career change. This was not a statistically significant sample, and was set in communities and not organizations, but as design innovation, it said to me: 'design across boundaries and connect to power'.

Based on the material from social identity theory (remembered from undergraduate textbooks) the issue that struck me was the impact of perceived status of an identity on how identity is enabled and enacted in the workplace. It also made me question the extent to which the current approaches to Employee Resource Groups (ERGs – the BN structure is one example) – have been informed (or not) by a thorough understanding of the identity complexity they activate. I then thought about basic undergraduate social psychology and the 'fact' of in-group/out-group processes (see Chapter 8) which made me consider how the use of an 'identity group' in an organization may provoke these boundaries and how we could design in helpful ways to work with this human reality (which was drawn from my general graduate texts and there is now the review by Haslam (2014) which provides a very practical consolidation of these issues).

Also of interest were studies of the impact on women and men from 'identity fractures' between work and home – which indicated that women are negatively impacted and men positively impacted from having both work and home, identities active (Rothbard 2001). I found nothing equivalent studying Black identity but extrapolated from the gender-based evidence on 'integrated identities'.

This is clearly not using the literature advocated in research endeavour, but I was not primarily concerned with the accuracy or the relevance of the literature but instead how the insights could inform my psychosocial design practice. Fully applied design thinking (see Chapter 4) would also recommend collecting pictures and stories to help with the insight process. I was not on the ground with the client at the time but was working at a distance so I could not employ these visual and narrative techniques in this circumstance. Instead I explored the realities of working in this context with my client (which was also critical for the coaching support offered) and used the evidence from this to integrate with the other literature driven insights generated.

Since design is always contextual, although these external insights were interesting and helpful, they did not provide sufficient evidence to be clear about the design challenge. Through coaching conversations with my client, we identified three critical integrated insights that needed to feed into the co-created design for this context:

1. Psychological safety had to be a predominant concern throughout the programme, which meant embedding as much as possible in the existing protocols, practices and habits of the organization – so only the topic felt disruptive.
2. The need to ensure that the approach designed was boundary-spanning and alliance-based rather than inwardly referent and so the first step was to create external power-based alliances.
3. The need to directly address the psychosocial processes around identity construction in a complex workplace and in this case to find a rapid way of disrupting the status quo of negative assignations for Black identity in this workplace.

Working with identity was particularly urgent as there was clear evidence of a negative identity dynamic associated with claiming Black identity in the UK workplace. There were also issues of psychological safety and a pattern of disaggregated identity leading to psychosocial fragmentation. Identities associated with home, work, brand, race, aspiration, profession, gender and friendship were all to a greater or lesser extent held separately. This fragmentation meant that there was extra workload on Black employees due to the self-management in and across roles required of them. The tension this created in attachment patterns due to never quite belonging as an integral person anywhere also needed to be addressed. This manifested in habits of avoidance around identity issues and the failure of previous approaches (no one joined the previous network that was set up) were attributed to it being unsafe to describe oneself as Black. The need to re-frame this was built into the programme through naming Black identity in the title.

Translation for implementation

One of the critical aspects for the implementation phase of translation (Chapter 1, Table 1.3, phase 4) is to shape the delivery approach for the field context, so ensuring that it is stabilized for that context. Large organizations are filled with people managing resources that do not belong to them, governed by a wide array of legal and economic frameworks established in different jurisdictions. This means that designing for accountability/authority is essential to enable implementation. Very often this can start with the development of a business case, outlining the financial and other considerations associated with the implementation of the design. However, in this case, because the design deliberately used the start small and leverage approaches (fail fast and prototyping) this was not required as the method involved minimal financial investment/risk at the outset. This meta-design for accountability/authority has been described as *design governance*, which articulates how the implementation will *stay on track with the intent* and not merely be run as a project or programme management process that can disconnect project activity from programme purpose. An associated need is to clearly articulate the benefits tracking approach to be used and the mechanisms to be used for course correction (Chapter 1, Table 1.3, phase 5). Effective design governance requires clarifying how accountability and authority works in the field context and being explicit about how the planned programme or intervention will be aligned with these existing accountability and authority dynamics.

Accountability/authority dynamics in implementation and course correction

To design and deliver an innovative approach of this nature required careful attention to the pressures and realities of the specific context. To summarize the requirements for governance, it requires attention to three factors and these always need to be bespoke:

- how accountability/authority flows in the context and how to work with this social norm;
- how impact is demonstrated in this context;
- what psychosocial and other insights have been built into the design and how you track these and course correct, to stay true.

To minimize unhelpful disruption (while accepting that disruption is the essence of innovation) the work needed to be as closely aligned with 'normal operating procedure' as possible. This is to ensure the point of disruption was the ethnicity focus and that this did not get lost in other concerns and reactions. This is a key aspect of effective translation for the implementation phase.

Critical to understanding intervention practice is the recognition that merely exporting the same approach outlined in this case to another context without accommodating the vicissitudes of a new context is not guaranteed to work. The assumption that one design solution could work anywhere is invalid, as shown by the previous translation failure of the US model to the UK business. A different context may not use the same programme structure for delivery or may not have the same history to work with and all these contextual factors shape how to work with insights to create effective designs.

Design governance for implementation and course correction in this case needed to engage with five aspects of this field context:

- anchoring the work in the US-based Black Leadership framework, forming close alliances with the BNs in the USA and having a UK voice on the Black Governance Structure;

- embedding recognition for the work done into the wider corporate performance management process;
- securing an executive sponsor for the programme who could authorize the emerging work and any course correction required (the sponsor very quickly put in place a wider committee structure around this programme to ensure a sustainable governance design across the complex organizational matrix);
- establishing a programme reporting protocol that mirrored the one used for other programmes in this organization;
- completing the relevant documentation to integrate the plan and the intended outputs of the design with the various strategic D&I goals already articulated for business (around recruitment, retention and diverse customers), to ensure that all stakeholders gained due credit for contributing to a corporate goal.

Implementation design

There was one 90-day 'intervention' planned for each of the three years, timed around the UK BHM (this took a while to get on the UK corporate calendar – and is again another story), which was fully active and fully reported. Symbolically this needed to represent the design challenges – positive identity, connection with power and psychologically safe – and so was a very demanding position for my client contact to hold. Coaching during these high profile stages was connected to the need for symbolic leadership – or in his words 'to keep it real' and running delivery for one season out of four ensured that stress levels were contained.

For the remainder of the year the general approach was to invest in building the environmental conditions for success, predominantly through the growth and activation of boundary-spanning alliances, such as working to be appointed as the first non-American on the Black Governance Structure of the BNs.

In keeping with the participate/orchestrate model of intervention (Chapter 3), the programme was codified into three one-year segments that helped articulate the pathway for delivering the change intended: build the internal network; connect with the community; and build the network of networks across businesses.

Within each segment, there was one 90-day intervention process run around the Black History Month date in the UK calendar (October) with maintenance, impact reporting and governance activities running for the remainder of the year.

Conclusion

This chapter has provided two accounts of the way in which the phases of knowledge translation unfold in client contexts, focusing upon concerns with complex belonging structure and the work with identity that is becoming of increasing relevance to complex workplaces.

It covered the importance of accessing contextual insights to frame how to approach a problem and the process of converting this into a design challenge through the engagement with insights rather than evidence. It then outlined the importance of issues of design governance and accountability/authority norms for containing disruption in implementation as a meta-design to ensure the principles are sustainable in action.

References

Atewologun, D. and Nitu, M. (2015) What is inclusive leadership? A systematic literature review of the empirical evidence. *DOP Conference Proceedings*. British Psychological Society, Glasgow, January.

Burt, R. S. (2000) The network structure of social capital. *Research in Organizational Behavior* 22: 345–423.

Farrands, R. (2013) *Design Rationality: Working with Donald Schon*. Vienna: EODF.

Granovetter, M. S. (1973) The strength of weak ties. *American Journal of Sociology* 78(6): 1360–1380.

Haslam, S. A. (2014) Making good theory practical: Five lessons for an Applied Social Identity approach to challenges of organizational, health and clinical psychology. *British Journal of Social Psychology* 53(1): 1–20.

Haslam, S. A., Reicher, S. D. and Platow, M. J. (2011) *The New Psychology of Leadership: Identity, Influence and Power*. Hove: Psychology Press.

Meyerson, D. and Scully, M. (1995) Tempered radicalism and the politics of ambivalence and change. *Organization Science* 6(6): 585–600.

Rothbard, N. (2001) Enriching or depleting? The dynamics of engagement in work and family roles. *Administrative Science Quarterly* 46(4): 655–684.

12

MEASUREMENT, SILENCE AND THE MECHANISMS OF COMPLIANCE

Introduction

The overarching issue in this chapter concerns how authority and accountability appear to have been disconnected in organizational design and practice. This disconnect can lead to cover ups, corporate collapses, complexities around managing financial risk, concerns about how reward structures encourage or discourage abuse of position and expertise, widespread organizational bystanding and the 'tyre blow out' of the whistleblowing manoeuvre.

Client questions about the risks associated with these accountability disorders are relatively new and most often expressed as reputational and risk management questions. This means they are sensitive and so difficult to cover with case material. Respect for obligations of confidentiality apply (when not displaced by an obligation of candour) which limits what can be written. For this reason the case illustrations have been constrained to:

- A consideration of an anonymous UK pay data-set that raises important questions about how we approach redressing unequal pay in our society.
- An exploration of the bystanding phenomenon in the UK NHS associated with its increasing reliance on whistleblowing. This is based upon public domain information coupled with insights from my pro bono psycho-legal work.

Resource distribution and equal pay: the role of measurement (case one)

This case illustration will both reinforce the importance of activism around the gender pay gap and also the importance of recognizing that this is not merely a gender issue but that there is also an ethnicity pay gap. Further it suggests that the intersections between these different drivers of marginalization work to hide the full extent of the pay disparity problem.

To contextualize this case on resource inequity in organizations, I have identified the three key resources that are unequally shared in complex workplaces: dignity; time; money. Much of the material so far outlined in this book is linked to the damaging impact that the uneven distribution of dignity generates. This is critical, as lack of dignity is the source of most conflict and is manifest in the unacceptable damage done to physical bodies, identities and communities. The inequality in distribution of dignity reinforces systemic patterns of marginalization and inequality and consequent organizational toxicity. However, this is not the whole story and we cannot allow ourselves to be seduced into concentrating our D&I efforts only to the 'dignity' resource.

The problem and the gender pay gap literature

We live in a world where marginalized sections of our communities are paid less than those in the mainstream, *despite making exactly the same contribution*. The underpinning meaning is that members of *marginalized groups are 'expected' to give a proportion of their effort without being paid for that work*.

While this topic could be 'written out' of a textbook on the social psychology of organizations, arguing it is a political issue outside our remit as practitioners, I would suggest the opposite. Working as an intelligent activist, fully driven by the psychosocial evidence we have to hand, with the intent to create more effective, prosperous and healthy environments for us all to work in, means we must fully engage with the causes and consequences of this resource inequity.

Pay dispersion is a significant psychosocial issue in workplaces as it strongly activates social comparison processes. Pay satisfaction is at its lowest when people consider that they are underpaid compared with upwards comparators (Brown 2001). The critical issue is the extent to which variability in pay, or pay dispersion, is justifiable or not (Shaw 2014). There appears to be an acceptance of difference in pay levels, but only some causes are felt fair. If pay differences are explicable there is a positive impact on productivity and workplace safety but if they are not it has a negative effect on overall organizational performance (Frederickson et al. 2010). Keeping pay secret does not manage these psychosocial factors as secrecy damages perceptions of justice in the workplace (Colella et al. 2007) which is implicated in work-induced mental ill health and organizational toxicity discussed in Chapter 6.

The European Commission (EC) revealed that women across the European Union (EU) earn 17.4 per cent less than men (Deschenaux 2009). Kandola and Kandola (2013) point to the universality of this gender difference in pay and the difficulty in really digging deep enough into the historical mud to elucidate the other drivers of this unacceptable status quo. At board level the existence of the gender pay disparities is well documented. Bonuses awarded to men are larger than those awarded to women and managerial compensation of male executive directors is much more performance-sensitive than that of female executives (Kulich et al. 2011). The level of satisfaction that women have with life and job are related to how their communities value the concept of equal pay (HBR 2010).

However, women spend a higher percentage of their income on family and community than men (Zelizer 2010). This identified gendered pattern of money use indicates that pay inequality is not just unfair, but probably has substantial and negative implications for the health and prosperity of our communities and societies.

There are a wide variety of different dynamics postulated. That deeply held stereotypical, discriminatory views of employers (and some employees) cause the gender pay gap (Penner et al. 2012) even in ostensibly 'progressive' contexts such as universities (Doucet et al. 2012). Increasingly organizations are using 'broad-banding' to structure jobs. This makes job comparison difficult. There is evidence that job evaluation schemes have built in gender bias (McShane 1990; Gilbert 2005) and that they have not helped generate equal pay, as the implicit biases built into valuing work are inherently discriminatory and stereotypical (Gilbert 2012). Increasingly temporary, marginal or 'liminal' work is strongly associated with secondary labour market characteristics (temporary contracts, 'non-western' citizenship) and impacts women to a greater extent than men (Kieldstad and Nymoen 2012).

Regularly the explanation for abiding gaps in pay level is linked to family responsibility (Datta et al. 2013). The area where individual case claims are relatively successful compared with all other discrimination claims is in the area of family responsibility or work–life balance. The number of these cases in the US context has jumped substantially over the past 15 years (Williams and Cuddy 2012). It suggests that if a woman draws attention to unfairness that aligns with the stereotype, she will get more attention than anything aimed at addressing the need to destabilize these stereotypes and to pay women equally. Tackling unequal pay through anti-discrimination legislation, which uses the individual case approach has not generated the systemic shift needed (Gow and Middlemiss 2011). Even when legal decisions change individual pay levels, these individual changes do not appear to be maintained over time (Connolly et al. 2012). The development of statute- and case-based legislation has failed to address this inequity. Also, and unfortunately, some trade union organizations, which emerged to address resource inequality, are now implicated in the maintenance of practices that sustain this pay inequality (Robins 2007).

At the moment there is so much legal fear about the possible consequence of admitting to such inequality that inquiry and action are blocked in organizations; it is almost better not to know for fear of what responsibility such knowledge would bring. Shifting the distribution of money is necessary, as it frees choice and works as a critical enabler to get different perspectives, different concerns and different questions being voiced, heard and actioned.

The following field evidence is used to bring the drivers of unfair pay to life in a single situation and to illustrate the complexities of intersecting fairness dynamics that disadvantage people based on gender and ethnicity, and how these together can work to hide the extent of both types of resource inequality.

Intersectionality in resource inequality dynamics

When one of our clients (as in the material shared below), has the courage to ask the question, we must be ready and able to help. This is commercially sensitive information for the UK division of this company as all of these gaps in pay are above the threshold of 2 per cent indicated by the UK Equalities Commission as cause for action. Asking questions about fair pay is risky and we need to use all our skills in creating psychological safety to support such courageous acts. By contrast, if one of our clients is complacent about the role of their institution in sustaining this inequity, given the negative social impacts from this ongoing problem, then we need to be placed to initiate a different response.

The case material used here is partial due to all the considerations of client confidentiality and commercial sensitivity outlined in Chapter 5. This means that what can be shared will not meet the standards of interrogation that 'academic' scrutiny would require of such knowledge (I am reminded of *The Handmaid's Tale* (Atwood 1985)). However scholarly uncertainty is something that we need to live and work with, as no academic is likely to be given the necessary access to such sensitive data for fear of where their account will end up and what damage it could do.

The standard metric approach used to assess the gender pay gap is to look at collated 'mean' differences in pay between men and women (descriptive statistical approach). This approach was applied to an in-company data-set and then the same data-set was subject to a multivariate analysis (inferential statistical approach). The simple descriptive statistical analysis of the pay data-set led to an account of there being a gender pay gap with 'issues' centred on part-time and full-time working, which was assumed to be about childcare – the stereotyped view of causes of the gender pay gap (see Table 12.1).

TABLE 12.1 What the 'mean' approach tells us about inequalities in pay

The simple statistical analysis using averages of pay inequality in the client data-set

Protected characteristic	The mean difference in pay
Based on averages, the biggest gap was between *part-time and full-time workers*	Just greater than a 10 per cent difference in pay
Based on averages the next biggest gap was between *men and women*	Just less than a 10 per cent difference in pay
Based on averages there was a smaller, yet clear gap between those with *disabilities* and those without	A 5 per cent difference in pay
Based on averages the smallest gap was between *BAME (Black and Minority Ethnic)* and *White* members of staff	A 2 per cent difference in pay

However the use of inferential statistics gave quite a different account. This indicated that while gender accounted for some non-legitimate variance in pay, the biggest source of variance on non-legitimate pay difference was being of Black African/Afro-Caribbean ethnicity and there was no difference in part-time and full-time pay once legitimate sources of pay variance were controlled for (see Table 12.2). The inferential tests gave us insights that completely displaced the gender stereotype explanation and pointed towards systemic patterns of marginalization and disadvantage in operation in the pay structures and practices.

The two steps in the analysis of variance are outlined in Figures 12.1 and 12.2. The first step was to factor in all those dynamics that would be expected to have a legitimate impact on pay levels in a living employment context to see what variance in salary these accounted for (Figure 12.1). Of these characteristics, location, seniority and length of service all had an impact on pay levels as would be expected. The purpose of this was to be able to remove the impact of the variance due to these factors in advance of the second analysis.

The second step was to factor in the protected characteristics to see how each protected characteristic was implicated in the variance in pay. This identified the scale of the non-legitimate sources of variance on pay, once the legitimate variance was controlled (Figure 12.2).

Both approaches showed significant variances in pay, but analysing causes of variance in pay rather than merely looking at the descriptive statistics gave very different insights into the dynamics at work. This requires a different set of questions

TABLE 12.2 Intersectionality and non-legitimate pay differentials

The impact of intersectionality (analysis of pay variance)

The protected characteristic	Associated variance in pay
Being Black (Afro-Caribbean or African) had the biggest and most significant negative impact on pay level	Converted into pay, this suggested that a Black employee would be paid 10 per cent less than expected once all other factors were accounted for
Being female had the next biggest and most significant negative impact on pay level	Converted into pay, this suggested that a female employee would be paid 3 per cent less than expected once all other factors were accounted for
Being disabled had a negative impact (non-significant) on pay level	Converted into pay, disability status did not account for any variance in pay
Being Asian had no impact on level of pay	Converted into pay, Asian ethnicity in this client context had no impact on pay level
Being part-time had a positive and significant impact on level of pay	Converted into pay, working part-time would mean a staff member was paid 3 per cent more than expected once all other factors were taken into account

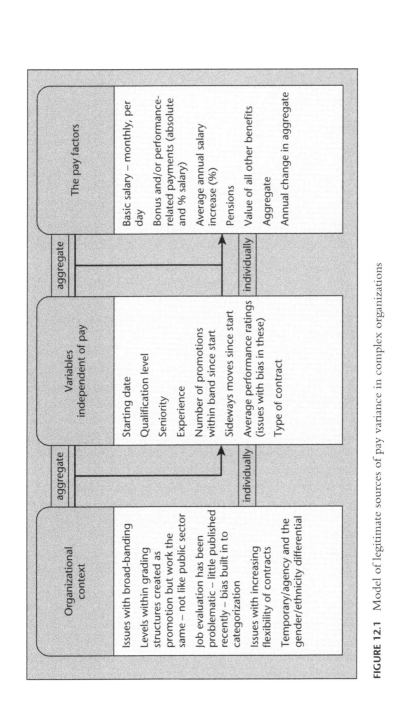

FIGURE 12.1 Model of legitimate sources of pay variance in complex organizations

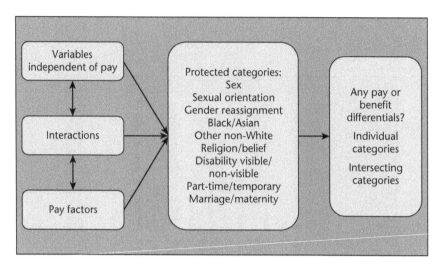

FIGURE 12.2 Model of protected characteristics and pay outcome

to be asked to be able to meet the requirements for transparency, and to deal with the root causes of unfair pay within this context:

- How do we re-frame this issue as one of pay inequality through marginalization and systemic inequality in organizational practices rather than the simplistic (and stereotypically comfortable) idea that this is about childcare?
- How can we sustain the 'gender pay gap' as the dominant cause for resource distribution inequity when the largest, non-legitimate variance in pay, was probably caused by racism against those of African and Afro-Caribbean heritage in the workplace?
- What impact does the evidenced pay disadvantage for Black employees in this context (given that for this client data-set the majority of Black employees were male) have on masking the full extent of the 'gender pay gap' in this context?
- What impact does the differential impact of ethnicity on variance in pay have on the gender pay gap (given that the majority of Asian employees were female)?

What this case illustration raises is two important insights to inform intelligent activism around systemic resource inequality:

- Recognizing the impact of intersectionality in the processes of marginalization and the full range of different variables that are implicated in pay inequality.
- Choosing to take a sophisticated approach to measurement and not accept simple target metrics to ensure that what we choose to look at generates 'transparency'.

Intersectionality

This refers to the 'double whammy' of gender with, for example, race, disability or sexual preference (Acker 2006) which contributes to gender pay disadvantage through multiple points of inequity as illuminated through the sharing of this field case. These are not made clear if we only ask specific questions about pay and gender. For a developing account of intersectionality and the dynamics in the workplace see Atewologun et al. (2015).

Transparency and measurement sophistication

Poor quality, unsophisticated measurement and tracking based on using simple metrics, are a key part of the problem. We all know the rich stories of intelligent 'gaming' of simple data (Osterloh 2014) to achieve 'political' outcomes. We know that deploying simple measures leads to unintended and negative consequences (Harris and Ogbonna 2002). This case also shows that using a single measure to create a 'target' approach is implicated in sustaining the very problem it seeks to change. When using 'measurement' to engage with a 'wicked problem' we need to explicitly work with the complexity of interrelating metrics and overall signal detection, if our system governance is going to be effective.

To adopt pay practices that remove this inequality we need sophisticated causal models to begin to design interventions that can generate change. How we measure things impacts the narratives we create, hence what we should do to intervene. There is substantial peer reviewed research evidence, consistent with this single case outline, that shows the subtle and interacting biases that impact pay systems (McShane 1990; Eremin et al. 2010; Kulich et al. 2011; Cortis and Meagher 2012; Fransen et al. 2012; Golman and Bhatia 2012). A more robust approach, that is, multivariate linear regression (Reese and Warner 2012), was deployed in this field illustration to provide more sophisticated understanding of the causes of variance in pay. This can be effectively deployed to understand what the key drivers of inequality are and so what interventions are needed and where they must focus (Moral-Arce et al. 2012).

Accounts of unequal pay as linked to childcare issues are currently dominating the rhetoric. This appears to centre on a particularly white middle class female experience and ignores the issue of intersectionality and marginalization dynamics. This case suggests we need to disentangle the discussion of the gender pay gap from issues of maternity. Is the difference between part-time and full-time pay averages a product of more complex organizational factors such as location, length of service or role; the legitimate causes of unequal pay? Overall it suggests that the approaches we need for the consideration of equal pay must be linked to issues of intersectionality, unequal progression masked by pseudo-rational assessment process (see Chapter 10) and to address the overall dynamics of marginalization.

We need to use psychosocial techniques, including our robust statistical prowess, to generate the evidence needed to support this social change. This is not only in the publication of evidence, but also in the nitty-gritty work of monitoring the important things, detecting changes and 'blips' in the emerging realities to keep our intent on track and tell better narratives about impact. This is a critical concern, not just for the health of organizations but for the social structure they operate within:

> We have reached a tipping point. Inequality in OECD countries is at its highest since records began. The evidence shows that high inequality is bad for growth. The case for policy action is as much economic as social. By not addressing inequality, governments are cutting into the social fabric of their countries and hurting their long-term economic growth.
>
> *(OECD 2015)*

Bystanding, blowing the whistle and the dynamics of silence (case two)

An emerging area of policy concern centres on the extent to which 'accountability disorders' or wrongdoing in complex workplaces can be addressed by encouraging more whistleblowing (Civil Service 2015). This is deeply problematic from a psychosocial perspective. The problem with identifying whistleblowing as a control mechanism for corporate wrongdoing is that psychosocially such acts will be experienced as a form of treachery based upon the insights from social identity theory. Backlash is therefore psychologically predictable and so it is sensible to consider such an act as a form of psychological suicide or martyrdom and to approach policy development and statutory provision from this full recognition.

Relying on people to make the individuated choice to be whistleblowing martyrs will also increase acts of bystanding and silence in an organization, which in turn will lead to organizational toxicity. When this 'solution' is directed at healthcare, as in the UK NHS (Francis 2015) it has significant and worrying social consequences. Whistleblowing needs to be considered, if at all, as a last resort in efforts to keep the population safe from corporate malfeasance, rather than a 'duty', because it generates such negative personal consequences.

Whistleblowing: the evidence

The examples from my recent experiences of working with individual whistleblowers in the UK NHS indicates that although many people in the impacted organization become involved in managing the whistleblower, no one appears to be charged with or feel confident to take authority for the situation, the content of the complaints or the means for resolution. Instead all around are 'turned' into bystanders who driven by fear and in-group 'loyalty' aid and abet (Linstead 2013). Accountability floats and slides and never gets handled, so investment is increasingly directed to dependency on external expert and internal compliance processes. As a practitioner, my experience is one of pain and suffering among all involved and a deep sense of learned helplessness.

The literature indicates that whistleblowing has serious negative consequences for individuals and organizations. The evidence of physical retaliation, dismissal actions and bullying against whistleblowers makes for very troubling reading: 22 per cent of whistleblowers report physical and violent retaliation; 75 per cent have a move to dismiss made against them; and nearly all report bullying after raising a concern (Parmerlee et al. 1982; Miceli and Near 1988; Bernstein et al. 2010; Katz et al. 2012; Verschoor 2012; Bjerkelo 2013). Just as significant however is the substantial research evidence which indicates that, while such public disclosures may improve governance practices in the short term, they have a serious detrimental impact on overall organizational and operational effectiveness over the medium to long term (Bowen et al. 2010; Dasgupta and Kesharwani 2010).

Generally whistleblowers are more likely to be highly educated, show good job performance and hold higher-level positions (Miceli and Near 1988; Vadera et al. 2010). Whistleblowing is much more likely to be undertaken against those who score low on likeability and on performance (Robertson et al. 2011). The psychosocial processes involved in such actions mean that this will not necessarily lead to balanced reporting of wrongdoing or error, which adds further complexity and concern to ideas that we should rely on this mechanism.

When the likelihood of speaking up is studied, it appears that there is a cost to benefit assessment (Robinson et al. 2012) made in each situation. This means that only profound wrongdoing will provoke such action, leaving many of the micro acts that lead to very dysfunctional workplace habits uncommented upon. Another critical consideration made in this cost–benefit assessment is whether it is likely that anything will be done about the problem (Keil et al. 2010; Waples and Culbertson 2011). It also appears that those who speak up are more likely to show high dominance and low agreeableness (Bjerkelo et al. 2010) suggesting that individual difference also impacts on the outcome of this cost–benefit assessment process.

The importance of social identity is highlighted in the evidence that it is more likely that people will speak up in organizations perceived by others to be open and responsive to complaints (Micelli and Near 1988; Loyens 2013). Sometimes being observed will make it more likely that a person will 'do the right thing' despite a potential personal detriment (Fischer and Greitemeyer 2013) particularly if it is linked to an active experience of positive social identity. However, if the social context is full of others ignoring the problematic situation, these social identity pressures work to generate a different outcome and pluralistic ignorance is more likely where assumptions that either silence is normal or it is someone else's problem will dominate action (or inaction) (Linstead 2013).

The NHS example: a system issue

There are three features of the NHS context (Gerada and Wilde 2015) that suggest bystanding is probable:

1. The psychological environment that NHS staff are expected to work within is not safe. Over a quarter of NHS staff report physical and psychological violence from patients and the same levels of psychological violence from other NHS staff members. The figures equate to 300,000 of NHS staff being bullied or hurt by patients or managers every year. Further 72 per cent do not believe that anything would be done if they spoke up about their concerns. Of these, 14 per cent believe they would be punished for speaking.

2. This complex NHS system works 24/7 and delivers exceptional levels of service to the UK. One million people are seen every 36 hours with an astounding 81 per cent of patients giving a very positive (always) response to the question 'are you treated with dignity and respect?' Any organization that works consistently with this amount of distress, pain and sickness inevitably becomes compassion depleted (see Chapter 8 for a review of compassion and also Gerada and Wilde 2015).

3. The use of simplistic externally defined targets and the fractured nature of the different approaches to regulation and assessment lead to 'gaming' decisions about how organizations in this structure are run.

I would suggest that these headline figures indicate a substantial 'compassion gap'; greater compassion is shown to patients than is shown to NHS staff. This compassion gap cannot be sustained without accepting a system that is draining those working within it. To disengage and withdraw commitment and compassion in unsafe environments is a deeply rational response. It is self-protective of individual psychological well-being. It is now substantially evidenced that work environments characterized by low levels of fairness and psychological safety are a serious risk factor for depression (see Chapter 6).

The inherent toxicity of 'quasi-judicial' procedures in organizations

A key concern that I have is the use of quasi-judicial processes for addressing employee grievances and concerns with discipline. Through considerable recent experience these appear to be as problematic for all concerned as the performance management systems that are critiqued in Chapter 10. These conflict-based, quasi-judicial procedures appear to be considered best practice in organizations to manage disputes and concerns from and about employees. These quasi-judicial processes appear to be functioning to suppress employees who raise moral and safety concerns. From a psychosocial perspective I consider that we need seriously to consider a re-design if we are to mitigate the current level of organizational toxicity from breaches of 'natural justice'. At the core for me is that perceptions of justice are inherently compromised when one party in a dispute (in this case the employer) also nominates the individual who holds the role of judge. Regularly the individual in the role of judge is subject to the authority of the organization and hence inherently financially dependent on one of the parties in dispute. There can be no 'natural justice' in such an arrangement and the long-term negative impact on effectiveness from whistleblowing is unsurprising.

Understanding acts of silence

In examining the NHS, the evidence that predictors of low psychological safety are deficiencies in work design, role ambiguity, high demands, deficiencies in leadership behaviour and evidence of tolerance for bullying, is relevant (see Chapter 7). In addition a history of 'organizational trauma' described as survivor syndrome is predictive of low safety. Re-structuring and redundancy are significant examples of this and the NHS was impacted by both of these in 2013. These experiences generate perceptions that the organization is dangerous, unfair and set in its ways. In such working contexts people will 'keep their heads down', 'keep their mouths shut' and 'turn a blind eye'. To repair NHS cultures that are currently 'silent' (Edwards et al. 2009) we must build psychologically safe work environments for the >1 million staff in the NHS. This includes all staff; those providing direct day-to-day care for patients, their managers and senior managers, the administrators that keep the services flowing, the clinical leaders, the commissioners of services and those who are asked to regulate these complex workplaces. These comments above are 'easy to say, hard to do' as they require a level of openness that is not currently safe. Broadly the psychological literature (see Chapters 6–8 for more details) indicate that openness will be enabled through:

- the compassionate moderation of counter-productive group processes that cause bias, silo thinking, groupthink, compliance, hostility, discrimination, apathy, learned helplessness and fear in the workplace;
- the design of grounded interventions that are high support, low hassle and have meaning for those impacted;
- the presence of active and accessible role models, ideally from those with authority in the system;
- the deployment of double loop responses to staff feedback –feedback is used productively, impact is shared and then is evaluated so the work of improvement become habitual – known as organizational learning.

Such psychological safety does not emerge 'naturally' but instead requires the active capability of people in the workplace deliberately setting the tone and actively crafting the environment in the day-to-day micro processes of relating.

Design challenges for reclaiming organizational voice

There are already various initiatives that are addressing this silence. Finding these and leveraging them is critical. Despite the NHS being a 'macro' concept, the reality of its effectiveness will be grounded in the multitude of micro processes that will vary widely based on context, task and history. The purpose in seeking ways to increase psychological safety for openness is not to suggest there is a universal solution; there never is. The belief that there is a single 'solution' comes from 'macro' only thinking and inherently operates from a position of power rather than understanding the accountability/authority dynamics across localized contexts.

The types of design challenges that could be trialled are given in the following six suggestions. These are not intended as a shopping list, but as a set of design ideas that need localized attention, to be tested and either rejected or used as effective in each local context, so they are outlined with the proviso that effective intervention needs to be grounded in the specific context, requiring resources to support them, rather than being designed and imposed from a distance.

Design challenge one

Create a system wide change platform: support the localized design of distributed, specifically situated short-term interventions, led by different people in different places and levels across a system, integrated through values. Avoid large-scale imposed complex over-planned change programmes, as such initiatives signal lack of control, increased demand and disempowerment for the majority. This requires resourcing for localized approaches, with some guidelines around types of approaches that could be trialled. This represents a significant shift in orientation and is consistent with the emphasis being developed at the NHS Institute for Innovation and Improvement, led by Helen Bevan (http://www.institute.nhs.uk/index.php?option=com_content&task=view&id=48&I temid=24). Such an approach could consider how to include the regulatory structures and practices.

Design challenge two

Compassionate regulation – role model psychological safety at regulatory level: develop 'compassionate regulation' approaches for commissioners and regulators, using the growing knowledge about organizational capabilities and routines that increase responsiveness and openness in a system. Regulatory bodies can then be required to work as effective stewards and culture change agents of the NHS rather as scrutineers: such stewardship requires inquiry skills, cross-cultural capability, political skill, requisite variety in team structures and fully developed diagnostic approaches to evidence that allows system pattern inferability. This approach needs to be informed by questions about how regulation could be re-constituted to be psychologically safe for all. An important consideration in connection with this is the impact of 'confirmatory bias'. This means people only see evidence that confirms what they already believe and is why culture change is so difficult. It will be necessary to do such role modelling for much longer than imagined. Once social norms have become established, as they have been across the NHS, only intelligent and subtle intervention will generate change to this very stable perceptual framework. The consistency, frequency and visibility of contradictory data needs to be high, constantly reinforced and sustained over an extended period to have any impact, as a half-hearted attempt merely creates more cynicism.

Design challenge three

Remove quasi-judicial grievance and disciplinary procedures. Instead design practices that enable those with authority and accountability to be honest with staff. They need to demonstrate what is realistic, what the constraints in the system are while being actively interested in the well-being of staff, so that employees are more easily supported to act compassionately and report concerns. This includes attention to approaches to participation that actively listen. For listening to be 'evidenced' to staff it needs two steps that loop together: the ability to *express*, for example, through surveys, Organization Development (OD) sessions or via 'yammer' type social media and the ability to see the *consequence in action*, for example through resourced action planning sessions with a choice of what to track and regular feedback. Currently most such participation attempts are partial, hence dysfunctional. Full double loop approaches are essential for organizational learning and to prevent bystanding.

Design challenge four

Make sure there is time to talk. This is important both as a significant mechanism to enable peer-to-peer compassion and support and also to be able to reflect upon, and improve work approaches and learn from errors. The current level of work overload in the NHS will mean that only the immediate work priority will get attention and the capacity for role improvisation in managing the unexpected is limited. Also make it safe to speak within the system about areas of concern through a confidential disclosure mechanism (Lowry et al. 2013; Loyens 2013). This needs to ensure there is appropriate sanction for really problematic actions in a way that treats the perpetrator with dignity – so not naming and shaming (Kahan 2006). This needs to be linked with the design of approaches for intervening with compassion in situations where individual or group behaviour is unacceptable. Such a mechanism also needs to both give confidence that action will be taken and ensure there is no reactive backlash consequent upon the raising of concerns. This removes reliance on external approaches to whistleblowing.

Design challenge five

Deploy 'free radicals' or brokers across the organization. The purpose is to model listening across all groups in the system and to act as connectors and cross-fertilizers. This work is focused upon interpreting and translating meaning across levels and disciplines and has been conceptualized as an equivalent role to that of the 'court jester', who served an integral role in keeping the 'king safe' through giving the truth a safe place. This could be something along the lines of the service user mentoring approaches being developed in NHS trusts where the CEO has a regular mentoring session with a service user, an internal OD consultant working across professional groups or an external provider of, for example, group facilitation or staff survey and action planning services. What is critical here is that the authority and accountability inherent in this role is provided by someone external to the system that has become silent, otherwise the same compliance pressures will be brought to bear on those in the 'court jester role' leading to an increase in cynicism and fear.

Design challenge six

The development of 'inquiry capability' across the system. This has been identified as a core organizational capability to mitigate confirmatory bias that leads to 'system blindness'. The introduction of cross-discipline peer review in the NHS is an example of an approach that can increase open inquiry skills as different ways of seeing are brought to bear on a situation. The literature on network structures, in this case the effectiveness of the 'brokering' role in the functioning of multi-disciplinary teams in the healthcare context (Currie and White 2012) also points to the positive impact of enabling loose boundaries around groups for overall system effectiveness. The introduction of sufficient levels of diversity in decision-making groups can disrupt this tendency to groupthink but as groups do not voluntarily invite this disruption, organizations need to have routines that make this the social norm.

Conclusion

The cases outlined in this chapter explore the meaning-making work inherent in intelligent activism and how this can interact with the regulatory framework, legal context, financial inequality and political environment. The legal, regulatory and statutory codes are a significant macro constraint on how we all can operate and can either be a source of toxicity in complex workplaces or provide the means of micro-level restitution and consequent positive symbolic actions that can be leveraged for macro impact. As intelligent activists we have the obligation to use our inquiry skills, our evidence base and our know-how to tell better stories about the processes of marginalization, privilege and prosperity and how they can be changed for the better. We must engage with meaning making to create the stories that make right action possible.

References

Acker, J. (2006) Inequality regimes: Gender, class, and race in organizations. *Gender & Society* 20(4): 441–464.

Atewologun, D., Sealy, R. and Vinnicombe, S. (2015) Revealing intersectional dynamics in organizations: Introducing 'intersectional identity work'. *Gender and Work Organization* DOI: 10.1111/gwao.12082.

Atwood, M. (1985) *The Handmaid's Tale*. Canada: McClelland & Stewart.

Bernstein, M. J., Sacco, D. F., Young, S. G. et al. (2010) Being 'in' with the in crowd. *Social Psychology Bulletin* 36(8): 999–1009.

Bjerkelo, B. (2013) Workplace bullying after whistleblowing: Future research and implications. *Journal of Managerial Psychology* 28(3): 306–323.

Bjerkelo, B., Einarsen, S. and Matthiesen, S. B. (2010) Predicting proactive behaviour at work: Exploring the role of personality as an antecedent of whistleblowing behaviour. *Journal of Occupational and Organisational Psychology* 83(2): 371–394.

Bowen, R. M., Call, A. C. and Rajgopal, S. (2010) Whistle-blowing: Target firm characteristics and economic consequences. *Accounting Review* 85(4): 1239–1271.

Brown, M. (2001) Unequal pay, unequal responses? Pay referents and their implications for pay level satisfaction. *Journal of Management Studies* 38(6): 879–896.

CivilService(2015)https://civilservice.blog.gov.uk/2015/08/12/whistleblowing-in-the-nhs/.

Colella, A., Paetzold, R. L., Zardkoohi, A. et al. (2007) Exposing pay secrecy. *Academy of Management Review* 32(1): 55–71.

Connolly, J., Rooney, T. and Whitehouse, G. (2012) Tracking pay equity: The impact of regulatory change on the dissemination and sustainability of equal remuneration decisions. *Journal of Industrial Relations* 54(2): 114–130.

Cortis, N. and Meagher, G. (2012) Recognition at last: Care work and the equal remuneration case. *Journal of Industrial Relations* 54(3): 377–385.

Currie, G. and White, L. (2012) Inter-professional barriers and knowledge brokering in an organisational context. *Organisation Studies* 33(10): 1333–1361.

Dasgupta, S. and Kesharwani, A. (2010) Whistleblowing: A survey of literature. *IUP Journal of Corporate Governance* 9(4): 57–70.

Datta, S., Guha, A. and Iskandar-Datta, M. (2013) Ending the wage gap. *Harvard Business Review* 91(5): 30.

Deschenaux, J. (2009) Pay gaps persist throughout Europe. *HR Magazine* 54(6): 97–104.

Doucet, C., Durand, C. and Smith, M. R. (2012) Pay structure, female representation and the gender pay gap among university professors. *Industrial Relations* 67(1): 51–75.

Edwards, M., Ashkanasy, N. M. and Gardner, J. (2009) Deciding to speak up or to remain silent following observed wrongdoing: The role of discrete emotions and climate of silence. In J. Greenberg and M. Edwards (eds) *Voice and Silence in Organizations*. Bingley: Emerald Group Publishing.

Eremin, D. V., Wolf, J. F. and Woodard, C. A. (2010) Systemic bias in federal performance evaluations. *Public Performance & Management Review* 34(1): 7–25.

Fischer, P. and Greitemeyer, T. (2013) The positive bystander effect: Passive bystanders increase helping in situations with high expected negative consequences for the helper. *Journal of Social Psychology* 153(1): 1–5.

Francis, R. (2015) Review of whistleblowing in the NHS. https://www.gov.uk/government/groups/whistleblowing-in-the-nhs-independent-review.

Fransen, E., Plantenga, J. and Vlasblom, J. D. (2012) Why do women still earn less than men? Decomposing the Dutch gender pay gap, 1996–2006. *Applied Economics* 44(33): 4343–4354.

Frederickson, J. W., Davis-Blake, A. and Sanders, W. M. G. (2010) Sharing the wealth: Social comparisons and pay dispersion in a CEOs top team. *Strategic Management Journal* 31(10): 1031–1053.

Gerada, C. and Wilde, J. (2015) Care, compassion and concern in the NHS. *Journal of Psychological Therapies in Primary Care* 4(S): 47–68.

Gilbert, K. (2005) Job evaluations. *Employee Relationships* 27(1): 7–19.

Gilbert, K. (2012) Job evaluation. *Industrial Relations Journal* 43(2): 137–151.

Golman, R. and Bhatia, S. (2012) Performance evaluation inflation and compression. *Accounting, Organizations & Society* 37(8): 534–543.

Gow, L. and Middlemiss, S. (2011) Equal pay legislation and its impact on the gender pay gap. *International Journal of Discrimination and the Law* 11(4): 164–186.

Harris, L. C. and Ogbonna, E. (2002) The unintended consequences of culture interventions: A study of unexpected outcomes. *British Journal of Management* 13(1): 31–49.

HBR (2010) The gender wage gap. *Harvard Business Review* 88(9): 22–27.

Kahan, D. M. (2006) What's really wrong with shaming sanctions. *Texas Law Review* 84: 2075–2103.

Kandola, B. and Kandola, J. (2013) *The Invention of Difference: The Story of Gender Bias at Work*. Oxford: Pearn Kandola Publishing.

Katz, M., LaVan, H. and Lopez, Y. P. (2012) Whistleblowing in organizations: Implications from litigation. *SAM Advanced Management Journal* 77(3): 4–17.

Keil, M., Tiwana, A., Sainsbury, R. et al. (2010) Toward a theory of whistleblowing intentions: A benefit-to-cost differential perspective. *Decision Sciences* 41(4): 787–812.

Kieldstad, R. and Nymoen, E. (2012) Part-time work and gender: Worker versus job explanations. *International Labour Review* 151(1/2): 85–107.

Kulich, C., Trojanowski, G., Ryan, M. K. et al. (2011) Who gets the carrot and who gets the stick? Evidence of gender disparities in executive remuneration. *Strategic Management Journal* 32(3): 301–321.

Linstead, S. (2013) Organizational bystanding: Whistleblowing, watching the work go by or aiding and abetting. *M@n@gement* 16(5): 680–696.

Lowry, P. J., Moody, G. D., Galletta, D. F. et al. (2013) The drivers in the use of online whistle-blowing reporting systems. *Journal of Management Information Systems* 30(1): 153–190.

Loyens, K. (2013) Towards a custom-made whistleblowing policy: Using grid-group cultural theory to match policy measures to different styles of peer reporting. *Journal of Business Ethics* 114(2): 239–249.

McShane, S. (1990) Two tests of direct gender bias in job evaluation ratings. *Journal of Occupational and Organisational Psychology* 63(2): 129–140.

Miceli, M. P. and Near, J. P. (1988) Individual and situational correlates of whistle-blowing. *Personnel Psychology* 41(2): 267–281.

Moral-Arce, I., Sperlich, S., Fernández-Saínz, A. I. et al. (2012) Trends in the gender pay gap in Spain: A semiparametric analysis. *Journal of Labor Research* 33(2): 173–195.

OECD (2015) In it together: Why less inequality benefits all. http://www.oecd.org/social/in-it-together-why-less-inequality-benefits-all-9789264235120-en.htm.

Osterloh, M. (2014) Viewpoint: Why variable pay for performance in healthcare can backfire. Evidence from psychological economics. *Evidence Based HRM* 2(1): 120–123.

Parmerlee, M. A., Near, J. P. and Jensen, T. C. (1982) Correlates of whistleblowers' perceptions of organizational retaliation. *Administrative Science Quarterly* 27(1): 17–34.

Penner, A. M., Toro-Tulla, H. J. and Huffman, M. L. (2012) Do women managers ameliorate gender differences in wages? Evidence from a large grocery retailer. *Sociological Perspectives* 55(2): 365–381.

Reese, C. and Warner, B. (2012) Pay equity in the States: An analysis of the gender–pay gap in the public sector. *Review of Public Personnel Administration* 32(4): 312–331.

Robertson, J. C., Stefaniak, C. M. and Curtis, M. B. (2011) Does wrongdoer reputation matter? Impact of auditor-wrongdoer performance and likeability reputations on fellow auditors' intention to take action and choice of reporting outlet. *Behavioral Research in Accounting* 23(2): 207–234.

Robins, J. (2007) Who's best at getting equal pay for women? *The Guardian*, 12 August. http://www.theguardian.com/money/2007/aug/12/discrimination.

Robinson, S. N., Robertson, J. C. and Curtis, M. B. (2012) The effects of contextual and wrongdoing attributes on organizational employees' whistleblowing intentions following fraud. *Journal of Business Ethics* 106(2): 213–227.

Shaw, J. D. (2014) Pay dispersion. *Annual Review of Organizational Psychology and Organizational Behaviour* 1: 521–544.

Vadera, A. K., Aguilera, R. V. and Caza, B. B. (2010) *Making Sense of Whistleblowing: Learning from Research on Identity and Ethics Programmes*. Champaign, IL: University of Illinois.

Verschoor, C. (2012) Retaliation for whistleblowing is on the rise. *Strategic Finance* 94(5): 13–69.

Waples, C. J. and Culbertson, S. S. (2011) Best-laid plans: Can whistleblowing on project problems be encouraged? *Academy of Management Perspectives* 25(2): 80–82.

Williams, J. C. and Cuddy, A. (2012) Will working mothers take your company to court? *Harvard Business Review* 90(9): 94–100.

Zelizer, V. A. (2010) *Economic Lives: How Culture Shapes the Economy*. Princeton, NJ: Princeton University Press.

CONCLUSION

Our workplaces are struggling to reclaim their humanity and the psychosocial knowledge we have, coupled with the developing practice skills, has a profound contribution to make.

We need to model the behaviour we want; we have to validate practice as well as knowledge production as distinct and intelligent work.

We need to ensure our workplaces are safe for all people regardless of status or identity.

These are substantial challenges but it is vitally important work. I hope this book contributes in some small way to this vital work.

INDEX